Health and the War on Poverty

Studies in Social Economics

TITLES PUBLISHED

STUDIES IN SOCIAL ECONOMICS

Karen Davis and Cathy Schoen

Health and the War on Poverty: A Ten-Year Appraisal

THE BROOKINGS INSTITUTION
Washington, D.C.

Library of Congress Cataloging in Publication Data:

Davis, Karen.
   Health and the war on poverty.

   (Studies in social economics)
   Includes index.
      1. Poor—Medical care—United States.   2. Poor—
Health and hygiene—United States.   3. Medical policy—
United States.   I. Schoen, Cathy, joint author.
II. Title.   III. Series.
RA418.5.P6D38   362.1'0973   77-91832
ISBN 0-8157-1758-X
ISBN 0-8157-1757-1 pbk.

9 8 7 6 5 4 3 2 1

THE BROOKINGS INSTITUTION is an independent organization devoted to nonpartisan research, education, and publication in economics, government, foreign policy, and the social sciences generally. Its principal purposes are to aid in the development of sound public policies and to promote public understanding of issues of national importance.

The Institution was founded on December 8, 1927, to merge the activities of the Institute for Government Research, founded in 1916, the Institute of Economics, founded in 1922, and the Robert Brookings Graduate School of Economics and Government, founded in 1924.

The Board of Trustees is responsible for the general administration of the Institution, while the immediate direction of the policies, program, and staff is vested in the President, assisted by an advisory committee of the officers and staff. The by-laws of the Institution state: "It is the function of the Trustees to make possible the conduct of scientific research, and publication, under the most favorable conditions, and to safeguard the independence of the research staff in the pursuit of their studies and in the publication of the results of such studies. It is not a part of their function to determine, control, or influence the conduct of particular investigations or the conclusions reached."

The President bears final responsibility for the decision to publish a manuscript as a Brookings book. In reaching his judgment on the competence, accuracy, and objectivity of each study, the President is advised by the director of the appropriate research program and weighs the views of a panel of expert outside readers who report to him in confidence on the quality of the work. Publication of a work signifies that it is deemed a competent treatment worthy of public consideration but does not imply endorsement of conclusions or recommendations.

The Institution maintains its position of neutrality on issues of public policy in order to safeguard the intellectual freedom of the staff. Hence interpretations or conclusions in Brookings publications should be understood to be solely those of the authors and should not be attributed to the Institution, to its trustees, officers, or other staff members, or to the organizations that support its research.

Foreword

Many of the federal health programs and policies begun in the 1960s reflected a desire to redeem the American promise of equal opportunity by improving access to services that help people lead healthy, productive lives. Medicare and Medicaid began in 1966 to pay the medical bills of the elderly and the poor; comprehensive community health centers opened their doors in many underserved and poor communities; and the maternal and child health program started new projects designed to serve the health care needs of disadvantaged mothers and children.

These programs expanded the role of federal and state governments in financing and delivering health care services. The reduction of financial barriers increased the use of such services by lower income groups and contributed to improved health. In recent years, however, the rapid increase in government expenditures on health care and the rapid inflation in health care costs have eroded these gains.

The authors of this study summarize the basic health and poverty issues and the public programs that have attempted to break the link between low income and poor health. They discuss the performance—the limitations and the strengths—of Medicaid, Medicare, the maternal and child health program, and the comprehensive health centers from 1965 to 1975. They conclude with recommendations for improving individual programs and for the ways in which public policy might be changed so as to make comprehensive health care accessible to all.

Karen Davis is Deputy Assistant Secretary for Planning and Evaluation/Health of the U.S. Department of Health, Education, and Welfare. Cathy Schoen is an economist with the Office of the Assistant Secretary for Planning and Evaluation of HEW. This study was completed while the authors were members of the Brookings Economic Studies program.

Roger A. Reynolds helped in the preparation of chapter 6; M. K. Carney of the University of Texas helped prepare chapter 5.

For reading and commenting on preliminary drafts, the authors are grateful to Rashi Fein of Harvard University; Lawrence Brown of the Brookings Institution; Howard Newman of the Hitchcock Medical Center at Dartmouth College; Stuart Altman of Brandeis University; Dorothy P. Rice of the National Center for Health Statistics in the Department of Health, Education, and Welfare; and Daniel I. Zwick of the Department of Health, Education, and Welfare. They are also grateful to Le-Chau Loc for research assistance and to Valerie J. Harris for typing the manuscript. The manuscript was edited by Elizabeth H. Cross and checked for accuracy and consistency by Evelyn P. Fisher, assisted by Kathleen M. Kane and Cynthia E. Nethercut. The index was prepared by Florence Robinson.

Preparation of this volume, the seventeenth in the Brookings series of Studies in Social Economics, was assisted by grants from The Robert Wood Johnson Foundation, Princeton, New Jersey.

The opinions, conclusions, and proposals are those of the authors and do not necessarily represent the views of The Robert Wood Johnson Foundation or of the officers, trustees, or staff members of the Brookings Institution.

BRUCE K. MAC LAURY
President

June 1978
Washington, D.C.

Contents

x

xi

xiii

Text Figures

chapter one   Public Policy and Health Care for the Poor

The decade 1965–75 brought a major expansion in federal responsibility for the health care of the poor and disadvantaged. Medicare, Medicaid, the comprehensive health center program, and an expanded maternal and child health program were among the many programs designed to help the poor, the aged, and the disadvantaged enjoy the fruits of a growing and prosperous economy. Of all the programs arising from the War on Poverty and the Great Society, those devoted to health care receive the largest and most rapidly growing share of budgetary resources.[1] *footnote does not document this assertion*

The Great Society and War on Poverty programs have been subjected to a barrage of criticism in recent years.[2] Because of their predominance in funding, health programs have received particularly critical attention, which has only been intensified by rapidly rising costs in the health care sector, tight budgetary pressures reflecting a sluggish economy, and frustration induced by the failure of the programs to achieve all that was expected of them.

Such criticism has obscured many of the programs' genuine accomplishments. Poor people's access to medical care has increased remarkably, and many families have been relieved of the financial burden of medical care for their aged parents. Although substantial lags occur in both the achievement and the reporting of improved health, it is apparent that

1. In fiscal year 1977 combined federal, state, and local funds for health care services totaled $57 billion. In fiscal 1966 public expenditures for health care totaled $8 billion. See unpublished preliminary data, and Marjorie Smith Mueller and Robert M. Gibson, "National Health Expenditures, Fiscal Year 1975," *Social Security Bulletin,* vol. 39 (February 1976), pp. 8, 17.

2. See, for example, Eli Ginzberg and Robert M. Solow, eds., *The Great Society: Lessons for the Future,* a special issue of *Public Interest,* no. 34 (Winter 1974); Robert H. Haveman, ed., *A Decade of Federal Antipoverty Programs: Achievements, Failures, and Lessons* (Academic Press, 1976); and Henry J. Aaron, *Politics and the Professors: The Great Society in Perspective* (Brookings Institution, 1978).

1

steady progress has been made—particularly in the kinds of poor health that are most prevalent among poor people and those that are most sensitive to improved medical care (see chapter 2). Experimental programs for the delivery of health services, which have combined medical and nonmedical attacks on the causes of poor health, though conducted on a limited scale, have demonstrated considerable success in improving the health of the poor (see chapters 5 and 6).

source?

But much remains to be done. The gap has been narrowed, but not eliminated. About 8 million to 10 million people below the poverty level, or about one-third of the poor, are not covered by current federal health care programs and their receipt of basic health care services lags behind that of the rest of the population. Poor residents of rural areas continue to encounter difficulty in obtaining health care, and their death rates, chronic and disabling conditions, and untreated acute conditions remain at disturbingly high levels.

The remaining task of bringing quality health care to all the poor and disadvantaged is not inconsequential, but neither is it insurmountable. The major problem is freeing additional resources to meet the needs of those not covered by federal health programs in the face of rising budgetary costs for those now covered. Growing numbers of older people who can be expected to contribute to even higher expenditures in current programs add to the difficulty of this task.

To meet this challenge changes are needed, such as (1) more attention to the causes of poor health, so that the necessity for using health care services is reduced for a longer period of time; (2) attempts to make the administration of current health care programs more effective; (3) major systemwide change in the health care sector to foster efficiency and productivity in the provision of services; (4) closer scrutiny and control of the level and distribution of health professionals entering the industry, the cost of health care services, and the types and numbers of health facilities constructed; and (5) tapping unused or underused resources of an economy operating at less than full capacity.

Poverty, Health, and Minimum Standards of Health Care

The terms "poverty" and "health" are generally understood (though hotly disputed), but greater specificity regarding their use in this book may be helpful. The terms "poverty income" and "poverty population" are based on the Bureau of the Census definition of poverty level income as three times the amount of money required to purchase an economy food plan. This plan, established by the Department of Agriculture in 1961, is based on a "basket" of food items required for a minimally adequate diet. Changes in the prices of these items result in an adjustment in the poverty income level. Since the economy food plan varies depending on family size, family composition, sex and age of the family head, and residence— farm or nonfarm—the poverty income level also varies according to these family characteristics.

In estimating the number of persons below the poverty income level, the Census Bureau counts all income from wages and salaries, self-employment, social security payments, public assistance payments, dividends, interest, rent, unemployment and workmen's compensation, government and private employee pensions, and other periodic income. It does not include the monetary value of in-kind transfer programs such as food stamps, medical care, or housing assistance.

In 1976 the poverty level income varied from $2,313 for a single farm woman aged sixty-five or over to an average of $9,588 for a two-parent, nonfarm family with six or more children. Table 1-1 indicates the trend in the poverty income threshold from 1960 to 1976 for a nonfarm family of four. In 1960 the poverty income threshold was set at approximately $3,000; by 1976 it had increased to about $5,815.

From 1960 to 1969 there was a fairly dramatic reduction in poverty: from almost 40 million people (22 percent of the civilian population) to 24 million (12 percent). Since 1969 the number of people with incomes below the poverty level has remained fairly stable.

Although no firm evidence is available, many of those who remained poor throughout this period probably have serious disabling health conditions. As poverty has declined, the average level of health of the poor may have worsened because relatively healthier people have moved into higher income classes.

There are some popular misconceptions about who the poor are. Half of them are children under twenty-two (see table 1-2). Fourteen percent are sixty-five or over, the group most likely to be covered by Medicare and Medicaid. Two-thirds of the poor are white, and two out of every five live in nonmetropolitan areas. They are concentrated disproportionately in the South, which has 31 percent of the total population but 44 percent of the poor and 60 percent of poor nonmetropolitan residents. Medicaid, a combined federal-state program, is much more limited in southern states

Table 1-1. Trends in Poverty Income Threshold, Consumer Price Index, and Poverty Population, 1960–76

Year	Poverty income threshold[a] (current dollars)	Consumer price index (1967 = 100)	Poverty population	
			Thousands	As percent of total civilian population
1960	3,022	88.7	39,851	22.4
1961	3,054	89.6	39,628	21.9
1962	3,089	90.6	38,625	21.0
1963	3,128	91.7	36,436	19.5
1964	3,169	92.9	36,055	19.1
1965	3,223	94.5	33,185	17.3
1966	3,317	97.2	28,510	14.7
1967	3,410	100.0	27,769	14.2
1968	3,553	104.2	25,389	12.9
1969	3,743	109.8	24,147	12.1
1970	3,968	116.3	25,420	12.6
1971	4,137	121.3	25,559	12.5
1972	4,275	125.3	24,460	11.8
1973	4,540	133.1	22,973	11.0
1974	5,038	147.7	23,370	11.1
1975	5,500	161.2	25,877	12.2
1976	5,815	170.5	24,975	11.7

Sources: U.S. Bureau of the Census and U.S. Bureau of Labor Statistics.
a. For a nonfarm family of four.

so that many of the gaps in coverage occur among poor southerners and residents of nonmetropolitan areas.

The family composition of the poor is important in the analysis of Medicaid, which bases eligibility, in part, on the presence of children and the absence of a father in the family. Half the states participating in Medicaid do not cover nonelderly two-parent families; the others cover two-parent families only if the father is unemployed and not receiving unemployment compensation.

The characteristics of the poverty population differ greatly by the area in which they live. The majority of the poor in central cities are members of single-parent families, but nearly three-fourths of those in nonmetropolitan areas are from two-parent families (see table 1-3). The Medicaid eligibility restrictions are therefore particularly onerous for the rural poor. The composition of poverty on the basis of race also varies by geographical location: 49 percent of the poor in central cities are black and 73 percent of the nonmetropolitan poor are white.

The Census Bureau's definition of poverty is the general basis for delineating the poor throughout this book. The statistics on health and the use of medical care presented in the following chapters, however, are guided by the availability of data. When the available statistics on income are not adjusted for family composition and residence, as is often the case, income levels of $3,000 in the early 1960s and of $5,000 in the mid-1970s are used to represent poverty. (These income levels correspond roughly to the poverty income thresholds for a family of four at these times.) In some cases, pertinent statistics for the 1970s are only available for those with family income below $6,000. This higher income cutoff takes in roughly 20 percent of the population, as did a $3,000 income level in the early 1960s. In describing these statistics, the terms "low-income" and "poor" are used interchangeably, even though the statistics do not correspond exactly to those that would come under the Census Bureau's definition. Tables presenting data, however, specify the exact income levels involved.

For comparative purposes, health care utilization and the health status of low-income families are contrasted with those of high-income families.

Table 1-2. Distribution of the Poor by Age, Area of Residence, and Race, 1974

Age and area of residence	Number (thousands)	As percent of total poor population		
		Total	White	Black and others
Age				
Under 6	3,294	13.6	8.6	5.0
6–15	6,026	24.8	15.0	9.9
16–21	2,953	12.2	7.5	4.7
22–44	5,192	21.4	15.0	6.4
45–64	3,487	14.4	10.3	4.1
65 and over	3,308	13.6	10.9	2.7
Area of residence[a]				
Metropolitan	14,588	60.1	38.1	22.1
North and West	9,644	39.8	27.0	12.7
South	4,944	20.4	11.0	9.4
Nonmetropolitan	9,672	39.9	29.1	10.8
North and West	3,855	15.9	14.9	1.0
South	5,817	24.0	14.2	9.8
United States	24,260	100.0	67.2	32.8

Source: Bureau of the Census. Figures are rounded.

a. As defined by the Census Bureau, "North and West" includes all states but the sixteen (plus the District of Columbia) of the "South": Alabama, Arkansas, Delaware, Florida, Georgia, Kentucky, Louisiana, Maryland, Mississippi, North Carolina, Oklahoma, South Carolina, Tennessee, Texas, Virginia, and West Virginia.

Table 1-3. Distribution of the Poor, by Type of Family, Race, and Area of Residence, 1974

Area of residence	As percent of all members of poor families		As percent of total poor population	
	Two-parent families	Single-parent families	White	Black and other
Metropolitan	46.0	54.0	63.3	36.7
Central cities	38.7	61.3	51.3	48.7
Outside central cities	57.1	42.9	81.5	18.5
Nonmetropolitan	70.3	29.7	73.0	27.0
United States	56.0	44.0	67.1	32.9

Source: Bureau of the Census.

High income is typically defined as $10,000 and above in the early 1960s; $15,000 and above in the 1970s. Since the consumer price index increased 59 percent between 1964 and 1974, an income of $10,000 in 1964 was roughly equivalent in purchasing power to one of $15,900 in 1974.

A broad definition of health is considered most suitable for this study. One of the broadest is that of the World Health Organization, which defines health as "a state of complete physical, mental, and social well-being."[3] At the other end of the spectrum, some analysts define health as longevity or survival and measure improvement by extended life expectancy or reduced mortality rates without taking into consideration functional status or other factors of health. In general, health is defined in this study as the absence of disease, illness, pain, or physical impairment. A healthy person is one who can expect to live a normal length of time and can function effectively, free of significant pain or suffering from physical causes. Because of the complexities of mental health and the special problems involved in its analysis, the study will concentrate primarily on physical health, although a complete analysis of health ideally should include all factors contributing to physical and mental well-being.[4]

In spite of the broad view taken here, health factors, when measured

3. World Health Organization, *Official Records of the World Health Organization, No. 2: Proceedings and Final Acts of the International Health Conference, New York, 19 June to 22 July 1946* (United Nations, 1948), p. 100.

4. For a treatment of poverty and mental health, see August de Belmont Hollingshead and Frederick C. Redlich, *Social Class and Mental Illness: A Community Study* (Wiley, 1958).

for evaluation purposes, must frequently be restricted to concepts that are readily quantifiable. (Some of the difficulties with widely used ways of measuring are discussed in the next chapter.) Our intention is to explore, where possible, disaggregated measures of health status with a view to isolating the components most susceptible to medical care intervention.

Health care is often distinguished from medical care. Medical care is limited to care provided by physicians or other types of health practitioners and takes place in doctors' offices, hospitals, nursing homes, or other places. Comprehensive health care, on the other hand, encompasses not only medical care but also dental care, mental health, home health care, drugs, health education of patients, nutrition, environmental health, transportation for health services, and other activities to promote good health.

There are two approaches to determining the minimum standard of health care that should be available to all. The first is to establish an absolute standard—similar, say, to the economy food plan used in establishing poverty levels. This standard would be set without reference to patterns of health care among various population groups, but it would be sensitive to the condition of patients and to health needs. In this approach a minimum standard of health care is defined as that which is medically necessary—presumably, anything a physician or other health professional feels is required for a patient. A more restrictive variation would be to include only the portion of medical care that could be demonstrated to significantly affect health.

A second approach is the establishment of relative standards—similar, for example, to setting the poverty level at some fraction of the median income level. This approach is predicated on the view that it is difficult, if not impossible, to measure health adequately and to assess the "need" for or the efficacy of medical care. Rather than establishing some absolute standard, therefore, this approach would establish a minimum standard based on the pattern of health care use of the average American. One minimum standard could be the level of care received by middle-income people for various degrees or kinds of health problems.

Why Is Health Care for the Poor a Social Concern?

Since wide support of health care for the poor is a relatively recent federal government activity, a systematic review of federal health programs should include an examination of the basis for social responsibility for the poor. Differing views of why government should be involved in this activity explain a large portion of the variation in appraisals of the success of the health care programs of the last decade.

To Improve Productivity and Human Potential

One argument for a major governmental role in the provision of health care for the poor is that it is a good investment but one that is unlikely to be undertaken by the poor without governmental support. It is generally conceded that poor health prevents the disadvantaged from competing equally in the marketplace. In some cases the disadvantaged are handicapped from birth, off to a slow start because of inadequate care and nutrition during pregnancy. Limited intelligence and slower rates of growth and development resulting from these prenatal factors lower the potential productivity of the labor force. Poor health care during childhood and adulthood is recognized as causing a rapid loss of functional ability (the ability to hear, move about with ease, lift objects, and so forth), and this loss becomes even more apparent as people move into middle and old age. Hampered by disabling or crippling conditions, many of the poor are unable to lead normally healthy, productive lives. Selected investment in improving the health of the poor can be expected to have a high social payoff in reduced income inequality, reduced economic dependency, and improved productivity and output.[5]

To Maintain Minimum Standards for Human Decency

One major justification for a federal role in ensuring that the poor receive adequate health care is that human beings should have the right not only to survive but to live with dignity. As Okun points out, "the case for a right to survival is compelling. The assurance of dignity for every member of the society requires a right to a decent existence—to some minimum standard of nutrition, health care, and other essentials of life. Starvation and dignity do not mix well."[6]

Unlike the investment motivation, which argues that better health will

5. For estimates of some of the expected benefits, see U.S. Department of Health, Education, and Welfare, Office of the Assistant Secretary (Planning and Evaluation), *Human Investment Programs: Delivery of Health Services for the Poor* (Government Printing Office, December 1967).

6. Arthur M. Okun, *Equality and Efficiency: The Big Tradeoff* (Brookings Institution, 1975), p. 17.

permit the poor to earn more, the human dignity argument requires no demonstrable link. It simply asserts that no one should die for lack of financial resources to obtain adequate nutrition or medical care, and further that no one should suffer desperation or pain for lack of the health care that money can buy. Although opinions might vary about where the line between dignity and luxury should be drawn and what the minimum standard should be, some minimum standard of health care for all seems essential to the preservation of social order and justice.

Closely tied to this rationale is the need to provide the poor and the elderly with a degree of financial security. Giving them a minimum level of income does not guarantee a minimum level of economic welfare, since large, unpredictable outlays caused by the incidence of disease, accidents, or infirmity can make any income level too low to cover the basic amenities.

but why not min income + let them buy insurance because no access to group plans?

To Correct the Failures of the Private Market

A strong role for the federal government in providing the poor with health care is indicated by the numerous failures of the private market. Merely guaranteeing the poor a minimum level of income is unlikely to fulfill social objectives concerning their health.

For example, a guaranteed income level might be sufficient to cover health care needs as well as other basic goods and services if the poor, the elderly, and the disadvantaged purchased insurance against the contingency of illness or accident. Unfortunately, however, private companies have been unable to furnish this protection at a cost many disadvantaged people can afford. Private companies have been reluctant to write comprehensive policies for the elderly for fear of taking on an excessive number of poor risks, which could not be screened effectively even by physical examination. The policies that are available are limited in coverage, exempt preexisting conditions, rarely cover nursing home care in the event of infirmity or senility, and are generally inadequate to protect the elderly and their children from the possibly crushing financial burden of medical catastrophe.

o.k.

Then min income isn't high enough.

The nonelderly poor are in a similar position today. Those who do not work cannot participate in group employment policies with relatively low premium rates. Private companies are reluctant to write comprehensive health insurance policies for the poor, who because of their multiple health problems are considered a bad risk. The few policies offered are

I wonder if it is really this bad?.

usually limited in benefits and require the payment of a premium far in excess of the expected benefits. Often riders attached to policies give companies the option of dropping coverage should the beneficiary become a poor risk. For the disabled poor or those with obviously identifiable poor health, companies are unwilling to provide any coverage at all.

how much is enough?

Other failures of the private market also dictate a more significant role for government. Communities characterized by poverty or racial discrimination do not have enough physicians, other health professionals, or health facilities. Insurance, whether publicly provided or publicly subsidized, cannot be expected to change this quickly. Physicians, attracted by the high incomes to be made in the relative comfort and safety of the suburbs, have been leaving central cities and rural areas for some time. Only a small number of students from minority groups are enrolled in medical and other health professional schools; this contributes to the scarcity of health professionals sensitive to the needs of, and willing to work in, communities dominated by minority groups.[7] To offset these trends, specific policies supplementary to financing—to create new resources in deprived communities and to remove racial and cultural barriers that would prevent the poor from obtaining adequate care even if money or insurance were not a major problem—are necessary.

The health problems of the poor and disadvantaged tend to be both more numerous and more complex than those of the middle and upper income groups. Poor nutrition, inferior housing, inadequate sanitation, and the physical and psychological stresses of unemployment and deprivation all interact to intensify the health problems of the poor. An attack on poor health that focuses exclusively on the medical treatment of illness will not be as successful as one that deals with both the causes and the symptoms of poor health.

In the view of some, the poor bear many social costs imposed on them by a negligent society. These result in poor health, which the poor are largely helpless to avoid. Many feel that the poor should be compensated for their limited access to decent jobs, for the inferior public services— from trash collection to education—furnished them, for the high risks of injury, sickness, or poor health they incur in risky and physically demanding jobs or through industrial pollution and waste in the communities in which they live.

7. According to the *Los Angeles Times,* minority health professionals tend to practice in needy neighborhoods: 80 percent of black physicians practice in rural or urban ghettos, and 50 percent of the patients of black physicians are poor. *Los Angeles Times,* August 4, 1977.

The rationales for social concern about health care for the poor are thus many and lead to a multitude of objectives that have been, and continue to be, embodied in health care programs. Some objectives are primarily concerned with improving the health and productivity of workers—by prolonging life, reducing disability or morbidity, or alleviating debilitating pain. Others emphasize the right of all human beings to minimum levels of the services essential for survival and living with dignity, or more generally the right to minimum levels of economic and social welfare. Still others are concerned with the inability of the private market to deliver efficient, effective, and equitable health care to the poor.

Alternative Courses for Public Policy

Several approaches to achieving these objectives are possible. One would be to provide the poor with sufficient income to spend as they wish, on the presumption that they would invest in their own health—purchasing private health insurance coverage and obtaining adequate health care—as well as buying the other goods and services they need.

Another strategy would be to give the poor vouchers covering health care services. Health insurance represents this approach. Either the poor could be induced by subsidized premiums to purchase private health insurance or it could be provided directly under a public program. With adequate insurance, the poor could obtain care from any physician, hospital, or other qualified health provider they chose.

A third way would be to make direct grants to the providers of health care allowing them to care for the poor free or at low cost. The comprehensive health center program and the Hill-Burton hospital construction program are examples of this approach.

Variations within these broad approaches are also possible. Insurance could be publicly or privately provided and direct grants made to either private or public institutions. Financing could come from the federal government or from a combination of earmarked federal, state, and local revenues.

Income Transfers versus Health Care Transfers

The growth of programs to help the poor buy essential services has led to questions about whether it is better to furnish direct income support to the poor ("Wouldn't the poor be better off if we just gave them the money?") or to support them indirectly through medical care, food stamps, housing allowances, and other in-kind programs.

Cash income maintenance programs (excluding the social security program) accounted for $34 billion of federal outlays in 1975 and in-kind programs to help the poor and elderly purchase essentials cost $33 billion. Public assistance income support of the aged, blind, disabled, and families with dependent children cost $9 billion in federal funds; Medicaid cost $6.5 billion.[8] Replacing Medicaid with higher income support would result in a 70 percent increase in cash to the poor with no additional federal expenditures.

Interesting effect to show on of this on income distribution

Those who favor greater reliance on direct income support advance three major arguments for their case. The first is that the poor are capable of determining their own needs and should be permitted to allocate their dollars among different goods and services in accordance with individual desires. Forcing them to use medical care makes them give up other goods and services—clothing, educational materials, food, the opportunity to live in a better neighborhood—that might bring some of them greater welfare than expenditures on medical care.

A second argument, closely related to the first, is that even if the objective of medical care programs is to improve the health of the poor money spent on nonmedical goods and services may do more to improve it than medical care. Better nutrition, improved housing, and the elimination of safety hazards may be more beneficial than visits to the doctor's office or prescription drugs.

Finally, it is argued that an excessive portion of the money spent on medical care programs winds up in the pockets of the nonpoor—physicians, hospitals, program administrators—and that few of the dollars actually go for the welfare of the poor. Giving the money directly to the poor would encourage them to seek out lower-cost sources of medical care, enabling them to obtain the same level of medical services and have money left over to purchase other goods and services. (Countering this argument is the possibility that the collective purchase of health care services for the poor might achieve a lower price for services than would be obtained if the poor "bargained" individually.)

There is considerable merit to these arguments. But a review of the kinds of services now purchased by medical care programs for the poor

8. Barry M. Blechman, Edward M. Gramlich, and Robert W. Hartman, *Setting National Priorities: The 1975 Budget* (Brookings Institution, 1974), p. 168.

and the objectives of these programs makes it evident that income transfers alone would not suffice.

Almost half of Medicaid funds, for example, go for medical care of the severely ill—those who are confined to nursing homes or who require extensive care because of a host of chronic health problems. Giving these people the average $400 to $500 per capita spent by medical care programs on the poor and disadvantaged would not go far toward meeting their health care needs, when an average hospital stay costs $1,400 and a year in a nursing home $5,000 to $10,000. Nearly all of the one million residents of nursing homes have multiple chronic conditions, averaging three per person, and require extremely costly nursing attention.[9]

Nor could such patients take the $400 to $500 cash grant and purchase a private health insurance policy that would cover their health care needs since most policies exclude both nursing home services and preexisting conditions. Clearly, for the poor with serious health problems, there is no alternative to meeting these costs directly through a public program.

Even if the aged and the disabled are excluded from consideration, income transfers cannot be expected to achieve all the objectives of the health care programs. Younger, healthier poor people may be able to purchase private health insurance, but it is not inexpensive. (Individual coverage involves relatively high administrative and sales costs.[10]) And policies can be complex, with numerous exclusions and limits to protect the insurance companies against bad risks. So long as there is substantial variation in the out-of-pocket medical expenses of the poor, some of them will find any moderate cash income grant insufficient to purchase a minimum level of housing, food, and other goods and services as well as to pay their health care bills.

Even when the variability of expenditures is not a concern—as in the case of routine health checkups, well-baby care, prenatal care, family planning services, routine dental care, and so forth—giving money directly to the poor may not achieve desirable results. The types of preven-

9. According to a 1977 HEW report, 36 percent of nursing home patients have heart trouble, 14 percent have diabetes, and 63 percent are senile. Thirty-one percent were confined to bed or unable to walk without help. Department of Health, Education, and Welfare, National Center for Health Statistics, *Health, United States, 1976–1977,* DHEW (HRA) 77-1232 (GPO, 1977), p. 10.

10. For those not covered by an employer's group insurance plan, each dollar of premium paid returns on the average only 53 cents in health expenditure benefits. Marjorie Smith Mueller, "Private Health Insurance in 1973: A Review of Coverage, Enrollment, and Financial Experience," *Social Security Bulletin,* vol. 38 (February 1975), p. 35.

tive services that have high social payoffs[11] may need to be subsidized to encourage their use.

The objectives of health care programs make it important to ensure that everyone can obtain some minimum level of health care. Simply giving money to the poor is unlikely to induce them to devote their income to this minimum level unless extremely high levels of income support are provided. A less costly method is to directly subsidize the purchase or provision of health care services.

Finally, objectives that require intervention in the types of services provided, and the manner in which they are provided, cannot be readily achieved through income transfers. For example, it is easier to alleviate shortages of health care resources in low-income neighborhoods brought about by long periods of poverty, unemployment, and racial discrimination by direct attacks on this problem than through the indirect method of increasing the purchasing power of the poor. Effective methods of dealing with the interrelated circumstances of limited education, poor nutrition, inadequate sanitation, environmental health problems, and other aspects of poverty require a planned, innovative, coordinated approach rather than simply providing the poor with money and hoping they can overcome the multitude of health problems they face. Compensating them for occupational health and safety hazards, environmental health hazards, and the stresses of unemployment and poverty requires a far finer policy tool than general income transfers.

Financing Health Care for Individuals versus Making Grants to Providers

There are many special health care programs and ways to accomplish these objectives. The poor can be protected from the financial hardship of medical care outlays by providing them with health insurance coverage. Another strategy would be to subsidize the providers of health care services by supporting either public or private institutions such as health care centers and community hospitals.

In 1973 the Nixon administration urged greater concentration on consumer subsidies through health insurance and reduced reliance on sub-

11. Preventive medicine often reduces the monetary (and social) costs of disease. For instance, prenatal care can prevent mental retardation and other birth defects. As society normally bears the costs of disabilities, preventive services are of social concern.

sidies to the suppliers of specific services.[12] There are many reasons for this switch in emphasis, ranging from the fragmentation and proliferation of supply programs that have made them difficult to administer effectively to the desire to give the poor more freedom in selecting a physician or hospital.

Direct assistance to families and individuals is particularly appropriate when consumer choice seems desirable and there is adequate competition among a number of providers of services. Then health insurance can be an efficient means of reducing the financial barriers to medical care utilization and preventing the hardship occasioned by medical care bills. Assisting people to meet medical expenses is a first step in achieving the objective of guaranteeing minimum levels of health services and of economic welfare.

Reliance on this method of support, however, hinges crucially on whether the private market automatically provides services in the most efficient manner. Direct assistance to individuals should be supplanted or supplemented when increased demand is likely to drive up the prices of particular services or induce more costly methods of treatment; when discrimination, scarcity of medical resources, or special difficulties in obtaining care prevent families from making effective use of health insurance; when the social benefits of particular types of medical services are so significant that their use needs to be specifically promoted; and when it is necessary to encourage the development of innovative methods of providing care.

The major difficulty in providing families and individuals with assistance is that the market may respond to their enhanced purchasing power by charging higher prices, thus canceling out the benefits of the subsidy. This danger is less probable—once the market has had a chance to adjust to purchasing power—when the services are competitive and many alternative sources of care are available—a condition that is not characteristic of medical care in most low-income communities. Unless policies are established to curb price increases, health insurance for the poor is likely to be both costly and ineffective.

Even insured families and individuals may be unable to obtain care because of discrimination or a scarcity of medical resources. Institutional rigidity may prevent the market from responding to increased purchasing

12. See *Caspar W. Weinberger to Be Secretary of Health, Education, and Welfare,* Hearings before the Senate Committee on Labor and Public Welfare, 93:1 (GPO, 1973), pt. 2, pp. 13a–55a.

power for long periods of time. Direct grants to develop health centers and facilities in underserved communities may therefore be required, even if consumers are subsidized. To provide medical services to all, some communities may also need other forms of assistance, such as improved transportation or other programs to encourage the use of services.

Subsidies to providers of services are particularly appropriate for making essential services, such as certain types of immunizations, available to all who require them. Drug abuse, alcoholism, venereal disease, and mental illness may not receive adequate attention, even if those suffering from them are insured, unless patients have access to special centers known for their sympathetic treatment of these problems.

Direct grants would also encourage innovation. Institutional barriers often thwart the development of alternative means of providing care at lower cost, particularly if new methods threaten the economic status or prestige of professionals and decisionmakers in the industry. For example, the use of health professionals other than physicians or the growth of organizations relying on such personnel may be minimal without developmental programs sponsored by the government. Coordination of medical care delivery with nonmedical intervention—for instance, specific environmental health activities such as rat control, lead paint poisoning control, mosquito spraying, and human waste disposal—may be the most effective means of making permanent improvements in health. If left to the private market, these public health activities are unlikely to be optimally pursued or integrated with health care delivery.

The advantages of this approach must be weighed against some distinct disadvantages. A proliferation of special purpose programs can greatly complicate administration. Currently, separate federal health programs cover alcoholism, drug abuse, mental health, community health centers, crippled children, maternal and child health, family planning, migrant health, health maintenance organizations, the National Health Service Corps, public health service hospitals, the Indian Health Services, emergency medical services, immunizations, urban rat control, venereal disease control, childhood lead-based paint control, Hansen's disease, Cooley's anemia, and sickle cell anemia. The government also funds separate health programs for welfare recipients, the medically needy, the elderly, the permanently disabled, and people with chronic kidney disease. Such an administrative maze can easily work a hardship on poor families, who do not understand the benefits to which they are entitled or the procedures for obtaining care.

Many of the poor find that their problems do not qualify them for assistance under any program. The crippled children's program covers hemophiliac children in some states but not in others. Children suffering from nutritional deficiencies, parasitic diseases, and ear, nose, and throat infections may receive no care while those with specific crippling conditions receive extensive care. Yet the permanent reduction of productivity and restricted potential for the enjoyment of life resulting from inadequate treatment of the former conditions may be equally great.

Subsidizing specific health care centers can lead to a less equitable distribution of benefits. Poor families living in a neighborhood without a governmentally funded health project may receive no benefits while needy families in a more fortunate community may receive comprehensive care. Similar inequities may also occur in programs that directly assist families. Insurance to pay for health care services does people little good if their community does not have a doctor or a health facility to which they can turn.

If the poor are restricted in their choice of health care providers and forced to turn to specific, limited means of receiving low-cost or free care, they may not be sensitively or responsively served. Political pressure and the risk of public exposé may curb the worst abuses. Greater emphasis might be placed on health care centers or organizations that are controlled by representative community or patient groups.

The multiplicity of objectives and the strengths and weaknesses of alternative approaches make it unlikely that any single strategy for meeting the health care needs of the poor will be adequate or effective. A mixed approach, modified to meet the unique needs of different population groups, is required.

chapter two **Health, Use of Medical Care, and Income**

Since improved access to medical care services for the poor is a common objective of many federal health care programs, it is useful to examine overall trends in medical care utilization and health status before analyzing individual programs. This chapter sets forth the best available evidence on the health problems of the poor, on how these problems differ in severity and type from those of other Americans, and on whether the poor receive adequate medical services. The care received by the poor is compared with that of others to determine whether the amount, type, convenience, quality, or setting of medical care differs by the patient's income. But more important, the *changes* in these differences between income classes from the early 1960s to the 1970s—the years during which so many new programs were introduced—are examined.

It is evident that the poor's access to medical services greatly improved between 1965 and 1975. At the same time, considerable progress was made in selected areas of health that have traditionally been poor for low-income people and that are amenable to medical care—infant mortality rates (particularly postneonatal mortality rates) and deaths from pneumonia and influenza, cervical cancer, cerebrovascular disease, diabetes mellitus, and accidents. It seems plausible, therefore, that in addition to providing the usual benefits of medical care—relief from acute conditions, management and amelioration of chronic conditions, preventive care, prenatal and well-baby care—improved access has contributed to a reduction in mortality from causes sensitive to medical intervention.

Caveats

An effort to document the effects over ten years of federal health care programs cannot be expected to complete the history of these programs. In many ways, an appraisal after only ten years is premature because both the occurrence of changes in health and the reporting of these changes frequently take place after considerable time has elapsed. For example, some studies have stated that the health of babies is dependent on how healthy their mothers were as young children.[1] Thus it takes more than a generation to detect the full effects of improved health. Shorter periods will do for other types of intervention, but still a considerable amount of time must pass before changes appear. Uncorrected ear infections are likely to produce hearing loss only after scar tissue has built up for five to seven years. Uncorrected urinary tract infections may take even longer to show up in permanent kidney damage. The long-term effects of untreated venereal disease, including sterility, blindness, and senility, do not become fully apparent for decades. Many of the untreated acute conditions of childhood and adolescence show up as debilitating and crippling chronic conditions only in middle and old age. The ability of the aged to move about with ease, retain their auditory, visual, and mental faculties, and care for themselves is related, in part, to the adequacy of health care in earlier years.

Systemic changes in the provision of health care also take place only after a considerable time. Programs to help the poor purchase medical services may have limited effects for residents of geographical areas with few physicians or other health professionals. Changes in the distribution of health professionals—brought about by increased emphasis on family practice in medical schools, admission of students from underserved areas, changed attitudes and value orientation, and the guarantee of adequate professional income provided by a medical care financing program—take time.

Another difficulty is that all new programs make jagged steps toward progress. Some efforts inevitably fail, and the experimental approach has to be altered and then tried again. Failures do not imply that the effort is impossible or unworkable but only that rethinking and improvements in design are required. Too precipitate a judgment about success or failure may preclude the growth of an effort that might be successful in the long run.

The Difficulty of Detecting and Measuring Changes

The science of detecting changes in health is inexact and imperfect. Evaluations of public programs are impeded by such obstacles as multiple

1. See, for example, Herbert G. Birch and Joan D. Gussow, *Disadvantaged Children: Health, Nutrition, and School Failure* (Grune and Stratton, 1970).

objectives, not all of which are quantifiable or measurable; crude measurements of even quantifiable effects; inadequate baseline and follow-up data; and the presence of countervening factors that make it difficult to isolate the effects attributable to specific programs.

Most of the literature on operational measurements of health employs a single or composite health index, such as life expectancy or expected disability-free days over the remaining life span.[2] These fail, however, to detect changes in health resulting from government medical care programs. To detect changes, it is important to look not only at overall measurements but also at disaggregated measurements that are expected to be particularly sensitive to improved access to medical care.

Disaggregated measurements of health would include infant and general mortality by cause of death; incidence and severity of acute conditions by type (infective and parasitic, ear, nose, and throat infections, respiratory, digestive, and urinary conditions, dietary deficiencies, skin infections, and so on); incidence of and degree of deterioration from chronic conditions (hypertension, diabetes, kidney disease, heart conditions, arthritis, asthma, and obesity, among others); pregnancy outcomes (prematurity, low birth weight, stillbirth, and miscarriage); functional capacity (disability, handicap, limitation of activity or mobility, inability to work, go to school, or care for oneself, loss of teeth, of hearing, or of vision, for example); accidental death and injuries; deviations from individually

2. See, for example, Warren Balinsky and Renee Berger, "A Review of the Research on General Health Status Indexes," *Medical Care,* vol. 13 (April 1975), pp. 283–93; Robert L. Berg, ed., *Health Status Indexes* (Chicago: Hospital Research and Educational Trust, 1973); J. W. Bush, W. R. Blischke, and C. C. Berry, "Health Indices, Outcomes, and the Quality of Medical Care," in Richard Yaffee and David Zalkind, eds., *Evaluation in Health Services Delivery, Proceedings of an Engineering Foundation Conference, South Berwick, Maine, August 19–24, 1973* (Engineering Foundation, n.d.), pp. 313–39; C. L. Chiang, *An Index of Health: Mathematical Models,* Vital and Health Statistics, series 2, no. 5 (GPO, 1965); S. Franshel and J. W. Bush, "A Health-Status Index and Its Application to Health Services Outcomes," *Operations Research,* vol. 18 (November–December 1970), pp. 1021–66; Seth B. Goldsmith, "A Reevaluation of Health Status Indicators," *Health Services Reports,* vol. 88 (December 1973; published by GPO), pp. 937–41; Donald L. Patrick, J. W. Bush, and Milton M. Chen, "Methods for Measuring Levels of Well-being for a Health Status Index," *Health Services Research,* vol. 8 (Fall 1973), pp. 228–45; Richard M. Scheffler and Joseph Lipscomb, "Alternative Estimations of Population Health Status: An Empirical Example," *Inquiry,* vol. 11 (September 1974), pp. 220–28; Daniel F. Sullivan, "A Single Index of Mortality and Morbidity," *HSMHA Health Reports,* vol. 86 (GPO, 1971), pp. 347–54; Daniel F. Sullivan, *Conceptual Problems in Developing an Index of Health,* Vital and Health Statistics, series 2, no. 17 (GPO, 1966); James E. Veney, "Health Status Indicators," *Inquiry,* vol. 10 (December 1973), pp. 3–4.

desired family sizes and spacing of children; unremedied health defects in children (hearing, visual, dental, growth and development); and level of preventive services (as indicators of the probability of future impairment or death).

Even if sensitive indicators of health could be isolated, gaps and deficiencies in the available data impede extensive analyses. Few data correlating health statistics with socioeconomic characteristics are available. Mortality data, for example, though based on one of the most clear-cut and measurable dimensions of health, are drawn from death certificate records, which do not indicate family income or socioeconomic status.

Nor are data often disaggregated by important subpopulations. Migrant workers, sharecroppers in the Mississippi delta, or mountaineers may have severe health problems or marked improvements in health, but these are not adequately captured by averages for the poor as a whole.

Measurements of health for those covered by public programs are particularly rare. For example, the infant mortality rate for mothers covered by Medicaid or by other health programs for the poor is not currently known and cannot be compared with the rate for low-income mothers not covered by a health program.

Clearly, the methodological difficulties of isolating the contribution of medical care to health are great. Interactions between indexes of health and medical care utilization make it difficult to disentangle the causes of change. Increases in life expectancy may lead to increases in chronic conditions and disability. Infant mortality may have been reduced because more premature or low-birth-weight babies survive, but their average health may be poorer than that of the babies who survived when many died at birth. As more people receive regular physical examinations, they may learn of health conditions of which they were previously unaware. Responses to household interview surveys are therefore likely to show increases in health problems for groups that are making increased use of medical care services.

The many factors that affect health make it difficult to isolate the contribution of any one, whether it is medical care, adequate income, diet and nutrition, housing, education, personal habits, sanitation, environmental conditions, or genetic factors. At a given time, the poor may be less healthy than others for several reasons: they are less able to pay for necessary medical care; medical care is less available in their communities; with limited education they are unaware of good health practices or unable to use the medical care system effectively; cultural barriers keep them from recognizing health problems and seeking care for them; they may work in jobs or live in communities that are deleterious to health because of occupational health and safety hazards or environmental conditions; conditions in the home related to family size, marital stability, and age and spacing of children may not be conducive to good health; and so forth.[3] The relation between poverty and health may also exhibit two-way causality, with poor health leading to a reduction in productivity and consequent diminished earning power and income.[4]

Detecting the contribution of changes in any of these elements to changes in health is also difficult, because past patterns of poor health or lack of medical care may have adverse effects that persist for a long time. For example, a chronic condition, once incurred, may not be reversible and may continue to deteriorate even with the best of ameliorative medical care.

There are many factors that may explain different changes in health among income classes: improved medical care received by the poor; reduction in poverty and higher real incomes among lower-income families; general economic conditions of unemployment and inflation; food stamp, nutrition, and other governmental programs to improve the economic and social well-being of the poor; better birth control methods; worsening environmental conditions such as air and water pollution, noise pollution, and the use of chemicals and food additives; and changes in personal

3. For annotated bibliographies of the extensive literature on health and poverty, see Robert L. Kane, Josephine M. Kasteler, and Robert M. Gray, eds., *The Health Gap: Medical Services and the Poor* (Springer, 1976); Lu Ann Aday and Ronald Andersen, *Development of Indices of Access to Medical Care* (University of Michigan, Health Administration Press, 1975); and James C. Stewart and Lottie Lee Crafton, *Delivery of Health Care Services to the Poor: Findings from a Review of the Current Periodical Literature, With a Key to 47 Reports of Innovative Projects* (University of Texas at Austin, Center for Social Work Research, School of Social Work, 1975), and Crafton and Stewart, *Delivery of Health Care Services to the Poor: Abstracts from Health Care Journals, 1967–1974* (University of Texas at Austin, Center for Social Work Research, Graduate School of Social Work, n.d.), boxed cards. Other general references on the subject include Ronald Andersen, Joanna Kravits, and Odin W. Anderson, eds., *Equity in Health Services: Empirical Analyses in Social Policy* (Ballinger, 1975); E. Gartly Jaco, ed., *Patients, Physicians, and Illness: A Sourcebook in Behavioral Science and Health* (Free Press, 1972); John Kosa and Irving K. Zola, eds., *Poverty and Health: A Sociological Analysis,* rev. ed. (Harvard University Press, 1975); Judith R. Lave and Samuel Leinhardt, "The Delivery of Ambulatory Care to the Poor: A Literature Review," *Management Science,* vol. 19 (December 1972), pt. 2, pp. P-78–P-99.

4. For an exploration of the effect of poor health on earnings, see Harold Stephen Luft, "Poverty and Health: An Empirical Investigation of the Economic Interactions" (Ph.D. dissertation, Harvard University, 1972).

habits such as diet, exercise, smoking, alcohol consumption, and drug usage.[5] Although some of them may affect all income groups, they are unlikely to do so equally. Not all of them can be expected to work in the same direction; some may improve health but others may undercut such improvements.

Does Medical Care Improve Health?

The combination of conceptual difficulties and inadequate data have led some investigators to conclude that medical care can do little to improve health.[6] Views range from the proposition that Americans now receive so much medical care that more would have little effect on health to the stronger assertion that medical care as a whole does little for health. The most extreme critics suggest that medical care does more harm than good—through excessive surgery, overmedication, adverse drug reactions,

5. Literature stressing one or another of these factors includes Leon Gordis, "Effectiveness of Comprehensive-Care Programs in Preventing Rheumatic Fever," *New England Journal of Medicine,* vol. 289 (August 16, 1973), pp. 331–35; Nedra B. Belloc and Lester Breslow, "Relationship of Physical Health Status and Health Practices," *Preventive Medicine,* vol. 1 (August 1972), pp. 409–21; David M. Kessner, project director, *Infant Death: An Analysis by Maternal Risk and Health Care* (National Academy of Sciences, 1973); M. Harvey Brenner, *Mental Illness and the Economy* (Harvard University Press, 1973); U.S. Environmental Protection Agency, *Pollution and Your Health* and *Health Effects of Air Pollution* (both EPA, Office of Public Affairs, 1976); World Bank, *The Assault on World Poverty: Problems of Rural Development, Education, and Health* (Johns Hopkins University Press, 1975).

6. See, for example, Victor R. Fuchs, *Who Shall Live? Health, Economics, and Social Choice* (Basic Books, 1974); Nathan Glazer, "Paradoxes of Health Care," *Public Interest,* no. 22 (Winter 1971), pp. 62–77; Leon R. Kass, "Regarding the End of Medicine and the Pursuit of Health," *Public Interest,* no. 40 (Summer 1975), pp. 11–42; *Economic Report of the President, January 1976,* chap. 3; and Lee Benham and Alexandra Benham, "The Impact of Incremental Medical Services on Health Status, 1963–1970," in Andersen and others, *Equity in Health Services,* pp. 217–28. A similar argument for Canada is presented in Marc Lalonde, *A New Perspective on the Health of Canadians* (Ottawa: Information Canada, 1975). Ivan Illich, *Medical Nemesis: The Expropriation of Health* (Random House, 1976), and Rick J. Carlson, *The End of Medicine* (Wiley, 1975), are among the most outspoken critics. Excesses of medicine and overuse are documented in John P. Bunker, "Surgical Manpower: A Comparison of Operations and Surgeons in the United States and in England and Wales," *New England Journal of Medicine,* vol. 282 (January 15, 1970), pp. 135–44; and *New York Times,* January 26–30, 1976: Boyce Rensberger, "Few Doctors Ever Report Colleagues' Incompetence"; Boyce Rensberger, "Unfit Doctors Create Worry in Profession"; Jane E. Brody, "Incompetent Surgery Is Found Not Isolated"; Boyce Rensberger, "Thousands a Year Killed by Faulty Prescriptions"; and Jane E. Brody, "How Educated Patients Get Proper Health Care."

and other such iatrogenic illnesses. Illich, for example, begins *Medical Nemesis* with the statement: "The medical establishment has become a major threat to health."[7]

In the abuse directed at the medical profession, fact, fiction, and fantasy are indiscriminately intertwined. Some claims are based on spotty or inaccurate evidence; contraindicative evidence is frequently ignored.[8]

The indisputable claims that have been made include: (1) historically, most of the reduction in death rates has resulted from public health and nonmedical improvements, such as immunizations, sanitation, and standard of living; (2) many of the leading causes of death today (suicide, homicide, accidents, cirrhosis of the liver, heart attacks, and some forms of cancer) are closely linked to environmental health hazards, life style, and personal habits, and thus for those currently receiving adequate medical care, the greatest contributions to better health are likely to be found in altered life styles and elimination of personal and occupational or environmental hazards; and (3) excessive confidence in the all-healing power of medicine has led in some instances to the provision of medical services of negligible benefit or demonstrable harm.

It is an overstatement, however, to assert that medical care does no good or that there are no groups in the United States that could benefit from improved access to it. There can be little doubt that for a wide range of conditions such care is essential to the preservation or restoration of health, as anyone who has ever suffered a broken bone, acute appendicitis, venereal disease, pneumonia, hypertension, or a ruptured spleen can attest. Nor is there much doubt that additional medical care would be of value to those who find it difficult to obtain even basic services—many poor people, members of minority groups, and residents of inner cities or rural areas. Even for these people, however, the most effective strategies for improving health may well be approaches that combine both medical care and attacks on the nonmedical causes of poor health.

A balanced assessment of the claims made about the relation of medical care to health requires evidence on the composition of medical care expenditures by kinds of care and on the kinds of improvements in health that can be reasonably expected. Much of the distortion of the discussion

7. Illich, *Medical Nemesis*, p. 3.

8. An evaluation of some of the econometric evidence—most of which is seriously flawed methodologically—is presented in the appendix. The rest of this chapter discusses the evidence on health trends by income class. Chapters 5 and 6 survey a number of case studies documenting the relation between the care provided by the comprehensive health centers and the health of the patients they served.

of health and medical care derives from a preoccupation with mortality. While medical care is essential to avert death in some emergencies, most medical expenditures are incurred in the diagnosis, treatment, and rehabilitation of acute and chronic conditions that are not immediately life-threatening (although without adequate care these conditions may result in avoidable pain and discomfort, gradual deterioration into more serious conditions, loss of functional capability, and shortened life span). Care that is largely informational (family planning, counseling, assessment of physical state and risks of future conditions) is also of considerable value and might appropriately be classified as a health benefit.

In short, the potential benefits of medical care vary from case to case. The effect of improved medical care on health can best be detected by looking at disaggregated measures of health status and the content of medical care.

The Human Side of Health

No examination of statistics depicting overall trends in health can reveal the human suffering and agony that lie behind them. One of the most poignant accounts of what it means to live in poverty and not receive adequate health care is contained in a report by Raymond Wheeler, M.D., who examined children in the South and in the ghettos of northern cities as a member of the Citizens Board of Inquiry into Hunger in the United States in the spring of 1970. He recounts:

Wherever we went, in the South, the Southwest, Florida or Appalachia, the impact was the same, varying only in degree or in appalling detail. . . .

We saw housing and living conditions horrible and dehumanizing to the point of our disbelief. In Florida and in Texas, we visited living quarters constructed as long cinder-block or wooden sheds, divided into single rooms by walls which do not reach the ceilings. Without heat, adequate light or ventilation, and containing no plumbing or refrigeration, each room (no larger than 8 x 14 feet) is the living space of an entire family, appropriately suggesting slave quarters of earlier days. . . .

In all of the areas we visited, the nearly total lack of even minimally adequate medical care and health services was an early and easily documented observation. Again, that which most Americans now agree to be a right of citizenship, was unavailable to most of the people whom we saw. . . .

We saw hundreds of people whose only hope of obtaining medical care was to become an emergency which could not be turned away. . . .

Most of these people live constantly at the brink of medical disaster, hoping that the symptoms they have or the pain they feel will prove transient or can somehow be survived, for they know that no help is available to them. . . .

For the majority of the hundreds of people we examined, it was a different, frustrating, and heartbreaking story. We saw people with most of the dreadful disorders that weaken, disable, and torture, particularly the poor.

High blood pressure, diabetes, urinary tract infections, anemia, tuberculosis, gall bladder and intestinal disorders, eye and skin diseases were frequent findings among the adults.

Almost without exception, intestinal parasites were found in the stool specimens examined. Most of the children had chronic skin infections. Chronically infected, draining ears with resulting partial deafness occurred in an amazing number of the smaller children. We saw rickets, a disorder thought to be nearly abolished in this country. Every form of vitamin deficiency known to us that could be identified by clinical examination was reported.[9]

Nor have these conditions been eradicated since 1970. A report on the Rio Grande valley in Texas in the fall of 1975 echoed many of the same problems:

Almost a decade later, conditions are still the same. The floor in de Hoyas's one-bedroom shack sags dangerously. A single 40-watt bulb burns in the tiny living room, which serves as the bedroom for the four de Hoyas children. A mosquito-infested drainage canal runs alongside the house. . . . Ninety-five percent of the homes have outdoor toilets. Most have been hand-built and are badly in need of repairs.

Balboans have to haul in household and drinking water in broken-down pickups and trailers from a faucet nearly a mile away. The water comes from an irrigation ditch with an abnormally high concentration of fecal organisms. . . . Farmworker Pablo Castañeda says that his children are sick much of the time from the *agua peligrosa.* "I feel anger and I feel pain," he says. "People want to shut their eyes and not think about us. But we have suffered for quite a while now." . . . There are diseases in the magic valley that were virtually wiped out years ago in other parts of the country—whooping cough, tuberculosis, typhus and amoebiasis. Infant mortality is also very high, and Dr. Paul Musgrave, medical director for twenty of Texas's southernmost counties, says, "We don't exactly advertise it, but it's not uncommon for us to have leprosy down here."[10]

Health Status: Trends in the Differences between Socioeconomic Groups

Although the gap between the health of the poor and that of others narrowed in the decade 1965–75, it has not disappeared. Of the health trends for which data are available, reduction in mortality rates was the most dramatic. Mortality data by income are available for the earlier period,

9. Raymond Wheeler, "Health and Human Resources," *New South,* vol. 26 (Fall 1971), pp. 3–4.
10. "Mañana," *Newsweek* (November 24, 1975), pp. 16, 21, 22.

but have not yet been reported for the mid-1970s. Strong evidence suggests, however, that reductions in mortality have been concentrated disproportionately in the lower income classes. Rates for blacks and Indians have declined at a faster rate than for whites. The rates for the causes of death that have traditionally been highest among the poor are the ones that have fallen the most rapidly.

By contrast, little progress in reducing the prevalence of chronic conditions was made from 1965 to 1975. Restriction of activity from acute and chronic conditions increased slightly, and the poor made no gains relative to others. Perhaps this is not surprising. Better medical care for the poor cannot be expected to show up in reduced prevalence of chronic conditions for decades yet. Most of the immediate benefit would take the form of amelioration or a more gradual deterioration of functional capability. Better medical care would also affect the incidence of only a small portion of acute conditions, those such as contagious diseases, which can be prevented by immunization. For most acute conditions, better medical care provides relief of pain and discomfort and lessens the probability that serious, chronic conditions will develop.

General Mortality by Cause of Death

One of the oldest and most common ways to measure health is mortality. Its popularity can be traced in part to the fact that counting deaths provides a readily quantifiable measure and one that is reported with reasonable accuracy over a long period of time. But it is also undeniable that extending life or averting death is one of the most socially valued "improvements" in health.

Several measures of mortality are available: the crude death rate, or simply the number of deaths divided by the population; age-adjusted death rates, which are based on a standard age composition of the population; and life expectancy rates, which indicate the average number of years remaining for an age group at different points in the life cycle.[11]

11. In recent years, there have been divergences between the crude death rate and the age-adjusted death rates. As birth rates decline, the average age of the population rises. With old people accounting for a larger share of the population, the proportion of deaths automatically rises. Therefore, in making comparisons over time or in comparing current populations with markedly different age distributions, it is important to look at age-adjusted death rates or life expectancy rates.

See, for example, U.S. Department of Health, Education, and Welfare, National Center for Health Statistics, *Mortality Trends: Age, Color, and Sex, United States— 1950–69,* Vital and Health Statistics, series 20, no. 15, DHEW (HRA) 74-1852 (GPO, 1973), pp. 11–13.

Table 2-1. Age-adjusted Death Rates per 100,000 Population, All Causes of Death and Fifteen Causes, Selected Years, 1950-74

Cause of death	1950	1960	1965	1969	1974	Percentage change	
						1950-74	1965-74
All causes[a]	841.5	760.9	741.8	730.9	666.2	-20.8	-10.2
Leading causes with a downturn in mortality							
Diseases of the heart	307.6	286.2	275.6	262.3	232.7	-24.3	-15.6
Cerebrovascular diseases	88.8	79.7	73.1	68.5	59.9	-32.5	-18.1
Accidents	57.5	49.9	53.4	55.3	46.0	-20.0	-13.9
Influenza and pneumonia	26.2	28.0	23.4	24.6	16.9	-35.5	-27.8
Certain causes of mortality in early infancy[b]	40.5	37.4	28.6	21.4	13.6	-66.4	-52.4
Diabetes mellitus	14.3	13.6	13.5	14.5	12.5	-12.6	-7.4
Arteriosclerosis	16.2	13.2	12.0	9.2	7.6	-53.1	-36.7
Congenital anomalies[b]	12.2	12.2	10.1	8.4	6.4	-47.5	-36.6
Nephritis and nephrosis	16.6	6.5	5.2	3.9	n.a.	...	...
Peptic ulcer	5.0	5.2	4.3	3.6	n.a.	...	...
Leading causes with an upturn in mortality							
Malignant neoplasms	125.4	125.8	127.9	129.7	131.8	5.1	3.0
Bronchitis, emphysema, and asthma	3.7	8.2	11.6	12.0	9.2	148.6	-20.7
Cirrhosis of the liver	8.5	10.5	12.1	14.2	14.8	74.1	22.3
Suicide	11.0	10.6	11.4	11.3	12.2	10.9	7.0
Homicide	5.4	5.2	6.2	8.6	10.8	100.0	74.2

Source: U.S. Department of Health, Education, and Welfare, Division of Vital Statistics.
n.a. Not available.
a. Includes causes not shown separately.
b. Crude death rates.

The twenty-five years from 1950 to 1974 were characterized by steady reductions in the age-adjusted death rate, which fell from 842 per 100,000 in 1950 to 666 per 100,000 in 1974, a decline of 21 percent (see table 2-1). From 1965 to 1974 the age-adjusted death rate declined by 10 percent, and deaths from ten of fifteen leading causes dropped. Between 1965 and 1974 deaths from diseases of the heart declined 16 percent; cerebrovascular diseases, 18 percent; accidents, 14 percent; influenza and pneumonia, 28 percent; diabetes mellitus, 7 percent; and arteriosclerosis, 37 percent. Since these causes of death are potentially amenable to medical intervention, it is plausible that increased use of medical care played a part in achieving the reduction.

Over this period the only increases in major causes of death were for cancer (up 3 percent), cirrhosis of the liver (up 22 percent), suicide (up 7 percent), and homicide (up 74 percent). Deaths from these causes are believed to be linked to personal habits or adverse environmental conditions—alcohol consumption, cigarette smoking, violence, stresses of urban living, pollution, use of hazardous chemicals and substances. Improved medical care could not be expected to reduce deaths from these causes substantially.

One important exception is cervical cancer. With early detection through Pap smears, a reduction in cancer of this type might be expected to follow greater use of medical services by women. The age-adjusted rate for deaths from malignant neoplasms of female genital organs did in fact decline steadily, down 10 percent for white women and 12 percent for women of other races from 1965 to 1969.

Data on trends in mortality rates by income classes are not yet available, but a common proxy for income differences is comparing mortality rates by race. Although a higher proportion of blacks than of whites are poor,[12] a minority of both races are poor, so differences by income may not be detected by racial comparisons.

Mortality rates for blacks and other nonwhites declined more than those for whites from 1965 to 1974. Age-adjusted death rates fell 10 percent for whites and 13 percent for blacks and others, but blacks continued to have substantially higher death rates than whites—more than 40 percent higher. Relative improvements for blacks and other nonwhites were

12. In 1973, 9 percent of the white population fell below the poverty level as against 32 percent of blacks and persons of other races. Bureau of the Census, *Current Population Reports,* series P-23, no. 46, "The Social and Economic Status of the Black Population in the United States, 1972" (GPO, 1973), p. 28.

particularly notable for cerebrovascular diseases and influenza and pneumonia. Rates for deaths from malignant neoplasms and cirrhosis of the liver increased more rapidly for nonwhites than for whites, however, widening the differences by race for these causes of death.

Statistics on American Indians suggest that, during a period of greatly increased expenditures for Indian health care, there have been quite astonishing drops in mortality rates from a number of causes amenable to better medical care. Between 1960 and 1974 crude death rates of Indians from influenza and pneumonia fell 68 percent and death rates from certain diseases of early infancy fell 81 percent. Infant mortality rates plummeted from 50 deaths per 1,000 live births in 1960 to 19 in 1974.[13] Between 1955 and 1971 death rates from tuberculosis fell 86 percent, and death rates from enteritis and other diarrheal diseases 89 percent. In 1971, however, both rates were still four times as high as those for the U.S. population.[14] Offsetting these declines somewhat was a tripling of the death rate from cirrhosis of the liver.

It is a well-documented fact that the poor and less educated have higher death rates than others.[15] A 1962–63 study of death rates by age, sex, and family income in the year before death showed that death rates of males and females under fifty-five were about six to ten times higher for those with family incomes below $2,000 than for those with family incomes above $8,000.[16] Some of the difference might be because people with long illnesses may have had abnormally low incomes in the year before death.

13. *Special Analyses, Budget of the United States Government, Fiscal Year 1978,* p. 222.

14. *Federal Health Policies in Rural Areas,* Appendix to Hearings before the Subcommittee on Family Farms and Rural Development of the House Committee on Agriculture, 93:2 (GPO, 1974), pt. 2, p. 88.

15. See, for example, Evelyn M. Kitagawa and Philip M. Hauser, *Differential Mortality in the United States: A Study in Socioeconomic Epidemiology* (Harvard University Press, 1973); HEW, National Center for Health Statistics, *Socioeconomic Characteristics of Deceased Persons, United States—1962–1963 Deaths,* series 22, no. 9 (GPO, 1969); NCHS, *Selected Vital and Health Statistics in Poverty and Nonpoverty Areas of 19 Large Cities, United States, 1969–71,* Vital and Health Statistics, series 21, no. 26, DHEW (HRA) 76-1904 (GPO, 1975); HEW, Office of the Assistant Secretary (Planning and Evaluation), *Delivery of Health Services for the Poor* (GPO, 1967); Lawrence Bergner and Alonzo S. Yerby, "Low Income and Barriers to Use of Health Services," *New England Journal of Medicine,* vol. 278 (March 7, 1968), pp. 541–46, reprinted in Kane and others, *The Health Gap,* pp. 27–39; Aaron Antonovsky, "Social Class, Life Expectancy and Overall Mortality," *Milbank Memorial Fund Quarterly,* vol. 45 (April 1967), pt. 1, reprinted in Jaco, *Patients, Physicians and Illness;* and NCHS, *Health, United States, 1976–1977,* DHEW (HRA) 77-1232 (GPO, 1977).

16. National Center for Health Statistics, *Socioeconomic Characteristics of Deceased Persons, United States—1962–1963 Deaths,* p. 21.

However, this seems less likely to explain high death rates among low-income younger women, since family income is not usually as dependent on the employability and health of female family members.

Kitagawa and Hauser matched death certificates with 1960 census records for deaths in the United States from May to August 1960. They found that age-adjusted mortality rates were 80 percent higher for white male family members twenty-five to sixty-four years old with family incomes under $2,000 than for similar males with family incomes of $10,000 or more. For white female family members, the mortality rate was 40 percent higher in the lowest family income class than in the highest.[17]

Kitagawa and Hauser also compared death rates by cause with educational levels (without holding income constant). They found that in 1960 for white males twenty-five years old and over those with less than eight years of education had higher death rates than those with a year or more of college from the following causes: tuberculosis (four times as high), malignant neoplasms (13 percent higher), diabetes mellitus (25 percent), cerebrovascular diseases (24 percent), hypertensive disease (23 percent), influenza and pneumonia (60 percent), accidents (71 percent), and suicide (87 percent). But college-educated white males had higher age-adjusted death rates than white males with less than eight years of education for malignant neoplasm of the prostate (95 percent) and cirrhosis of the liver (6 percent). Deaths were not appreciably different for many types of cardiovascular and renal diseases. Among white women, those with a college education tended to have similarly lower death rates with the exception of malignant neoplasms of the breast, where death rates were 42 percent higher for college-educated women than for women with less than eight years of education, and cirrhosis of the liver, where death rates were about the same for both groups.[18]

Conclusive evidence on trends in mortality rates by income and educational class from the mid-1960s to the mid-1970s will have to await follow-up studies linking death certificate information with other sources of data on socioeconomic characteristics. It is interesting to note, however, that the death rates that have declined most rapidly over this period are those for the same causes that have traditionally had the highest incidence among the poor and less educated. This strongly suggests that when follow-up data do become available a narrowing of the differences in death rates by income and education will be found.

17. *Differential Mortality in the United States,* pp. 8–10, 18.
18. Ibid., pp. 76–77.

Infant Mortality, Maternal Mortality, and the
Deaths of Young Children

A second, widely used way of measuring health status is infant mortality. This way of measuring is popular because it has been recorded over long periods of time for many subpopulations of the United States. Beyond these advantages, however, the infant mortality rate is believed to be especially sensitive to the adequacy of medical care and thus a good indicator of the influence of improved medical care on health.[19]

Table 2-2. Infant and Maternal Mortality Rates in the United States, by Race, Selected Years, 1950–74

Rate per 1,000 live births

							Percentage change	
Age and race	*1950*	*1955*	*1960*	*1965*	*1970*	*1974*	*1965–74*	*1950–74*
				Infant mortality				
Under 28 days								
White	19.4	17.7	17.2	16.1	13.8	11.1	−31.1	−42.8
Nonwhite	27.5	27.2	26.9	25.4	21.4	17.2	−32.3	−37.5
All races	20.5	19.1	18.7	17.7	15.1	12.3	−30.5	−40.0
28 days to 1 year								
White	7.4	5.9	5.7	5.4	4.0	3.7	−31.5	−50.0
Nonwhite	16.9	15.6	16.4	14.9	9.5	7.7	−48.3	−54.4
All races	8.7	7.3	7.3	7.0	4.9	4.4	−37.1	−49.4
Total, under 1 year								
White	26.8	23.6	22.9	21.5	17.8	14.8	−31.2	−44.8
Nonwhite	44.5	42.8	43.2	40.3	30.9	24.9	−38.2	−44.0
All races	29.2	26.4	26.0	24.7	20.0	16.7	−32.4	−42.8
				Maternal mortality				
White	0.6	0.3	0.3	0.2	0.1	0.1	−50.0	−83.3
Nonwhite	2.2	1.3	1.0	0.8	0.6	0.4	−50.0	−81.8
All races	0.8	0.5	0.4	0.3	0.2	0.1	−66.7	−87.5

Source: HEW, Division of Vital Statistics.

Infant mortality rates are defined as the number of babies alive at birth who die within the first year. Neonatal death rates measure deaths under the age of twenty-eight days per 1,000 live births; postneonatal death rates measure deaths between the ages of twenty-eight days and one year.

Infant mortality rates dropped markedly from 1965 to 1974, from 24.7 deaths per 1,000 live births in 1965 to 16.7 in 1974 (see table 2-2). This

19. See, for example, Kessner, *Infant Death*.

followed a period of relative stability from 1950 to 1965. From 1965 to 1974 postneonatal death rates fell slightly more rapidly than neonatal rates—37 percent and 30 percent, respectively. Infant mortality rates for several gastrointestinal diseases declined markedly, as did those for influenza and pneumonia and for prematurity. Maternal deaths resulting from complications of childbirth—much rarer than infant deaths—declined by two-thirds between 1965 and 1974 and by almost 90 percent between 1950 and 1974.

These improvements were also shared by young children. Death rates for children one to four years old fell by 14 percent from 1965 to 1973 (table 2-3). An increasing number of small children as well as of children aged five to fourteen died in motor vehicle accidents. Deaths from influenza and pneumonia, however, declined dramatically for both age groups from 1965 to 1973. In contrast to trends for older people, malignant neoplasms took a smaller toll among children during this period, perhaps because of the breakthroughs made ten years ago in the treatment of acute leukemia.

Table 2-3. Death Rates of Children per 100,000, All Causes of Death and Five Leading Causes, Selected Years, 1950–73

Age and cause of death	1950	1960	1965	1970	1973	Percentage change 1950–73	Percentage change 1965–73
One to four, all causes	139.4	109.1	92.9	84.5	79.5	−43.0	−14.4
Motor vehicle accidents	11.5	10.0	10.5	11.5	12.3	7.0	17.1
Accidents other than motor vehicle	25.3	21.6	21.3	20.0	19.6	−22.5	−8.0
Congenital anomalies	11.1	12.9	10.2	9.7	9.6	−13.5	−5.9
Malignant neoplasms	11.7	10.9	8.6	7.5	6.4	−45.3	−25.6
Influenza and pneumonia	18.9	16.2	11.4	7.6	5.9	−68.8	−48.2
Five to fourteen, all causes	60.1	46.6	42.2	41.3	41.0	−31.8	−2.8
Motor vehicle accidents	8.8	7.9	8.9	10.2	10.6	20.5	19.1
Accidents other than motor vehicle	13.8	11.3	9.8	9.9	10.2	−26.1	4.1
Congenital anomalies	2.4	3.6	2.8	2.2	2.2	−8.3	−21.4
Malignant neoplasms	6.7	6.8	6.5	6.0	5.4	−19.4	−16.9
Influenza and pneumonia	3.2	2.6	2.1	1.6	1.4	−56.2	−33.3

Source: Department of Health, Education, and Welfare, National Center for Health Statistics, *Health, United States, 1975*, DHEW (HRA) 76-1232 (NCHS, 1976), pp. 359, 361.

As is the case for general mortality rates, data on trends in mortality rates for infants and young children by income group are not yet available. Indirect evidence, however, suggests that the poor may have experienced relatively more improvement than others. Infant mortality declined for both whites and nonwhites, but declined somewhat more rapidly for non-whites between 1965 and 1974 (see table 2-2). In 1965 the infant mortality rate for blacks and other nonwhites was 87 percent higher than for whites; by 1974 it was 68 percent higher. Nearly all of the improvement in the infant mortality rate of nonwhites relative to whites occurred in the postneonatal period.

Other indirect evidence on trends in infant mortality rates by socio-economic class is discovered when trends in infant mortality rates are broken down by states. Table 2-4 shows total, neonatal, and postneonatal infant mortality rates by states arranged in groups of ten according to the incidence of poverty. In 1965 the infant mortality rate in the ten states with the highest rates of poverty was 29.5 deaths per 1,000 live births, 1.3 times that of the ten states with the lowest rates of poverty. Between 1965 and 1974 infant mortality declined more rapidly in the ten highest-poverty states than in most of the other states, reducing this ratio to 1.19 by 1974. The neonatal and postneonatal components of the total infant mortality rate make it apparent that the major gains in the high-poverty states rela-tive to the low-poverty states came in postneonatal death rates.

Several studies have documented the wide variation in infant mortality rates by the socioeconomic characteristics of families.[20] One study for the period 1964–66 found that infant mortality rates were 61 percent higher for families with incomes below $3,000 than for families with incomes of $10,000 and above. Furthermore, the date of death and cause of death differed greatly among families. The death rate for infants seven to twenty-seven days old in low-income families was 2.7 times higher than for those in high-income families, and the death rate for infants of one to five months in low-income families was four times as high as for those in high-income families.[21] Babies of low birth weight are also more common in

20. National Center for Health Statistics, *Infant Mortality Rates: Socioeconomic Factors, United States,* Vital and Health Statistics, series 22, no. 14, DHEW (HSM) 72-1045 (GPO, 1972); NCHS, *Health, United States, 1975;* NCHS, *Trends in "Prematurity," United States, 1950–67,* Vital and Health Statistics, series 3, no. 15, DHEW (HSM) 72-1030 (GPO, 1972); NCHS, *Selected Vital and Health Statistics in Poverty and Nonpoverty Areas of 19 Large Cities, 1969–71;* and Kessner, *Infant Death.*

21. National Center for Health Statistics, *Infant Mortality Rates.*

low-income families, with a concomitantly higher risk of death, mental retardation, and other crippling defects.[22]

Causes of infant deaths that are more prevalent in low-income families are infective and parasitic diseases, influenza, pneumonia and other respiratory diseases, accidents, and gastritis, duodenitis, and other diseases of the digestive system. These types of conditions are the most dangerous for babies who have been discharged from the hospital and taken home. Improper sterilization of bottles, impure water, or unsafe sanitation may cause diarrhea, which can quickly lead to severe dehydration, hospitalization, and death. Crowding, inadequate heating and ventilation, and the presence of siblings increase the incidence of respiratory illness. These illnesses, which strike babies during vulnerable, formative stages, can in many cases be effectively combated by prompt medical attention. Delay in seeking medical care is probably more common among low-income families.

Chronic Conditions and Limitation of Activity

There is little evidence that the poor experienced any reduction in the incidence of long-term chronic health problems in the ten-year period. For people between forty-five and sixty-four, the prevalence of chronic conditions such as arthritis, diabetes, hearing and visual impairments, heart conditions, and hypertension remains two to three times higher for those with low incomes than for others.[23]

It would be incorrect to conclude, however, that medical care programs for the poor have had no effect. As the death rate falls, the incidence of chronic conditions can be expected to increase.[24] Thus the relative stability of the prevalence of chronic conditions during a period when the death rate declined may be a significant achievement.

Improved medical care, moreover, can be expected to reduce the prev-

22. National Center for Health Statistics, *Health, United States, 1975*, p. 371.

23. National Center for Health Statistics, *Current Estimates from the Health Interview Survey, United States*, Vital and Health Statistics, series 10, various issues; NCHS, *Health, United States, 1975*, pp. 247, 487, 557. For those sixty-five and over, the gap narrows. The National Center for Health Statistics considers a condition chronic if it has existed for three months or more or if it falls within a list of defined chronic conditions ranging from allergies to strokes.

24. For example, as the number of deaths from heart attacks is reduced, the incidence of heart conditions among the living may increase. As more people receive regular medical care, they may also become more aware of the existence of chronic conditions such as hypertension, which is probably underreported by those not seeing a physician regularly.

Table 2-4. Average Infant Mortality Rates by States in Groups of Ten, in Descending Order of the Poverty Rate, 1965 and 1974

Mortality rates = deaths per 1,000 live births

States grouped from highest to lowest poverty rates	Poverty rate, 1969[a] (percent)	Mortality, all infants[b]			Neonatal mortality[b]			Postneonatal mortality[b]		
		Rate		Percentage change, 1965–74	Rate		Percentage change, 1965–74	Rate		Percentage change, 1965–74
		1965	1974		1965	1974		1965	1974	
Group 1 Mississippi, Arkansas, Louisiana, Alabama, South Carolina, Kentucky, New Mexico, West Virginia, Tennessee, Georgia	24.9	29.5	19.0	−35.6	19.3	13.7	−29.0	10.2	5.3	−48.0
Group 2[c] North Carolina, Oklahoma, Texas, South Dakota, District of Columbia, Florida, North Dakota, Virginia, Arizona, Missouri, Maine	16.8	25.8	18.2	−29.5	17.9	13.5	−24.6	7.9	4.7	−40.5

Group 3 Montana, Idaho, Nebraska, Kansas, Alaska, Colorado, Vermont, Wyoming, Iowa, Oregon	12.4	24.1	15.6	−35.3	16.8	11.5	−31.5	7.3	4.1	−43.8
Group 4 Utah, California, New York, Rhode Island, Delaware, Minnesota, Pennsylvania, Illinois, Washington, Maryland	10.7	22.6	15.6	−31.0	16.6	11.6	−30.1	6.0	4.0	−33.3
Group 5 Ohio, Wisconsin, Indiana, Michigan, Hawaii, Nevada, New Hampshire, Massachusetts, New Jersey, Connecticut	9.0	22.6	15.9	−29.6	17.0	11.7	−31.2	5.6	4.2	−25.0
United States	13.7	24.7	16.7	−32.4	17.7	12.3	−30.5	7.0	4.4	−37.1
Ratio, group 1 to group 5	2.77	1.30	1.19	...	1.14	1.17	...	1.82	1.26	...

Sources: U.S. Bureau of the Census, *Statistical Abstract of the United States, 1974* (GPO, 1974), p. 391, and HEW, Division of Vital Statistics.

a. Percentage of people below the official poverty level for 1969.
b. All infants, under one year; neonatal, under twenty-eight days; postneonatal, twenty-eight days to one year.
c. The District of Columbia is included as the eleventh unit.

alence of chronic conditions only after considerable time has elapsed. No amount of medical care will eliminate chronic conditions for those who already have visual and hearing impairments, arthritis, diabetes, or heart conditions. Improved medical care or other types of intervention may affect the future incidence of these conditions, but such changes cannot be expected to become evident for decades. For many of those with chronic conditions, greater access to medical care can mean the relief of pain or discomfort and the ability to function more capably (through corrective visual and hearing assistance, regulation of blood pressure and diabetes, control of hernias and ulcers, relief of asthmatic symptoms, and the like).

Table 2-5. Prevalence of Selected Chronic Conditions, by Family Income Class, Fiscal Years 1964 and 1965 and Calendar Year 1971[a]

Rates per 1,000 population

Chronic condition and income class[b]	All ages		65 and over	
	1964 and 1965	1971	1964 and 1965	1971 ·
Visual impairment				
All incomes	28.8	47.4	145.6	204.6
Lowest	71.2	96.3	177.5	232.1
Lower middle	21.7	37.7	115.4	163.2
Upper middle	14.3	28.9	110.1	181.3
Highest	15.2	34.5	105.7	169.2
Hearing impairment				
All incomes	45.7	71.6	216.3	294.3
Lowest	90.0	132.9	242.5	323.0
Lower middle	38.2	63.3	199.4	271.4
Upper middle	30.4	49.4	173.3	247.3
Highest	32.4	48.6	190.4	259.2
Impairment of back or spine[c]				
All incomes	34.7	39.6	55.4	67.1
Lowest	45.0	57.6	67.1	78.6
Lower middle	33.1	37.7	52.2	51.2
Upper middle	32.5	34.0	34.3	30.0
Highest	31.4	32.1	25.6	27.7

Sources: HEW, National Center for Health Statistics, *Prevalence of Selected Impairments, United States, July 1963–June 1965*, Vital and Health Statistics, series 10, no. 48 (GPO, 1968), pp. 28, 34, 55; and NCHS, *Prevalence of Selected Impairments, United States, 1971*, Vital and Health Statistics, series 10, no. 99, DHEW (HRA) 75-1526 (GPO, 1975), pp. 24, 27, 32, 36.

a. Data in the first and third columns based on interviews conducted from July 1963 through June 1965; data in the second and fourth columns based on interviews conducted during 1971.

b. Income classes (in dollars) are as follows:

	1964 and 1965	1971
Lowest	Under 3,000	Under 5,000
Lower middle	3,000–6,999	5,000–9,999
Upper middle	7,000–9,999	10,000–14,999
Highest	10,000 and over	15,000 and over

c. Excludes paralysis.

While the limited data on trends in chronic conditions convey an over-all picture of little change, there are isolated, modest improvements. The aged, poor or not, experienced a reduction in limitation of activity caused by chronic conditions.[25] And although children as a group experienced slightly increased limitation of activity, poor children were less affected than other children.

For the most part, data on selected chronic conditions are not com-parable over time because of a change in reporting methods in 1968.[26] Roughly comparable data by family income are available only for visual, hearing, and back or spine impairments. Table 2-5 shows that the prev-alence of selected chronic impairments increased between 1964–65 and 1971. In both periods low-income persons experienced higher rates of impairment of vision, hearing, and the back or spine than high-income persons.

Incidence of Acute Conditions and Restricted Activity

There has also been little change in the incidence of acute conditions (such as respiratory or gastrointestinal diseases) in the last ten years. These conditions are more prevalent among the poor, who reported slightly more acute illness and injury in 1973 than they did in 1964.[27]

Suffering an acute illness or injury, with the exception of certain types of contagious diseases, has little to do with the receipt of medical care. Most medical care for acute conditions provides relief of pain or discom-fort, lessens the severity (though not usually the duration) of illness, and

25. These statistics are based on the noninstitutionalized population. For example, more elderly people were cared for in nursing homes in 1973 than in 1964. Since nursing home patients may be expected to have more chronic conditions and more limitation of activity, it is possible that the rates for all elderly people did not change markedly over the period.

26. The major information on chronic conditions by income comes from the household health interview surveys conducted annually by the National Center for Health Statistics. Unfortunately, the center changed its reporting procedures in 1968; before the change it collected information on all chronic conditions, but afterward it reported them only if they resulted in a limitation of activity or caused the patient to seek medical attention. The center also selected one major type of chronic condition for more detailed reporting each year after 1968. The impairment data in table 2-5 are based on detailed reporting in 1971 but on the more general approach for fiscal years 1964 and 1965.

27. Some studies have shown, however, that people are more likely to report an acute condition if they have seen a physician. With the greater use of physicians' services by the poor over this period, some of the increase in acute conditions may reflect higher reporting rates rather than a change in incidence.

in some cases halts the development of long-term chronic conditions. Unfortunately, there are few statistics that capture these benefits of medical care. Instead, the duration of restriction of activity (that is, confinement to bed or home, inability to work or go to school) is the major fact routinely reported.

The number of days of restricted activity resulting from acute and chronic conditions increased among the poor between 1964 and 1973. Only for the aged did significant declines occur. Fewer days of restricted activity were reported for poor children than for nonpoor children in 1964, but by 1973 more restricted activity days were reported for poor than for nonpoor children. Among the communicable diseases, there were declines in the incidence of measles, German measles, and whooping cough.[28]

Use of Medical Care

One of the most striking changes to occur between 1964 and 1974 was the increased use of medical care services by low-income people. Historically, the poor have been much sicker than other Americans but have had less care from physicians. The period 1964–74 brought a major reversal in this pattern of abnormally low use, and for the first time the poor began to visit physicians as frequently as the nonpoor. To a lesser extent the poor also made greater use of dental services. Their hospitalization rate increased by 40 percent, far surpassing that of other income classes.

Since increasing the access of the poor to health care services was a common objective of many of the federal health care programs instituted in the mid-1960s, this change suggests that progress has been substantial and that the health programs of the Great Society and the War on Poverty have been largely successful in this respect.

It does not detract from this achievement to probe for possible shortcomings. Various questions should be raised. Has the increased use of services been shared equally by all the poor? Is the job of improving their access to medical services completed? Has their receipt of health care services brought tangible or intangible benefits? Do some of them now receive too much medical care, and are economic incentives to treat them so strong that they have become vulnerable to excessive testing, hospitalization, and surgery? Is the care they receive of the same quality and convenience, and in the same type of setting, as that of others? Although

28. National Center for Health Statistics, *Health, United States, 1976–1977,* pp. 248–49.

not all of these questions can be answered adequately because of incomplete data and information, the evidence currently available is summarized below.

Physicians' Services

In 1964 the nonpoor saw physicians about 20 percent more frequently than the poor. In the 1970s the poor overtook those with higher incomes—by 1975 they saw physicians 18 percent more frequently than the nonpoor (see table 2-6). These gains by the poor were true of every age group from 1964 to 1975.

The average annual number of visits to physicians by poor children increased from 2.7 in 1964 to 4.7 in 1975. Higher-income children's use of physicians' services dropped during this period, eliminating the difference by income of 89 percent in 1964: by 1975 lower-income children visited physicians as frequently as children in high-income families.

Increases in visits to physicians may occur either because more people go to see physicians or because those who go do so more frequently, or both. The proportion of the poor seeing a physician over a two-year interval rose: in 1964, 28 percent had not seen a physician for two years or more; by 1973 this percentage was only 17. Progress was especially evident for poor children, one-third of whom had not seen a physician for two years or more in 1964. By 1973 this figure was reduced to one-fifth. Despite this gain, poor children were still 57 percent less likely to have seen a physician in the two years before 1973 than nonpoor children.[29]

Since periodic examinations by physicians are considered good medical practice, the reduction in the number of those who have not had recent contact with the medical care system is a particularly good indicator of progress. Unlike the annual number of visits, however, this way of measuring utilization indicates that the poor still lag somewhat behind the nonpoor in access to physicians' services for all age groups except young adults.

While data on the trend in preventive examinations are not available, recent statistics indicate that the poor are still considerably behind others. Fifty-seven percent of low-income women but only 34 percent of high-income women did not have a Pap smear between 1971 and 1973; similar differences occur for breast examinations. Forty-five percent of the low-

29. National Center for Health Statistics, *Health, United States, 1975*, pp. 289, 409, 507, 509, 569.

Health and the War on Poverty

Table 2-6. Physicians' Visits per Person per Year, by Age Group and Family Income, Fiscal Year 1964 and Calender Year 1975

Income in dollars

	1964		1975	
Age group	Income	Number of visits	Income	Number of visits
All ages	All incomes	4.5	All incomes	5.1
	Under 4,000	4.3	Under 5,000	6.0
	4,000–6,999	4.5	5,000–9,999	5.2
	7,000–9,999	4.7	10,000–14,999	4.8
	10,000 and over	5.1	15,000 and over	4.9
	Ratio, highest to lowest	1.19	Ratio, highest to lowest	0.82
Under 15	All incomes	3.8	All incomes	4.4
	Under 4,000	2.7	Under 5,000	4.7
	4,000–6,999	3.8	5,000–9,999	4.0
	7,000–9,999	4.1	10,000–14,999	4.4
	10,000 and over	5.1	15,000 and over	4.7
	Ratio, highest to lowest	1.89	Ratio, highest to lowest	1.00
15–44	All incomes	4.5	All incomes	4.8
	Under 4,000	4.1	Under 5,000	5.7
	4,000–6,999	4.5	5,000–9,999	5.0
	7,000–9,999	4.7	10,000–14,999	4.5
	10,000 and over	4.9	15,000 and over	4.7
	Ratio, highest to lowest	1.20	Ratio, highest to lowest	0.82
45–64	All incomes	5.0	All incomes	5.6
	Under 4,000	5.1	Under 5,000	7.4
	4,000–6,999	5.0	5,000–9,999	5.8
	7,000–9,999	5.3	10,000–14,999	5.5
	10,000 and over	5.1	15,000 and over	5.3
	Ratio, highest to lowest	1.00	Ratio, highest to lowest	0.72
65 and over	All incomes	6.7	All incomes	6.6
	Under 4,000	6.3	Under 5,000	6.5
	4,000–6,999	7.0	5,000–9,999	7.2
	7,000–9,999	7.0	10,000–14,999	6.9
	10,000 and over	7.7	15,000 and over	6.4
	Ratio, highest to lowest	1.22	Ratio, highest to lowest	0.98

Sources: Department of Health, Education, and Welfare, National Center for Health Statistics, *Volume of Physician Visits by Place of Visit and Type of Service, United States, July 1963–June 1964*, Vital and Health Statistics, series 10, no. 18 (GPO, 1965), pp. 18, 19, 29; and National Center for Health Statistics, *Health, United States, 1976–1977*, DHEW (HRA) 77-1232 (GPO, 1977), p. 265.

income adult population had not had a physical examination in the previous two years as against 31 percent of high-income adults.[30]

Another indicator of the increased use of medical care is the percentage of pregnant women receiving early prenatal care. Low-income women who saw a physician early in pregnancy increased from 58 percent in 1963 to 71 percent in 1970, although high-income women were still 20 percent more likely to have sought early care.[31]

Dental Services

Most of the federal health programs of the last decade have been primarily concerned with medical care, but some programs also include dental care. Most of the comprehensive health centers provide routine dental care. The federal Medicaid program covers dental care as an optional service, and most states have elected to extend at least some dental services to Medicaid recipients.

The dental health of the poor has long been shockingly bad. In 1971 low-income adults between the ages of forty-five and sixty-four were almost three times as likely to have lost all their own teeth as were adults of the same age with incomes above $15,000. Among the aged, almost 60 percent of those with incomes below $3,000 had lost their teeth but only 35 percent of those with incomes above $15,000 had lost them.[32]

Poor dental health begins in childhood. In the mid-sixties among children between six and eleven, those whose family's income was less than $3,000 had an average of 3.4 decayed, unfilled teeth, but children in families with incomes of $15,000 or more had an average of only 0.7. Nearly four times as many low-income children as high-income children between twelve and seventeen had decayed or missing permanent teeth.[33]

30. Ibid., p. 273.

31. Ronald Andersen and others, *Health Service Use: National Trends and Variations, 1953–1971,* DHEW (HSM) 73-3004 (HEW, Health Services and Mental Health Administration, 1972), p. 22.

32. National Center for Health Statistics, *Edentulous Persons, United States—1971,* Vital and Health Statistics, series 10, no. 89, DHEW (HRA) 74-1516 (GPO, 1974), pp. 9, 11.

33. HEW, Health Resources Administration, *Decayed, Missing, and Filled Teeth Among Children, United States,* Vital and Health Statistics, series 11, no. 106, DHEW (HRA) 74-1003 (HRA, 1974); National Center for Health Statistics, *Decayed, Missing, and Filled Teeth Among Youths 12–17 Years, United States,* Vital and Health Statistics, series 11, no. 144, DHEW (HRA) 75-1626 (GPO, 1974), pp. 19, 20.

Although the dental health of the poor remains at substandard levels, they made steady progress in availing themselves of dental services from 1964 to 1975. In 1964 those with high incomes visited the dentist 3.5 times as often as those with low incomes. By 1974 this had been reduced to 2.0 times as often.

For poor children the average annual number of dental visits increased from 0.5 to almost one visit per child. Despite this, about 58 percent of poor children had not seen a dentist in the two years before 1973.[34]

Hospital Services

Because the poor are afflicted with more chronic conditions than others and because their health problems are generally more severe, it is not surprising that low-income people are hospitalized more than others. The period 1964–73 brought a fairly sharp increase in low-income people receiving hospital care; in 1964 discharges from short-stay hospitals averaged fourteen for every hundred low-income people; by 1973 this had risen to twenty-four per hundred people, a 70 percent increase over the period.[35] At the same time there was only a moderate increase in the hospitalization rates of higher-income people.

A major shift in the hospitalization rate also occurred for older people. In 1964 there were nineteen hospital discharges for every hundred people sixty-five or over; this had increased to thirty-five discharges in 1973.

An Assessment of Trends

These trends in the use of medical care by the poor make it clear that there has been a significant narrowing of the gap in opportunity to receive medical care. Some observers conclude that medical programs for the poor have been so successful that the job is complete and there is no longer cause for special concern about the health care of the poor. Others cite

34. Ronald W. Wilson and Elijah L. White, "Changes in Morbidity, Disability, and Utilization Differentials between the Poor and the Nonpoor: Data from the Health Interview Survey, 1964 and 1973," *Medical Care*, vol. 15 (August 1977), table 5.

35. National Center for Health Statistics, *Health, United States, 1975*, p. 309; and NCHS, *Hospital Discharges and Length of Stay: Short-Stay Hospitals, United States—July 1963–June 1964*, Vital and Health Statistics, series 10, no. 30 (GPO, 1966), p. 36.

Table 2-7. Number of Physicians' Visits per Capita Adjusted for Health Status of Patient, by Family Income, Public Assistance Status, and Age Group, 1969

Family income (dollars)	All ages	Under 17	17–44	45–64	65 and over
All incomes	4.6	3.8	4.4	4.9	6.6
Under 5,000	3.7	3.0	4.2	4.0	6.1
Aid	4.5	3.5	5.9	5.2	6.4
No aid	3.6	3.0	4.1	3.9	6.1
5,000–9,999	4.6	3.9	4.5	5.2	6.8
10,000–14,999	4.9	4.2	4.6	5.1	7.5
15,000 and over	5.2	4.5	4.8	5.5	10.4
Ratio, aid to no aid, income under 5,000	1.25	1.19	1.42	1.32	1.05
Ratio, income of 15,000 and over to income of under 5,000, no aid	1.44	1.53	1.17	1.40	1.72

Source: Estimated from National Center for Health Statistics, 1969 Health Interview Survey. For a discussion of the method of adjustment for health status, see Karen Davis and Roger Reynolds, "The Impact of Medicare and Medicaid on Access to Medical Care," in Richard N. Rosett, ed., *The Role of Health Insurance in the Health Services Sector* (Neale Watson Academic Publications for National Bureau of Economic Research, 1976), pp. 391–425 (Brookings Reprint T-013). Figures are rounded.

instances in which the poor now surpass others in the use of health care services and suggest that perhaps the poor use them excessively.[36]

Neither of these conclusions is warranted by the evidence gathered so far. When the poor make greater use of services than others, it can be attributed to the greater incidence of illness and injury among them.[37]

The claims that access to health services for the poor is now adequate are also premature. Significant groups of the poor have not shared equally in the advances that have been achieved. About one-third of the poor are excluded from the Medicaid program. Low-income people not covered by public assistance use physicians' services much less frequently than other people (table 2-7).

Minority groups and residents of rural areas, where poor people are heavily concentrated, continue to lag well behind others in using physi-

36. Thomas W. Bice, Robert L. Eichhorn, and Peter D. Fox, "Socioeconomic Status and Use of Physician Services: A Reconsideration," *Medical Care*, vol. 10 (May–June 1972), pp. 261–71; Myron J. Lefcowitz, "Poverty and Health: A Re-examination," *Inquiry*, vol. 10 (March 1973), pp. 3–13; Martin S. Feldstein, "The Medical Economy," *Scientific American*, vol. 229 (September 1973), pp. 151 ff.; and *Economic Report of the President, January 1976*, pp. 121–22.

37. When adjustment is made for this greater incidence, the poor visit physicians slightly less frequently than others with comparable health problems (see table 2-7).

cians' services. By 1973 whites averaged 5.1 visits to physicians a year; blacks and other races averaged 4.5 visits. Differences by race are particularly marked for children.[38] Since blacks and other minority groups tend to have more severe health problems than whites, disparities in the use of physicians' services relative to health needs are even greater than these figures suggest. There were substantial improvements for blacks and other races relative to whites, however, between 1964 and 1973. In 1964 whites averaged 42 percent more visits to physicians than blacks and others; by 1973 the gap had been narrowed to 13 percent.[39]

Rural residents, representing 55 million people, continued to lag behind urban residents in using physicians' services, and the differences remained remarkably stable for a fairly long time. Some increases occurred for nonmetropolitan children between 1964 and 1973, but elderly people in nonmetropolitan areas fell even further behind the aged in metropolitan areas.

Although data indicating trends in the frequency of visits to physicians by race and income or by residence and income are not currently available, the overall trends suggest that not all poor people have made equal progress in gaining access to physicians' services. Instead, some groups that face special barriers—whether of distance, physical availability, cultural attitudes, or discrimination—continue to lag well behind in the use of medical services.

And even though the poor as a whole receive more care from physicians than formerly, major differences do remain in the setting, continuity, and type of health care available to them. In 1974 almost 27 percent of families earning less than $5,000, but 15 percent of families earning over $15,000, had no "usual" place for obtaining care. Eight percent of the low-income families used hospital emergency rooms as usual sources of care; only 2 percent of those earning over $15,000 used hospitals regularly.[40] Care is usually less convenient for the poor. They spend 58 percent more time than those with higher incomes traveling and waiting to see a physician.

It is not possible to conclude from the evidence currently available whether the care the poor receive is as good as, the same as, or inferior to

38. National Center for Health Statistics, *Health, United States, 1975*, pp. 291, 295, 405.

39. Ibid.; NCHS, *Volume of Physician Visits*, p. 17.

40. National Center for Health Statistics, *Health, United States, 1976–1977*, p. 213.

that received by others.[41] Apparently the poor go to physicians and hospitals for much the same reasons as other people. The Georgia Medicaid program, for example, found that the ten most frequently reported conditions of patients visiting physicians were acute upper respiratory infection, high blood pressure, acute tonsillitis, bronchitis, diabetes mellitus, kidney infection, otitis media, acute pharyngitis, heart disease, and abdominal pain.[42] The ten most common final diagnoses of Kentucky Medicaid hospital patients in fiscal 1972–73, in order of declining frequency, were childbirth, pneumonia, gastroenteritis and colitis, hypertrophy of the tonsils and adenoids, chronic ischemic heart disease, diabetes mellitus, bronchitis, false labor, acute bronchitis and bronchiolitis, and asthma.[43] In the absence of any definitive evidence to the contrary, it must be assumed that physicians and other health care providers treat these conditions when encountered in the poor as professionally as they do when encountered in other patients. The poor presumably benefit from the relief of pain or discomfort, cure of acute conditions, control of chronic conditions, and return to normal functioning as much as any other patients who receive medical treatment for similar conditions.

More information on the content and style of care the poor receive would be desirable, however. Economic incentives in public medical programs, as well as in private health insurance plans, frequently reward unprofessional practice. There is some danger that when there are alternative methods of treating a condition a physician or other health provider might be influenced to select the method of diagnosis or treatment that is most remunerative. Some conditions, for instance, can either be treated surgically or be monitored over longer periods of time and treated with nonsurgical techniques. One report on surgical procedures among Medicaid patients found high rates of tonsillectomies, hysterectomies, and

41. For a survey of the available evidence, see Avedis Donabedian, "Effects of Medicare and Medicaid on Access to and Quality of Health Care," *Public Health Reports,* vol. 91 (July–August 1976), pp. 322–31; and Robert H. Brook and Kathleen N. Williams, *Evaluating Quality of Health Care for the Disadvantaged: A Literature Review,* R-1658-HEW (Rand Corp., 1975).

42. Letter from Sam T. Thurmond, Director, Georgia Medicaid Program, to William C. Pembleton, Social and Rehabilitation Service, Department of Health, Education, and Welfare, January 23, 1976.

43. Kentucky Bureau for Social Insurance, *The Kentucky Medical Assistance Program: Report of Services Rendered, Fiscal Year 1972–73* (Frankfort: Department for Human Resources, 1973), p. 70.

**Table 2-8. In-Hospital Surgical Procedures per 100 People a Year, by
Family Income, United States, 1963 and 1970**

Family income (dollars)	1963	1970
Under 2,000	3	7
2,000–3,499	4	6
3,500–4,999	4	7
5,000–7,499	6	7
7,500 and over	6	5
All incomes	5	6
Ratio, under 2,000 to 7,500 and over	0.5	1.4

Source: Ronald Andersen and others, *Health Service Use: National Trends and Variations, 1953–1971,*
DHEW (HSM) 73-3004 (HEW, Health Services and Mental Health Administration, 1972), p. 21.

cholecystectomies.[44] Other data bear out the claim that Medicaid may
have caused physicians to select surgical methods of treatment more frequently than they did in the past. Table 2-8 shows that in 1963 the number
of surgical procedures per capita performed on low-income people was
half that performed on high-income people, but by 1970 surgical procedures performed on the poor had doubled. The number performed on the
elderly also rose after the introduction of Medicare. One study found that
hospital admissions for surgery rose 30 percent in the first year; admissions for gall bladder operations tripled.[45]

A higher rate of surgery does not, in itself, suggest poor care. Survival
rates, relief of pain or discomfort, and recovery times may be favorably
affected by better surgical care. This is an area, however, where further
exploration would clearly be of value.

44. *Getting Ready for National Health Insurance: Unnecessary Surgery,* Hearings
before the Subcommittee on Oversight and Investigations of the House Committee
on Interstate and Foreign Commerce, 94:1 (GPO, 1975), pp. 263–67. Data in this
report for some states are questionable because of a misunderstanding of the term
"surgical procedures." Some states reported every bill for a surgical procedure separately (including those of anesthesiologists, hospitals, surgeons, attending physicians,
and others), which led to overcounting of surgical procedures.
45. Regina Loewenstein, "Early Effects of Medicare on the Health Care of the
Aged," *Social Security Bulletin,* vol. 34 (April 1971), pp. 8–9. See also Donabedian,
"Effects of Medicare and Medicaid on Access to and Quality of Health Care," p. 327.

chapter three **Medicaid: Successes and Problems**

The Medicaid program was enacted in 1965 as an amendment to the Social Security Act of 1935. Its expenditures and the number of people it covers make it the largest governmental health care program for the poor. It provides a wide range of medical services to those on welfare and to some of the medically needy as well (those who would be on welfare if their incomes were a little lower).

It has never been a popular program, in large part because of its high cost. Medicaid expenditures quadrupled between 1968 and 1976. Yet although the Medicare program, enacted at the same time to help pay for medical care for the aged, has experienced very similar cost increases, it has been spared much of the opprobrium heaped on Medicaid.

Medicaid has benefited one out of every five Americans at one time or another (Medicare reaches one in nine). Most of its beneficiaries, however, are children and cannot vote; all of its beneficiaries are poor. Attacks on the program may result, in part, from the lack of a powerful interest group to defend it and press for improvements in coverage.

Unlike Medicare, Medicaid is a federal-state program. Administrative responsibility and about half the financial burden are borne by state and local governments. Much of the discontent with the program can be traced to the inability of the states to cope with both its rising cost and the political consequences of increases in expenditures for the poor. Faced with rising expenditures, limited tax revenues, and constitutional requirements to balance state budgets, state fiscal managers have had an impossible job. Their attempts to contain costs have resulted in curbs on primary health care services for the poor but left largely untouched the expensive provision of hospital and nursing home services. These actions have not only failed to curtail costs but may even contribute to rising costs over time as early primary care is neglected.

Frustration with rising costs has eclipsed some substantial achievements of the program. Most of the recent gains of the poor—greater access to adequate health care services, reduced mortality rates, and other improvements in health—must be credited to Medicaid. Thanks to the program, many poor patients and their families, relatives, and friends have been spared burdensome medical expenditures.

The desperate attempt to find the "villain" responsible for rising costs has diverted attention away from some of the underlying flaws in the structure of Medicaid as well. Attention has been focused on fraud and abuses by the poor and by physicians and others providing health care under the program. Little serious attention has been given to the failure of Medicaid and Medicare to make any attempt to change the health care system or improve its efficiency. Instead, both programs have accepted existing organizational arrangements and methods of compensation. Medicaid must share the blame with Medicare and private health insurance plans for much of the continuing inflation in health care costs. Policymakers have also been unwilling to consider genuinely needed changes in Medicaid that would require additional outlays—extension of coverage to all the poor and needy, maintenance of minimum, uniform benefits for all those covered, incentives for health care providers to participate in the program and provide quality care, and vigorous use of the financing mechanism to support the development of additional health care resources in underserved areas.

Medicaid's Link with the Past

Medicaid's roots go back to the Social Security Act, which established a program of public assistance for those unable to work.[1] Cash assistance from the states, with federal sharing of the cost, was extended to the needy, the aged, the blind, and single women with children, and later, to the disabled. Although the act did not provide direct assistance for medical ex-

1. For more detailed information on Medicaid history, coverage, and benefits, see Robert Stevens and Rosemary Stevens, *Welfare Medicine in America: A Case Study of Medicaid* (Free Press, 1974); U.S. Department of Health, Education, and Welfare, Health Care Financing Administration, *Data on the Medicaid Program: Eligibility, Services, Expenditures, Fiscal Years 1966–77* (Institute for Medicaid Management, 1977); John Holahan, *Financing Health Care for the Poor: The Medicaid Experience* (Heath, 1975); Allen D. Spiegel and Simon Podair, eds., *Medicaid: Lessons for National Health Insurance* (Rockville, Md.: Aspen Systems Corp., 1975); and Sydney E. Bernard and Eugene Feingold, "The Impact of Medicaid," *Wisconsin Law Review,* vol. 1970, no. 3 (1970) (Brookings Reprint 192).

penses, these expenses were included in determining the amount of support necessary. Participation by the states was optional, and medical care was only a small part of welfare assistance.

The Social Security Amendments of 1950 provided federal matching funds for medical payments to hospitals, physicians, and other providers of medical care to those on public assistance. By 1960 about forty states were participating, spending half a billion dollars on medical care.

The Social Security Amendments of 1960, known as the Kerr-Mills Act, greatly expanded federal involvement. The federal share was increased, an open-ended commitment to pay for an established set of services was made, and coverage was extended (at the discretion of the state) to the medically needy elderly who did not require cash assistance. By the end of 1965 all the states were participating, and forty-seven had added the optional coverage of the medically needy aged.

Medicaid replaced the Kerr-Mills Act, expanded the scope of eligibility and benefits, and attempted to impose more uniformity on state programs. However, it followed many of the general principles of earlier welfare-linked programs of medical assistance for the poor. It preserved a joint federal-state responsibility, with federal matching funds and broad, federally established requirements. State governments were given administrative responsibility and discretion to set eligibility standards and benefit coverage.

Medicaid expanded and improved the existing program of medical care for the poor and the aged. It increased federal sharing (which in 1976 ranged from 50 to 78 percent of the total depending on a state's per capita income), required states to cover everyone eligible for cash assistance (the aged, the disabled, and families with dependent children), and permitted states to extend coverage to all the medically needy. It delineated a mandatory set of medical services that each state was to provide and an optional set of services for which federal sharing was available. It initially required all states to have comprehensive health benefits by 1975. The additional annual cost of the program was estimated to be $250 million above the $1.3 billion already being spent under the existing program in 1965.

The unanticipated growth in the cost of the program led to subsequent attempts to trim costs. Amendments in 1967, 1969, and 1972 set curbs on the coverage of the medically needy, established procedures for quality and utilization review, allowed states to drop optional services if necessary because of budgetary pressure, and removed the requirement that states move toward a comprehensive program. Other cost-reducing provisions permitted states to assess patients on welfare some charge for optional services and to assess medically needy patients some charge for both basic and optional services.

Medicaid Coverage and Benefits

Eligibility for Medicaid is linked to eligibility for welfare and shares the complexity of that system. States must cover all families covered by the aid to families with dependent children (AFDC) program. They may also cover all aged, blind, and disabled recipients of supplemental security income (SSI),[2] or they may restrict coverage to SSI recipients meeting the more restrictive state Medicaid eligibility requirements of January 1, 1972 (before the implementation of SSI). All but fifteen states have elected to cover all SSI recipients.

In addition to covering cash assistance recipients, states may provide Medicaid coverage to the medically needy.[3] Twenty-eight states and four jurisdictions (the District of Columbia, Guam, Puerto Rico, and the Virgin Islands) extend coverage to the medically needy.

AFDC is limited in a majority of states to families without a father at home. Twenty-four states and two jurisdictions also extend AFDC and Medicaid coverage to families with unemployed fathers who are not receiving unemployment compensation. Seventeen states and three jurisdictions cover all children in families with incomes below the AFDC eligibility level, regardless of the employment status of the parents or the family composition.

To be eligible for welfare, families must have incomes falling below a standard of need established by each state. These standards range from $2,244 for a four-person family in Texas (as of July 1975) to $5,967 in Hawaii (slightly above the poverty level of $5,500 for a nonfarm family

2. The SSI program replaced the public assistance programs for the aged, the blind, and the disabled in 1972. It is entirely federally funded and administered, with uniform eligibility and benefit standards.

3. Currently, people must have incomes after medical expenses that are 133⅓ percent or less of the AFDC eligibility income level in each state to qualify as medically needy. It should also be emphasized that only the medically needy who are aged, blind, disabled, or constitute families with dependent children and who meet certain asset tests are eligible for coverage.

of four in 1975). Each state may also set limits on assets (homes, automobiles, savings, and so on) in determining eligibility.

States covering the medically needy establish income, asset, and family composition tests similar to those for public assistance recipients. Medically needy income levels for a family of four as of July 1976 ranged from $1,400 in North Carolina to $5,600 in Wisconsin. Families with incomes above these levels may also be eligible if their incomes fall below this level after deducting medical expenses incurred (the so-called spend-down provision).

As a result of this complex set of restrictions, the following low-income individuals are not eligible for Medicaid assistance:

—widows and other single persons under sixty-five and childless couples;
—most two-parent families (which constitute 70 percent of the rural poor and almost half the poor families in metropolitan areas);
—families with a father working at a marginal, low-paying job;
—families with an unemployed father in the twenty-six states that do not extend welfare payments to this group; and unemployed fathers receiving unemployment compensation in other states;
—medically needy families in the twenty-two states that do not voluntarily provide this additional coverage;
—single women pregnant with their first child in the twenty states that do not provide welfare aid or eligibility for the "unborn child";
—children of poor families not receiving AFDC in the thirty-three states that do not take advantage of the optional Medicaid category called "all needy children under 21."

With all the holes a needy family can fall through when trying to get help in meeting its medical care costs, it is not surprising that a large number of the poor are not covered by Medicaid.

The magnitude of these gaps in coverage is not well documented. There are few estimates of the proportion of Medicaid recipients with incomes above or below the poverty level, and little information on the number eligible for Medicaid at any one time. In 1976 an estimated 24 million people received services covered by Medicaid—a number similar in size to the poverty population, which was estimated at 25 million that year. Some Medicaid recipients, however, have incomes above the poverty level —because of certain earnings that may be disregarded and the spend-down provision. The Council of Economic Advisers estimated that 30 percent of all Medicaid recipients had incomes above the poverty level in 1973.[4] This suggests that only 17 million people, or two-thirds of the poor, were covered by Medicaid in 1976 and that approximately 9 million poor people were excluded. This estimate may be somewhat conservative, however, since Medicaid data are for persons covered at any time during the year whereas the poverty population is based on the number at a given time. Estimates of Medicaid recipients during a year therefore overstate the number covered at any given time. Adjusting for movements in and out of Medicaid suggests that perhaps no more than half of the poor population is covered by Medicaid at any one time.[5]

In some states, coverage of the poor is particularly restricted. In 1970 only one poor child in ten was covered by Medicaid in Alabama, Arkansas, Louisiana, Mississippi, South Carolina, and Texas. The Medical Services Administration of the Department of Health, Education, and Welfare estimated that fewer than one-third of the poor received Medicaid assistance in seventeen states.[6]

Who, then, is covered by Medicaid? The stereotype of a Medicaid recipient is a black welfare mother. This does not fit with the facts that almost half the recipients of Medicaid are children and that three out of every five people covered are white. Twenty-seven percent of the recipients are aged or disabled.[7] For them Medicaid is largely supplementary to the Medicare program.[8] Almost two-thirds of recipients, however, are female, and three out of every four recipients are on welfare.

The complexity of eligibility is matched by the complexity of the Medic-

4. *Economic Report of the President, February 1974,* table 45, p. 168.

5. The author is indebted to Nancy Amidei of HEW for this observation. See also Amidei, "The Children Left Behind: A Report on Medicaid and Child Health" (1974; processed).

6. The seventeen are Alabama, Alaska, Arkansas, Florida, Idaho, Indiana, Louisiana, Mississippi, Montana, New Mexico, North Dakota, South Carolina, South Dakota, Tennessee, Texas, Virginia, and Wyoming. HEW, Medical Services Administration, "Medicaid, 1977–1981: Major Program Issues" (MSA, July 1975; processed), p. 13.

7. HEW, National Center for Social Statistics, *Numbers of Recipients and Amounts of Payments under Medicaid, Fiscal Year 1973,* DHEW (SRS) 76-03153, NCSS Report B-4 (FY 73) (NCSS, 1975); NCSS, *Medicaid Recipient Characteristics and Units of Selected Medical Services, 1972,* DHEW (SRS) 75-03153, NCSS Report B-4 (FY 72) Supplement (NCSS, October 1974).

8. States may purchase Medicare coverage of care by physicians for Medicaid recipients by paying the Medicare premium on their behalf. States also pay the deductible and coinsurance amounts charged by Medicare. A large proportion of Medicaid payments for the aged go for nursing home care, which is covered to only a limited extent under Medicare.

aid benefit structure. Although a major objective of the original legislation was to make benefits more uniform and comprehensive among states, attempts by state governments to cut costs have largely undermined this objective.

States are required to cover the following basic services: inpatient and outpatient hospital care, physicians' services, family planning, laboratory and X-ray, skilled nursing facility and home health care for individuals twenty-one years old and over, and early and periodic screening, diagnosis, and treatment for individuals under twenty-one.

Some states have weakened this requirement in two ways. First, each state may set limits on the amounts of basic services covered. Only ten states do not place limits or restrictions on hospital, physicians', and nursing home services. Most states choose to be fairly restrictive. Alabama and Tennessee, for example, limit hospital stays to twenty days a year; Oklahoma to ten days per admission. A few states restrict care from a physician to one visit a month regardless of the health condition or illness.[9]

Second, states may indirectly limit the level of services received by those eligible for Medicaid by discouraging physicians and other health care providers from accepting Medicaid patients. Reimbursement of physicians may be set at low rates and not adjusted upward over time. Delays in payments, changing regulations, and extensive red tape, including prior authorization, all further discourage participation in the program.

Besides the required services, states may cover a wide range of optional services with federal matching assistance. These include drugs, eyeglasses, private duty nursing, intermediate care facility services, inpatient psychiatric care for the aged and persons under twenty-one, physical therapy, dental care, and other services. Forty-one or more states and jurisdictions add clinic services, prescribed drugs, prosthetic devices, emergency hospital services, skilled nursing care facility services for patients under twenty-one, care for patients sixty-five and over in institutions for mental diseases, and institutional services in intermediate care facilities.

When the 1972 Social Security Amendments allowed the states to charge patients for optional services, a number of states introduced copayment charges for prescription drugs, averaging 50 cents a prescription. Copayments for other services such as eyeglasses are also occasionally imposed.

Optional services account for a small portion of total Medicaid expen-

9. For more details on benefits offered by the states, see Health Care Financing Administration, *Data on the Medicaid Program . . . 1966–77.*

ditures. Most Medicaid dollars are spent on basic services and intermediate care facilities (nursing homes). In fiscal year 1976 inpatient hospital
care accounted for 32 percent of expenditures; nursing home and intermediate care, 38 percent; and physicians' services, 10 percent. Optional
coverage of drugs and dental care represented another 10 percent, with
all remaining services accounting for 10 percent.[10]

Why Does Medicaid Cost So Much?

Perhaps the best-known fact about the Medicaid program is that its
cost has grown rapidly throughout its history, far outpacing original cost
estimates. Combined federal and state-local expenditures increased from
$3.5 billion in 1968 to an estimated $17 billion in fiscal 1977 (see table
3-1).

**Table 3-1. Number of Recipients, Total Payments, and Payment per Recipient under
Medicaid, Fiscal Years 1968–77**

Fiscal year	Number of recipients[a] (millions)	Total federal and state payments[b] (billions of dollars)	Payments per recipient (dollars)	Medical care price index[c] (1968 = 100)	Payments per recipient (constant 1968 dollars)
1968	11.5	3.45	300	100.0	300
1969	12.1	4.35	361	106.9	338
1970	14.5	5.09	351	113.7	309
1971	18.0	6.35	353	121.0	292
1972	18.0	7.35	408	124.9	327
1973	18.8	8.71	463	129.8	357
1974	20.8	9.74	467	141.8	329
1975	22.1	12.09	547	158.9	344
1976	23.9	13.98	585	173.9	336
1977[d]	24.7	17.16	696	192.9	361

Source: U.S. Department of Health, Education, and Welfare, Health Care Financing Administration,
Data on the Medicaid Program: Eligibility, Services, Expenditures, Fiscal Years 1966–77 (Institute for
Medicaid Management, 1977), p. 34.
  a. Includes some recipients of aid under assistance programs that do not receive federal matching funds.
  b. Includes payments in 1968–70 for medical care programs enacted under the Social Security Amendments of 1960.
  c. U.S. Bureau of Labor Statistics medical care price index adjusted to make 1968 = 100; estimated for
fiscal year 1977 and for November and December 1976.
  d. Figures for 1977 estimated by HEW, Medical Services Administration, budget office.

But the fear that the costs of welfare and of medical care for the poor
have gone berserk and threaten to bankrupt state and local governments

10. Ibid., pp. 44–45.

as well as to dominate the federal budget is unfounded. Medicaid payments have not risen much faster than government expenditures generally: through the years they have accounted for roughly 2 percent of the federal budget and 2 percent of state and local government expenditures. This percentage increased to 2.8 percent of the federal budget in 1976; for state and local governments it reached 2.7 percent in 1974, then fell to 2.2 percent in 1976.[11] The cost of Medicaid thus represents a fairly small, though politically vulnerable, part of government budgets.

Surprisingly little is known about the reasons for the unanticipated high cost of Medicaid and its continued growth. Was the original cost estimate (of combined federal and state-local expenditures of $1.5 billion) unrealistic? Have providers of medical services taken unfair advantage of the program to increase their incomes exorbitantly? Have beneficiaries of the program used medical care services excessively? Has the program been incompetently administered? Or has it served far more people than anticipated?

The media have focused attention on charges and countercharges of various groups affected by Medicaid. Doctors making $300,000 a year have been blamed by some as responsible for high costs. Huge nursing home profits and kickbacks to state officials have been cited by others. Medicaid patients have come in for their share of attack, as they have been accused of taking joyrides in ambulances, obtaining prosthetic shoes for normal feet, and having extensive gold dental work done. Arrangements between laboratories and physicians for fraudulent billing or overcharging for laboratory services have been uncovered.

These abuses and inefficiencies may be unavoidable in a program as large as Medicaid. Corrective action should obviously be taken to uncover and attempt to eliminate them. But there is little evidence that fraud and abuse constitute a significant portion of total Medicaid costs. Effective control of Medicaid costs must look to the real causes of increased cost.

Since Medicaid is a federal-state program, with most decisions left to state governments, certain sources of growth in the cost of Medicaid are undoubtedly more important in some states than in others. On the whole, however, three factors explain almost all the growth: the increase in the number of Medicaid recipients covered under the AFDC program; the rise in medical care prices; and the high cost of nursing home care for the impoverished aged and disabled.

11. "National Health Expenditures," annual article in *Social Security Bulletin*, 1970–76 issues, and *Economic Report of the President, January 1977*, p. 270.

Figure 3-1. Number of People Receiving Medicaid Services, by Basis for Eligibility, Selected Months,ᵃ 1968–76

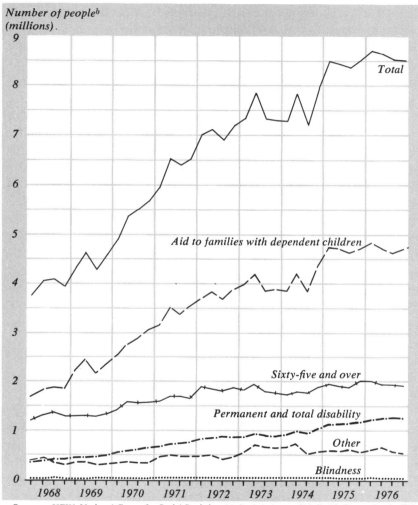

Sources: HEW, National Center for Social Statistics, *Medical Assistance (Medicaid) Financed under Title XIX of the Social Security Act*, NCSS Report B-1, various issues; NCSS, *Medicaid and Other Medical Care Financed from Public Assistance Funds*, NCSS Report B-6, various issues.
a. February, May, August, and November in each year.
b. Number of people whose bills for medical care were paid by Medicaid in the month indicated.

The rapid growth in the welfare rolls in the late 1960s and early 1970s accounted for a large portion of the increased cost of Medicaid. Between 1968 and 1972 the average number of people receiving Medicaid benefits each month doubled (see figure 3-1). While many explanations for this have been advanced, there is considerable agreement that most of the increase in the welfare rolls is the result of an increase in the number of eligible people applying for benefits. Estimates indicate that the percentage of eligible people actually participating in the welfare program increased from 60 percent to more than 90 percent.[12]

After this rise in the welfare rolls, the number of people eligible for Medicaid stabilized from mid-1972 to the fall of 1974. This period was also characterized by relatively stable unemployment, with rates averaging 4.9 percent in 1973 and hovering at the 5.0 level through the first half of 1974. By December 1974, however, the unemployment rate had shot up to 7.2 percent, and it continued to rise, reaching 9.0 percent in May 1975. This was promptly reflected in a new spurt in the number of welfare and medically needy recipients of Medicaid—by early 1975 the average monthly number of AFDC and medically needy recipients had increased by almost 20 percent over the mid-1974 figure. After unemployment peaked in May 1975, the number of AFDC recipients per month remained relatively stable.

The second major contributing factor has been the inflation in medical care prices faced by all Americans. Unfortunately, the bout of medical care price inflation in the mid-1970s coincided closely with rising unemployment and placed a double burden on Medicaid expenditures. After the removal of wage and price controls on the health industry in April 1974, the medical care price index rose at an annual rate of 13 percent—in sharp contrast with the rate of 4 percent when the economic stabilization program was in effect.[13] Hospital costs went up at the even faster annual rate of 16 percent. These higher prices promptly showed up in Medicaid expenditures.

Annual Medicaid payments per recipient in constant 1968 "medical dollars" (expenditures divided by the consumer price index for medical care services) averaged $361 per person in fiscal year 1977 as against $338 in 1969 (table 3-1).[14] That is, from 1969 to 1977, almost all of the growth in Medicaid costs could be traced to the rise in medical care prices

12. See, for example, John L. Palmer, "Government Growth in Perspective," *Challenge,* vol. 19 (May–June 1976), p. 43.

13. HEW, Social Security Administration, Office of Research and Statistics, *Medical Care Expenditures, Prices, and Costs: Background Book,* DHEW (SSA) 75-11909 (GPO, 1975), p. 22.

14. Use of the medical care consumer price index is only a crude estimate of the prices paid for Medicaid services. It probably overstates the rise in the prices of physicians' services since Medicaid's reimbursement rates to physicians have not kept pace with inflation. On the other hand it may understate the much faster rate of increase in hospital and other institutional costs. Hospital and nursing home care represent 70 percent of Medicaid expenditures and 50 percent of total U.S. personal health care expenditures.

Table 3-2. Medicaid Expenditures per Recipient and Health Care Expenditures per Capita in the United States, by Age Group, Fiscal Year 1975
Dollars

Type of expenditure	Children[a]	Adults[b]	Aged[c]	All ages
Medicaid recipients	210	432	1,257	548
On welfare	193	423	556	391
Medically needy and others not on welfare	319	491	2,665	1,039
Personal health care for total population	212	472	1,360	476

Source: Marjorie Smith Mueller and Robert M. Gibson, "Age Differences in Health Care Spending, Fiscal Year 1975," *Social Security Bulletin*, vol. 39 (June 1976), p. 20; and HEW, unpublished data.
a. Medicaid data are based on children under twenty-one in the aid to families with dependent children program; total population data on children under nineteen.
b. Medicaid data are based on adults in the AFDC program, excluding the blind and the disabled, for whom average payments were $779 and $1,245, respectively. Total population data are based on adults nineteen to sixty-four.
c. Sixty-five and over. Medicaid figures do not include the blind and the disabled.

and to the increased number of people receiving services. On the average, Medicaid beneficiaries were receiving approximately the same real services as in the early years of the program.

The average medical expenditure for Medicaid recipients is roughly the same as for the population as a whole (see table 3-2). In fiscal 1975 the average payment for services under Medicaid for children was slightly less than the average for all American children. Similarly, average Medicaid payments for adults compared reasonably with the amount spent by all Americans in that age group either directly or through private insurance and public programs. The aged on welfare received medical services costing an average of $556. For the elderly who were medically needy and in nursing homes costs were considerably higher, averaging $2,665.

These figures illustrate the third source of cost increase in Medicaid during recent years—the high cost of institutionalization for an impoverished elderly and disabled population that is unable to meet the demands of daily living without nursing assistance. The aged are the only sizable group for which there has been any substantial increase in real service costs in the last few years (see figure 3-2). The tendency to place large numbers of the elderly in nursing homes—where average Medicaid expenditures were $3,000 a person in fiscal year 1974—accounts for a major portion of Medicaid costs. Thirty-eight percent of all Medicaid payments, amounting to $7 billion in fiscal 1977, go for services provided by nursing

Figure 3-2. Average Medicaid Expenditures per Recipient in Constant 1967 Medical Dollars,ᵃ by Basis for Eligibility, Selected Months,ᵇ 1968–76

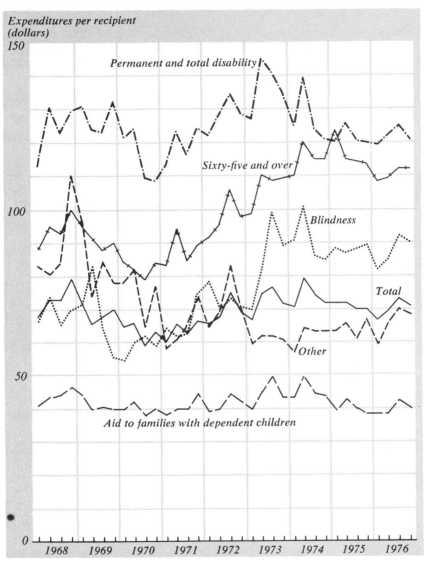

Sources: Same as figure 3-1.
a. Deflated by the consumer price index for medical care.
b. February, May, August, and November in each year.

homes and intermediate care facilities. Three of every five Medicaid dollars pay for services to aged or disabled adults.

Far from being a program for welfare mothers, Medicaid has been the primary vehicle by which society has helped assist those who are no longer able physically or mentally to care for themselves. Much of this responsibility has been assumed by Medicaid rather than Medicare, which has limited long-term-care benefits.

Medicaid costs are therefore high not because people get too much care or because the government pays higher rates for it than do other patients or third-party payers, but because (1) 25 million people received Medicaid services in fiscal 1977 (up from 11.5 million in 1968); (2) medical care costs are high whether the patient is covered by Medicaid or not; and (3) Medicaid has assumed the responsibility for meeting the health care costs of many elderly and disabled people who are confined to nursing homes. To restrain future Medicaid costs, these underlying causes must be recognized.

The Use of Medical Services and the Health of the Poor, 1964–74

From its initiation, the Medicaid program has had two major objectives: to ensure that those eligible receive adequate medical care, and to reduce the burden of medical expenditures for those with limited financial resources. Before the introduction of Medicaid, many of the poor, who had little or no private insurance, went without needed care. Some appealed to charity—from a doctor, a public hospital, or friends and relatives. Others attempted to pay all or part of their medical costs despite great hardship to themselves or their families. Medicaid was designed to alleviate this situation—if not for all the poor, at least for those on welfare and the medically needy.

It is difficult to separate the effect of Medicaid from that of other health programs for the poor and the changing conditions that influence them. The sheer size of the Medicaid program in relation to other health programs for the poor strongly suggests that Medicaid is largely responsible for the increased use of medical services by the poor. It may also deserve much of the credit for improvements in health conditions that are particularly sensitive to better medical care—such as infant mortality rates and deaths from influenza and pneumonia.

One approach to assessing the independent contribution of Medicaid

Table 3-3. Use of Physicians and Hospitals by Low-Income People, by Health Status and Welfare Eligibility, 1969

Number per person

| | Health status[a] | | | | | |
| | Public assistance recipients | | | Other low-income people | | |
Service used	Good	Average	Poor	Good	Average	Poor
Visits to physicians	4.09	4.95	7.10	2.69	3.36	5.12
Admissions to hospital	0.14	0.16	0.21	0.09	0.11	0.15
Days in hospital	2.40	2.72	3.47	1.18	1.42	2.04

Source: Karen Davis and Roger Reynolds, "The Impact of Medicare and Medicaid on Access to Medical Care," in Richard N. Rosett, ed., *The Role of Health Insurance in the Health Services Sector* (Neale Watson Academic Publications for National Bureau of Economic Research, 1976), p. 404, table 5 (Brookings Reprint T-013).

a. Average health status is defined as being at the mean level of two variables of health status—restricted activity days and chronic conditions—for all low-income people. Good health is that at half the mean; poor health, that at twice the mean.

is to compare the use of medical services by Medicaid recipients with that of other poor people. To do this, an econometric analysis of the use of hospital and physicians' services by recipients of public assistance and other low-income people was conducted.[15] The empirical estimation was based on data from a 1969 household interview survey of 3,163 public assistance recipients and 25,673 other persons with family incomes below $5,000. Receipt of public assistance was used as a crude proxy for Medicaid eligibility.[16] The empirical model adjusted for systematic differences between the two groups in such characteristics as health status, age, sex, education, family size, race, geographical location, and availability of medical resources.

Summary findings of the study are presented in table 3-3. The use of the services of physicians and hospitals by both public assistance recipients and other low-income people was found to be extremely sensitive to health status (as measured by the number of days of restricted activity and the

15. Karen Davis and Roger Reynolds, "The Impact of Medicare and Medicaid on Access to Medical Care," in Richard N. Rosett, ed., *The Role of Health Insurance in the Health Services Sector* (Neale Watson Academic Publications for National Bureau of Economic Research, 1976) (Brookings Reprint T-013).

16. True differences between Medicaid recipients and other low-income people may be obscured by this classification, however, since some public assistance recipients were not covered by Medicaid in the year studied (1969) and the low-income group included some medically needy Medicaid recipients, some working poor with private health insurance, and some poor with neither public nor private coverage. This overlapping of the two groups makes it difficult to detect actual differences.

Table 3-4. Average Number of Visits to and from Physicians per Medicaid Recipient of Physicians' Services, by Basis for Eligibility and Place of Visit, Fiscal Year 1974[a]

Basis for eligibility	Total number of visits to and from physicians per recipient	Percentage distribution			Number of noninstitutional visits to physicians per recipient	Percentage distribution			
		Hospital inpatient	Nursing home	Noninstitutional		Office	Home	Hospital outpatient	Other[b]
All Medicaid recipients	5.38	18.7	2.3	78.9	4.29	78.6	1.2	14.8	5.3
Children covered by AFDC	3.92	13.2	0.4	86.4	3.39	75.0	0.5	20.3	4.2
Adults covered by AFDC	6.34	18.5	0.2	81.3	5.15	80.9	0.6	13.3	5.3
Sixty-five or over	6.85	24.8	7.8	67.3	4.62	83.9	3.1	3.8	9.2
Blindness	6.55	20.0	4.4	75.6	4.95	87.5	2.9	5.9	3.8
Permanent and total disability	8.38	26.3	3.5	70.2	5.89	83.6	1.9	8.9	5.6

Source: Calculated from HEW, National Center for Social Statistics, *Medicaid Recipient Characteristics and Units of Selected Medical Services, Fiscal Year 1974*, DHEW (SRS) 75-03153, NCSS Report B-4 (FY 74) Supplement (NCSS, February 1977), tables 35–40.

a. Excludes Arizona, which had no program, and nonreporting states Colorado, Maine, Massachusetts, New York, North Carolina, and Rhode Island. Includes the District of Columbia. The data for other states were sometimes incomplete.

b. Includes clinic, intermediate care facility, and miscellaneous services.

number of chronic conditions). For every level of health status, public assistance recipients made greater use of services than others with low incomes. For example, a recipient with average health would visit a physician 50 percent more often and spend nearly twice as many days in the hospital as a similar poor person not on welfare. By reducing the price of care to zero, Medicaid has thus substantially increased utilization by those eligible for Medicaid benefits. In another comparison, it was found that public assistance recipients used medical services about as often, on average, as middle-income people with similar health status, but that the poor not on welfare continued to lag well behind.

Statistics from the Medicaid program provide some additional evidence on the use of physicians' services. These data are not strictly equivalent to those obtained from the Health Interview Survey because the Medicaid data include physicians' visits to hospital and nursing home patients and exclude telephone calls from patients to physicians.

The annual rate of Medicaid recipients' visits to physicians may be understated, since some recipients are covered for only a portion of the year. This is offset by the fact that Medicaid recipients tend to have more health problems; adjusting the rates would reduce utilization by Medicaid recipients relative to others.

Table 3-4 indicates that Medicaid recipients averaged 5.4 visits to or from physicians in 1974. If physicians' visits to institutionalized patients are excluded, Medicaid recipients averaged 4.3 visits—somewhat lower than the 5.1 visits (excluding telephone calls) averaged by the whole population in 1975. The noninstitutional visits to physicians of dependent children covered by Medicaid averaged 3.4, the same as the visits of all U.S. children in 1973. Aged Medicaid recipients averaged 4.6 visits in ambulatory settings, considerably less than the 5.8 average of the entire elderly population.[17] These statistics, while not exactly comparable, support the conclusion that Medicaid recipients now use physicians' services at about the same level as most Americans.

Other studies have examined the use of medical care services by Medicaid recipients over time or in relation to other population groups. Rabin and Albert found that in the Baltimore standard metropolitan statistical area from June 1968 to May 1969 Medicaid recipients were more likely

17. U.S. population averages are based on data from the Health Interview Survey reported in HEW, National Center for Health Statistics, *Health, United States, 1975,* DHEW (HRA) 76-1232 (NCHS, 1976), pp. 291, 293, 405, 407, 565, 567. All rates for visits to physicians cited here exclude telephone "visits."

to visit physicians than other residents of the area.[18] (The health problems of Medicaid recipients were also more serious—for example, 37 percent were chronically ill as against 22 percent of the middle- and upper-income people covered in the study.) Low-income people not covered by Medicaid visited physicians about as often as middle- and upper-income people, even though low-income people had more health problems. The study concluded that Medicaid appeared to be successful in attaining its objective of making the use of physicians by the indigent more consistent with health needs. Rabin and Albert also found some indication of increased use of preventive services by Medicaid recipients.

Roghmann and others found that an increasing number of children covered by Medicaid in Rochester, New York, were immunized between 1967 and 1969; by 1969 their immunization rates were comparable to those of children not covered by Medicaid.[19] They also found that Medicaid did not result in greater use of private physicians. Instead, many Medicaid recipients switched from private care to care from a neighborhood health center between 1967 and 1969. They attribute this change to a reduction in the reimbursement rates for private physicians under Medicaid and to vigorous efforts on the part of newly established neighborhood health centers to help people find out about and use their services.

A longitudinal study of welfare recipients in New York City by Olendzki found that welfare recipients did not increase their use of physicians' services in the two years after the introduction of Medicaid over that in the two years before Medicaid.[20] This result is perhaps not surprising since welfare recipients in New York were eligible for free medical care before Medicaid. Some increases were noted for children and for adults with less severe health problems. Welfare recipients enrolled in a comprehensive care project sponsored by the New York Hospital–Cornell Medical Cen-

18. David L. Rabin and Mary A. Albert, "Use of Physician Services by Medicaid Recipients," in Spiegel and Podair, *Medicaid: Lessons for National Health Insurance*, pp. 209–18; see also Thomas W. Bice, "Medical Care for the Disadvantaged: Report on a Survey of Use of Medical Services in the Baltimore SMSA, 1968–1969" (Johns Hopkins University, 1971; processed).

19. Klaus J. Roghmann, Robert J. Haggerty, and Rodney Lorenz, "Anticipated and Actual Effects of Medicaid on the Medical-Care Pattern of Children," *New England Journal of Medicine*, vol. 285 (November 4, 1971), pp. 1053–57.

20. Margaret C. Olendzki, "Medicaid Benefits Mainly the Younger and Less Sick," paper presented at the 100th Annual Meeting of the American Public Health Association, November 1972.

ter took advantage of physicians' services more frequently than other welfare recipients in both periods.

The Federal-State Partnership and the Distribution of Medicaid Benefits

The average experience of Medicaid recipients obscures many important variations within the program. Because Medicaid is a federal-state program that allows state governments freedom to determine eligibility, the range and level of Medicaid benefits, and reimbursement levels of health care providers, Medicaid benefits vary widely from state to state. These variations raise questions about the equity of Medicaid, in that the program treats similarly situated poor people differently depending on their geographical location.

Medicaid expenditures are concentrated in a few large industrial states outside the South. New York spends over one-fifth of all Medicaid funds. California has the second largest program and spends another 13 percent. These two states, together with Michigan, Illinois, and Pennsylvania, account for half of Medicaid expenditures.[21]

Such distribution of funds is not rationally related to the incidence of poverty or to the health problems of the poor. The South, which has 45 percent of the nation's poor, receives 22 percent of all combined federal-state Medicaid funds (and 26 percent of federal Medicaid funds).[22]

Differences between states arise because some states cover a greater fraction of their poor population and because some have more comprehensive benefits for covered Medicaid recipients. Table 3-5 shows the ratio of Medicaid recipients to the poverty population of each state. In 1970 in the entire country there were 59 Medicaid recipients (more than 70 percent of whom fell below the poverty level) for every 100 poor people. But in Arkansas there were 10 Medicaid recipients for every 100 poor people, and in California 174 people were Medicaid recipients for every 100 poor people. Only about one poor child in ten is covered in Alabama, Louisiana, Mississippi, South Carolina, and Texas.

21. National Center for Social Statistics, *Numbers of Recipients and Amounts of Payments under Medicaid, Fiscal Year 1973,* table 3.
22. HEW, Health Care Financing Administration, *Medicaid Management Reports: Annual Report, Fiscal Year 1976* (HCFA, n.d.), table 1.

Health and the War on Poverty

Table 3-5. Medicaid Recipients as a Percentage of the Poverty Population, by State and Age Group, 1970

State[a]	Total	Children under 21	Adults 21–64	Adults 65 and over
United States[a]	59	55	61	69
Alabama	17	10	11	49
Arkansas	10	6	10	19
California	174	133	173	317
Colorado	61	40	55	134
Connecticut	75	104	53	51
Delaware	61	81	48	28
District of Columbia	91	110	72	67
Florida	27	20	25	43
Georgia	35	26	31	71
Hawaii	95	92	101	96
Idaho	27	26	29	26
Illinois	55	70	50	34
Indiana	24	26	22	21
Iowa	36	43	32	32
Kansas	45	51	45	36
Kentucky	43	38	37	68
Louisiana	23	8	18	94
Maine	44	48	46	32
Maryland	76	73	83	68
Michigan	54	51	62	47
Minnesota	57	72	40	55
Mississippi	16	11	7	49
Missouri	38	33	33	55
Montana	28	28	26	31
Nebraska	33	31	31	39
Nevada	44	47	34	55
New Hampshire	45	46	37	52
New Jersey	55	70	63	22
New Mexico	28	26	29	37
New York	156	168	172	102
North Dakota	24	20	22	40
Ohio	36	40	36	29
Oklahoma	46	37	43	64
Oregon	38	35	47	31
Pennsylvania	93	97	128	38
Rhode Island	96	72	102	130
South Carolina	16	9	19	38
South Dakota	17	14	14	28
Tennessee	19	16	17	32
Texas	18	8	9	66
Utah	46	27	73	50
Vermont	71	80	60	72
Virginia	21	20	18	28
Washington	84	70	113	67
West Virginia	35	38	39	19
Wisconsin	59	66	47	62
Wyoming	19	18	18	24

Sources: Health Care Financing Administration, *Data on the Medicaid Program . . . 1966–77*, pp. 58–59; and Karen Davis, *National Health Insurance: Benefits, Costs, and Consequences* (Brookings Institution, 1975), pp. 48–49.

a. Does not include Alaska and Arizona, which did not have Medicaid programs in 1970, or North Carolina and Massachusetts, which did not report 1970 data.

Even for those covered by Medicaid, there are wide differences in benefit levels from state to state. Average payments per Medicaid recipient in fiscal 1974 ranged from $214 in Missouri to $911 in Minnesota (see table 3-6). For dependent children, payments ranged from a low of $62 in Wyoming to $326 in New York. The aged in Missouri received services costing Medicaid an average of $303 per person, but in Connecticut they cost Medicaid $2,709 apiece.

Part of this variation occurs because not all states cover the medically needy, whose health expenditures typically are higher. But even for welfare recipients Medicaid expenditures still vary widely. Annual Medicaid payments in fiscal 1975 per family eligible for AFDC, for instance, averaged $279 in Wyoming and $1,824 in New York, though the national average was $995.[23]

These wide differences would not be distressing if there were reason to believe that they reflected differences in the price of medical care or the health needs of the poor in each state. Unfortunately, this is not the case—benefit patterns bear no obvious relation either to the level of need or to health care costs.

For example, the average payment for physicians' services in fiscal 1974 ranged from $177 per recipient in Alaska to $26 in Pennsylvania (see table 3-7). In Delaware, 11 percent of the state's Medicaid recipients were hospitalized; in Nevada and Oklahoma, 24 percent. Oklahoma and Iowa place few of their elderly in nursing homes, but over half of the elderly Medicaid patients in Connecticut are in nursing homes. Average payments for nursing home services are less than $600 in Louisiana, New Mexico, and Iowa, about $5,900 in the District of Columbia, and $4,300 in North Carolina and Alaska.

It is difficult to explain the wide variation—it does not fit preconceived notions about generous and ungenerous Medicaid states. It may be systematically related to limitations on services. It may reflect differences in the efficiency of operation and monitoring of the program, political pressure on state governments that leads to reimbursement levels for some services being more generous in some states than in others, or ignorance on the part of some states of typical patterns of utilization. Some variation may be caused by the availability or lack of different types of services; some may simply be attributable to inaccurate statistical reporting. Whatever the causes, these statistics hardly provide reassurance that Medicaid

23. Health Care Financing Administration, *Data on the Medicaid Program . . . 1966–77*, p. 83.

Table 3-6. Average Payment per Medicaid Recipient, by State and Basis for Eligibility, Fiscal Year 1974

Dollars

State[a]	Total	Children covered by AFDC	Adults covered by AFDC	Sixty-five or over	Blindness	Permanent and total disability
United States[a]	390[b]	174	378	970	586	1,048
Alabama	256	104	307	305	299	389
Alaska	739	182	444	2,168	1,096	1,991
Arkansas	459	119	254	644	680	1,148
California	360	177	369	427	491	645
Colorado	570	162	334	1,091	1,429	1,229
Connecticut	710	180	512	2,709	1,420	1,727
Delaware	257	97	254	903	317	945
District of Columbia	499	275	572	671	1,101	1,540
Florida	313	115	247	656	334	451
Georgia	391	129	364	654	576	982
Hawaii	385	154	352	1,641	571	1,110
Idaho	513	135	380	1,451	606	1,169
Illinois	530	199	510	1,584	1,089	1,424
Indiana	598	146	397	1,962	1,310	2,058
Iowa	461	142	359	1,252	734	1,397
Kansas	560	154	476	1,191	1,036	1,710
Kentucky	236	99	235	362	306	588
Louisiana	358	95	244	576	592	977
Maine	466	161	391	1,171	592	1,163
Maryland	431	181	432	1,032	673	1,050
Massachusetts	411	160	382	962	752	941
Michigan	595	217	514	1,739	861	1,568
Minnesota	911	175	468	2,102	1,052	3,081
Mississippi	277	91	238	468	401	543
Missouri	214	92	234	303	361	431
Montana	515	162	351	1,276	886	1,060
Nebraska	670	151	377	1,366	1,113	1,638
Nevada	588	174	573	1,145	1,144	2,682
New Hampshire	492	138	374	1,074	1,084	1,085
New Jersey	523	192	453	2,410	991	967
New Mexico	353	142	381	666	1,258	820
New York	834	326	612	2,303	1,602	1,808
North Carolina	512	163	459	668	572	858
North Dakota	634	184	447	1,329	821	1,177
Ohio	426	156	379	1,210	871	1,153
Oklahoma	513	195	331	744	809	1,085
Oregon	389	128	203	1,132	1,114	993
Pennsylvania	296	99	186	1,039	198	784
Rhode Island	560	164	296	879	1,207	1,977
South Carolina	271	74	266	589	472	536
South Dakota	569	146	292	1,407	658	1,184
Tennessee	335	107	264	647	411	706
Texas	535	150	421	948	794	1,195
Utah	445	121	340	1,271	596	970
Vermont	576	203	393	1,487	731	997

Table 3-6 (*continued*)

State[a]	Total	Children covered by AFDC	Adults covered by AFDC	Sixty-five or over	Blindness	Permanent and total disability
Virginia	428	166	378	818	671	1,000
Washington	466	153	303	1,148	694	862
West Virginia	224	112	217	420	351	391
Wisconsin	731	286	425	1,432	1,917	2,048
Wyoming	225	62	149	627	1,161	374

Source: Health Care Financing Administration, *Data on the Medicaid Program: Eligibility, Services, Expenditures, Fiscal Years 1966–77*, pp. 77, 81.

a. Does not include Arizona, which did not have a Medicaid program in fiscal 1974; includes Puerto Rico and the Virgin Islands.

b. Includes "all other," not shown separately in this table.

money is being distributed according to the health needs of the poor throughout the United States.

Apparently, the federal-state partnership has not worked well. The intent of the legislation—to bring general medical care to the nation's poor—has been thwarted by the way in which the states have used their discretionary power to determine the level and types of benefits available to the poor and medically needy within their borders.

Equity Implications of a Financing Approach

Medicaid represents a financing approach to health care for the poor. It pays for services that those covered are expected to seek out and obtain. It was hoped that this approach would enable the poor to use private, "mainstream" health facilities instead of public hospitals or clinics. But for some groups, removing the financial barrier to medical care services is not enough to enable them to use medical services commensurate with their health needs. Other barriers to obtaining care—such as lack of transportation, long distances to travel, discrimination by facilities and personnel, limited patient education and information about the desirability and efficacy of medical treatment—frequently prevent the appropriate use of medical services, even when these services are free. Increased ability to pay for medical care may change some of these nonfinancial problems, but unless specific efforts are made to solve them the changes are likely to come slowly and with limited effect.

Table 3-7. State Variations in Medicaid Services and Average Payments for Services, Fiscal Year 1974[a]

Type of service, extent of use, and average payment	Average for total population	Average for three highest states	Average for three lowest states
Private physicians			
Percent receiving services under Medicaid	73	Pennsylvania, 95; Alaska, 89; Idaho, 85	Louisiana, 47; Florida, 51; Wyoming, 52
Visits per recipient[b]	4	Michigan, 10; Texas, 9; Arkansas, 8	Indiana, 1; Illinois, 2; Tennessee, 2
Payment per recipient (dollars)	69	Alaska, 177; District of Columbia, 132; Michigan, 122	Pennsylvania, 26; Oregon, 42; Kentucky, 49
General hospitals			
Percent receiving services under Medicaid	15	Nevada, 24; Oklahoma, 24; South Dakota, 22	Delaware, 11; California, 13; Virginia, 13
Length of stay per discharged patient[b] (days)	8	Illinois, 11; New Jersey, 10; Pennsylvania, 10	Idaho, 4; Washington, 4; Oregon, 5
Payment per hospital stay (dollars)	674	Maryland, 1,038; District of Columbia, 1,022; California, 982	Wyoming, 262; South Dakota, 312; Texas, 325
Nursing homes			
Percent of aged receiving services under Medicaid	14	Connecticut, 51; Idaho, 40; Pennsylvania, 34	Oklahoma, 0.7; Iowa, 0.8; Tennessee, 1.1
Length of stay[b] (days)	189	Connecticut, 283; Ohio, 270; South Dakota, 264	New Mexico, 25; Louisiana, 29; Tennessee, 37
Payment per recipient (dollars)	2,493	District of Columbia, 5,865; North Carolina, 4,336; Alaska, 4,311	Louisiana, 261; New Mexico, 342; Iowa, 585

Source: National Center for Social Statistics, *Medicaid Recipient Characteristics and Units of Selected Medical Services, Fiscal Year 1974.*

a. Excludes Arizona, which had no program, and nonreporting states Colorado, Massachusetts, New York, and Rhode Island.

b. Total use of service (visits, days) divided by total number of recipients of any Medicaid service.

The nonfinancial considerations are particularly important for residents of rural areas and for minorities in both urban and rural areas. Such groups are likely to receive a less than proportionate share of Medicaid benefits and to continue to use medical services they need less intensively than other covered Medicaid recipients.

Poor people in rural areas are at a disadvantage because of the Medicaid program's restrictions on eligibility. Only 40 percent of the poor in nonmetropolitan areas are elderly or members of one-parent families— the groups most likely to qualify for Medicaid. In metropolitan areas, 55 percent of the poor fall into the aged or one-parent welfare-eligibility category.[24]

Minorities and the Distribution of Medicaid Benefits

The most recent national data on the distribution of Medicaid payments and recipients by race are for 1974 and are based on the experience of forty-two programs reporting Medicaid data by race in that year. The data show disturbing inequities in the distribution of Medicaid benefits. Medicaid payments per white recipient were 74 percent higher than payments per black recipient (see table 3-8). There are large differences in all geographical regions except region 3, where payments to nonwhite recipients were slightly higher than to white recipients. Data for 1969 revealed that disparities in Medicaid benefits by race were smallest for children and largest for the elderly. For adults under sixty-five, payments for whites were more than 31 percent higher than payments for non-whites.[25] Differences are most extreme in rural southern and western areas, where whites receive more than twice the benefits received by blacks.

Receipt of individual medical services varied greatly by race too (see table 3-9). White recipients, for example, were more than four times as likely to receive nursing home services as black recipients.

Much more needs to be learned about the factors underlying these differences. Hearings before the House Committee on the Judiciary suggested that overt racial discrimination in nursing homes is widespread.[26] Referral patterns of physicians appear to be a factor behind segregated nursing home care—for instance, physicians referring white patients to one set of nursing homes and blacks to another set. Some of the difference may be due to the age composition of black Medicaid recipients. Blacks tend to

24. Some two-parent, nonelderly poor families may qualify because of blindness, disability, or an unemployed parent. Most states with high concentrations of rural poor, however, do not cover families with unemployed parents.

25. HEW, National Center for Social Statistics, unpublished state Medicaid reports.

26. *Title VI Enforcement in Medicare and Medicaid Programs,* Hearings before the Subcommittee on Civil Rights and Constitutional Rights of the House Committee on the Judiciary, 93:1 (GPO, 1974), especially pp. 2–29.

Table 3-8. Average Medicaid Payment per Recipient, by Race and Region, Fiscal Year 1974

Payments in dollars

Region (states reporting and not reporting)ᵃ	White	Nonwhite	Ratio, white to nonwhite
United States	560	321	1.74
1. Connecticut, Maine, New Hampshire (Vermont, Massachusetts, Rhode Island)	641	377	1.70
2. New Jersey (New York)	643	385	1.67
3. Delaware, District of Columbia, Maryland, Pennsylvania, Virginia (West Virginia)	351	356	.99
4. Alabama, Florida, Georgia, Kentucky, Mississippi, North Carolina, South Carolina, Tennessee	451	226	2.00
5. Illinois, Indiana, Michigan, Minnesota, Ohio, Wisconsin	717	393	1.82
6. Arkansas, Louisiana, New Mexico, Oklahoma, Texas	619	302	2.05
7. Iowa, Kansas, Missouri, Nebraska	430	261	1.65
8. Montana, North Dakota, South Dakota, Utah (Colorado, Wyoming)	679	261	2.60
9. Hawaii, Nevada (California)	567	379	1.50
10. Alaska, Idaho, Oregon, Washington	465	302	1.54

Source: Tabulated by National Center for Social Statistics, Social and Rehabilitation Service.

a. States in parentheses did not report data by race for fiscal 1974. Arizona, which had no Medicaid program, is in region 8.

die at an earlier age than whites and thus constitute a much smaller proportion of the very old people found in nursing homes.

In 1974, 74 percent of the whites and 67 percent of the blacks covered by Medicaid were cared for by private physicians. (The lack of data by race on payments to physicians for 1974 makes it impossible to determine whether white Medicaid recipients continued to incur higher expenses per person for physicians than blacks, as they did in 1969.) A much higher fraction of blacks than of whites used hospital outpatient services. This may reflect either the greater concentration of black Medicaid recipients in central cities where outpatient departments are a major source of care or the refusal of physicians in private practice to accept black patients in some areas.

Table 3-9. Percentage of Those Covered by Medicaid Receiving Selected Services, by Race, Fiscal Year 1974[a]

Type of service	White	Nonwhite	Ratio, whites to nonwhites
General hospital	18.1	16.3	1.11
Nursing home	4.5	1.0	4.50
Private physician	74.1	67.0	1.11
Dental	16.3	14.7	1.11
Outpatient hospital	30.9	39.6	0.78
Prescription drugs	68.2	66.5	1.03

Source: National Center for Social Statistics, *Medicaid Recipient Characteristics and Units of Selected Medical Services, Fiscal Year 1974*, tables 11 and 12.

a. Does not include Arizona, which had no program, and nonreporting states California, Colorado, Massachusetts, New York, Rhode Island, West Virginia, and Wyoming. Includes the District of Columbia.

Data from the Georgia Medicaid program for 1974 reveal more detailed differences by race. White Georgians covered by Medicaid averaged payments of $587 apiece; black Georgians averaged only $271—less than half as much as whites. Although white recipients averaged higher benefits than blacks, blacks were somewhat more likely to be covered than whites (Medicaid covered 54 percent of poor blacks and 42 percent of poor whites in Georgia).[27] This is probably because a higher proportion of poor black families than poor white families are headed by women, and thus more poor blacks are eligible.

The differences between the races in the type of medical service received are much the same in Georgia as those indicated by the 1969 national data. A higher proportion of the whites covered by Medicaid are hospitalized, but the hospital stays of blacks tend to be somewhat more expensive than those of whites. White Medicaid recipients in Georgia are almost six times as likely as black recipients to be in nursing homes. Slightly more white recipients see private physicians, and payments per recipient of the services of physicians are 28 percent higher for whites. Blacks in Georgia did receive more dental care than whites in 1974 (a Medicaid benefit that has since been discontinued by the state). As was the case in the national data, blacks in Georgia make greater use of hospital outpatient facilities than white Medicaid recipients.

In the econometric analysis of the health care utilization patterns of

27. Derived from "Statistical Report on Medical Care: Recipients, Payments, and Services," Georgia Form SRS-NCSS-2082, copies for fiscal 1974 (based on a 5 percent sample), provided by National Center for Social Statistics; and U.S. Bureau of the Census, *Census of Population, 1970, General Social and Economic Characteristics,* Final Report PC(1)-C12, *Georgia* (GPO, 1972), table 58.

public assistance recipients mentioned earlier,[28] it was found, when other factors were held constant, that black public assistance recipients in all areas received less ambulatory care than whites and that hospitalization rates for blacks also were lower in the South. Blacks on public assistance did receive more medical care than other low-income blacks, suggesting that Medicaid is of some help in overcoming racial barriers to care.[29]

While it is not possible to determine from these analyses exactly what accounts for racial differences, some explanations are ruled out. For example, since education, income, age, family size, health status, working status, and availability of medical resources were held constant, racial differences cannot be traced to these factors. Cultural attitudes may account for some of the differences. Discriminatory practices are still prevalent in many rural southern communities. A study of rural health in the South found numerous instances of insensitive or discriminatory practices in areas serving blacks and Mexican-Americans.[30] In one Alabama town, the four white physicians all maintained segregated waiting rooms, kept black patients waiting until all the white patients had been seen, and then allocated the remainder of the working day to the care of black patients—any for whom time did not permit treatment had to return the following day. Waiting times for black patients averaged between four and six hours. In some communities blacks are seen by local physicians, but the quality of care is poor. Many physicians do not ask black patients to undress for physical examinations, and make only cursory checks of the mouth, nose, and ears. Such discriminatory practices obviously limit utilization by blacks.

This kind of overt discrimination is readily documented. Frequently, however, discrimination is institutionalized, arising from segregated housing or past discriminatory practices that have led to current patterns of the location of physicians, hospital staffing, referral practices, and patient preferences. Some of the causes cited are the distance of hospitals and other facilities from black communities, familiarity with certain hospitals from

28. Davis and Reynolds, "The Impact of Medicare and Medicaid on Access to Medical Care."

29. Similar effects by race were found in an econometric investigation of interstate differences in Medicaid expenditures by Holahan. When income, education, and other factors were held constant, black children covered by Medicaid were found to be less likely than white children under Medicaid to use hospital inpatient services. Holahan, *Financing Health Care for the Poor*.

30. Karen Davis and Ray Marshall, "Rural Health Care in the South," preliminary summary report prepared for presentation at the meeting of the Task Force on Southern Rural Development, Atlanta, October 1975.

past association, lack of private physicians causing patients to turn to charity hospitals, scarcity of physicians in minority neighborhoods, and patients' lack of information or awareness that Medicaid benefits are available in private hospitals. These are not overt discriminatory practices.[31] Some practices, such as ambulance drivers taking black accident victims to charity hospitals and the restriction of hospital staffs to specialists (black physicians tend to be general practitioners), may be either overt or "statistical" discrimination depending on whether the rules governing these decisions are devised for the express purpose of excluding blacks from certain facilities or simply work on balance to exclude blacks.

Rural Residents and the Distribution of Medicaid Benefits

Rural residents, both white and black, face special barriers to receiving medical care. Medicaid often does not cover rural families at all because in typical poor rural families both parents are present and so do not qualify for AFDC in most states. Limited availability of medical personnel and lack of transportation also deter some of the rural poor from needed medical services. Rural blacks may be even more affected by discrimination than urban blacks, since there are so few sources of care.[32]

Again, Medicaid statistical reporting has been deficient, and current data are not broken down by residence. A nationwide household survey suggests that there are sizable disparities in Medicaid benefits between urban and rural areas. Andersen and others found that average Medicaid expenditures (and other, minor sources of free care) were $76 per poor child in central cities and $5 per poor child in rural areas (see table 3-10). Urban-rural differences also exist for other age groups; benefits for the elderly poor in central cities are twice as large as for those in rural areas.

One possible factor explaining the higher expenditures in urban areas is that urban Medicaid recipients are disproportionately concentrated in northern industrial states with generous Medicaid programs whereas rural Medicaid recipients are concentrated in southern states with limited programs. However, data for New York, an urban-industrial state with the

31. For a discussion of different trends of discrimination, see Ray Marshall, "The Economics of Racial Discrimination: A Survey," *Journal of Economic Literature,* vol. 12 (September 1974), pp. 849–71.

32. In 1969 average Medicaid payments for nonmetropolitan whites were more than double those for blacks, but for whites in large metropolitan areas they were 1.5 times higher. HEW, National Center for Social Statistics, unpublished state Medicaid reports.

**Table 3-10. Expenditures per Low-Income Person for Medicaid and All
Other Free Personal Health Services, by Age Group and
Area of Residence, 1970ᵃ**

Dollars

Age group	Central city of standard metropolitan statistical area	Other urban	Rural
Under 18	76	58	5
18–64	158	83	52
65 and over	54	38	27
All ages	44	43	13

Source: Ronald Andersen and others, *Expenditures for Personal Health Services: National Trends and Variations, 1953–1970*, DHEW (HRA) 74-3105 (HEW, Health Resources Administration, 1973), p. 52.
a. Low income in this table is income below $6,000 for a family of four.

largest Medicaid program, and for Kentucky, a predominantly rural state with a small Medicaid program, indicate that substantial intrastate variations in Medicaid benefits exist.

As shown in table 3-11, Medicaid expenditures in New York City averaged $1,272 per person eligible, $1,068 in six large urban counties, and $828 in small counties in the state. The number of people eligible for Medicaid in New York City at the end of 1974 was equal in size to the poverty population.[33] In the smaller counties of New York, 73 out of every 100 poor people were eligible. This helps explain why the average Medicaid payment per poor person in New York City was twice what it was for residents of the smaller counties.

Medicaid expenditures for hospital care were three times as high per eligible person in New York City as in the smaller counties of the state. Nursing home and other institutional care, on the other hand, was higher outside New York City.[34] Although expenditures for the services of private physicians were higher in New York City than in the smaller counties, people eligible for Medicaid in New York City also made much greater use of clinic services, averaging expenditures ten times as high. Combined

33. These data are based on the number of persons *eligible* for Medicaid at any one time. Other reported data count the number of persons receiving Medicaid at any time throughout a year. The size of the turnover in Medicaid enrollment is shown by the fact that 2.9 million people in New York State received Medicaid benefits during 1974, but only 1.8 million were eligible at the end of 1974.

34. This may be because the elderly in New York City are placed in nursing homes in rural areas.

Table 3-11. Number of People Eligible for Medicaid and Medicaid Payments in Relation to Poverty Population, by Type of Medical Service and Area of Residence, New York, 1974[a]

Payments in dollars

Description	Total, New York State	New York City	Large urban counties[b]	Small counties	Ratio, New York City to other counties
Medicaid payments per person eligible	1,155	1,272	1,068	828	1.54
Medicaid payments per poor person	1,068	1,273	988	603	2.11
Medicaid payments per person eligible by type of service					
Hospital care	429	549	257	181	3.03
Nursing home care, public infirmary, and intermediate care facility	310	293	489	466	.63
Physicians' services	81	88	76	59	1.49
Dental care	22	21	26	17	1.24
Drugs and supplies	49	48	54	49	.98
Clinic care	127	172	78	17	10.12
Number eligible for Medicaid per 100 poor people	92.5	100.0	92.6	72.9	1.37

Sources: New York State Department of Social Services, "Statistical Supplement to Annual Report for 1974," pub. no. 1053 (n.d.; processed), tables 19, 21, 24; and Bureau of the Census, *Census of Population, 1970, General Social and Economic Characteristics*, Final Report PC (1)-C34, *New York* (GPO, 1972), tables 58, 124.

a. Those eligible for Medicaid as of December 31, 1974 (includes those on welfare and the medically needy); poverty population from the 1970 census.

b. Includes Erie, Monroe, Nassau, Onondaga, Suffolk, and Westchester counties.

clinic services and private physicians' services were 3.4 times higher in New York City than in the smaller counties.

Similar intrastate Medicaid differences also exist for the predominantly rural state of Kentucky. As shown in table 3-12, 63 percent of the poor in metropolitan areas of Kentucky but only 39 percent of those in nonmetropolitan areas were eligible for Medicaid in 1973. Payments per person eligible were 1.6 times higher in metropolitan areas than in nonmetropolitan areas and payments per poor person 2.5 times higher, showing the

Health and the War on Poverty

Table 3-12. Number of People Eligible for Medicaid and Medicaid Payments in Relation to Poverty Population, by Type of Medical Service and Area of Residence, Kentucky, Fiscal Year 1973

Payments in dollars

Description	Total	Standard metropolitan statistical areas	Outside SMSAs	Ratio, SMSAs to outside SMSAs
Medicaid payments per person eligible	213	281	178	1.58
Medicaid payments per poor person	95	178	70	2.54
Medicaid recipients per 100 people eligible by type of service				
Physicians' services	61.4	56.6	63.5	.89
Hospital outpatient services	23.6	40.4	16.2	2.49
Hospital inpatient care	17.0	21.4	15.1	1.42
Nursing home care	1.9	2.9	1.5	1.93
Medicaid payments per person eligible by type of service				
Physicians' services	30	28	31	.90
Hospital outpatient services	8	16	4	4.00
Hospital inpatient care	69	118	47	2.51
Nursing home care	50	73	40	1.82
Number eligible for Medicaid per 100 poor people	44.5	63.2	39.4	1.60

Sources: Kentucky Bureau for Social Insurance, *The Kentucky Medical Assistance Program: Report of Services Rendered, Fiscal Year 1972–73* (Frankfort: Department for Human Resources, 1973); and Bureau of the Census, *Census of Population, 1970, General Social and Economic Characteristics*, Final Report PC(1)-C19, *Kentucky* (GPO, 1972), tables 58, 80.

combined effect of the more limited coverage and more limited benefits in nonmetropolitan areas.

Nonmetropolitan residents use the services of private physicians about as often as metropolitan residents, but metropolitan residents use more hospital outpatient services—40 percent of those eligible for Medicaid as against 16 percent. Metropolitan residents eligible for Medicaid also receive more institutional care than nonmetropolitan residents—21 percent of metropolitan residents, but only 15 percent of nonmetropolitan residents, are hospitalized. And average payments for hospital care are two and a half times higher for metropolitan residents. Nursing home care goes disproportionately to metropolitan residents, too—those eligible for Medicaid in metropolitan areas are nearly twice as likely to receive it as nonmetropolitan Kentuckians.

Econometric analyses of the use of medical services shed additional light on metropolitan-nonmetropolitan differences. Davis and Reynolds, in the analysis mentioned earlier,[35] examined the use of physicians' and hospital services by public assistance recipients. When the same factors as before were held constant, it was found that nonmetropolitan welfare recipients in the South visited physicians less frequently than other welfare recipients. The use of physicians' services was not significantly different, however, when adjustment was made for the availability of physicians, which suggests that the lesser use by welfare recipients in the South resulted from fewer physicians per capita.[36] No significant differences in the use of hospital services between metropolitan and nonmetropolitan public assistance recipients were found.[37]

Lower Medicaid benefits for rural families are thus partly a reflection of the urban focus of the program. Many of the rural poor simply do not qualify for Medicaid because they do not fall into the narrow eligibility categories established for welfare: only 40 percent are aged or members of one-parent families. The urban poor may also take greater advantage of Medicaid because they tend to be better organized and more informed about eligibility for assistance.

The lower benefits of rural residents also reflect the scarcity of medical resources and the difficulty of obtaining transportation to receive medical care. In most states, Medicaid will not pay for services provided by a nurse practitioner or physician's assistant unless a physician is present. Health professionals other than physicians have proved to be one means of pro-

35. "The Impact of Medicare and Medicaid on Access to Medical Care."

36. This result is weak, however, because of the manner in which the number of physicians per capita was constructed.

37. Holahan investigated the use of medical services in the California Medicaid program. He found that Medicaid expenditures per eligible person were significantly higher in urban cities for physicians' services, hospital outpatient services, drugs, and surgery, but he found no association between expenditures for inpatient hospital care per eligible person and urban-rural residence. A greater number of physicians per capita tended to increase the proportion of eligible persons using their services, but this effect was confined to urban counties. John Holahan, *Physician Supply, Peer Review and Use of Health Services in Medicaid* (Urban Institute, 1976). In his study examining interstate differences in Medicaid expenditures for 1969–70, Holahan found that urban residents received more hospital outpatient services than rural residents and equivalent amounts of private physicians' services. Holahan, *Financing Health Care for the Poor*, pp. 59–60, 68–69.

viding quality medical care in rural areas that cannot attract or support a physician. But they are hampered by the requirement that they work under the supervision of a physician and by legal restrictions and the failure of third-party payers, such as Medicaid, to develop adequate methods of reimbursement for their services. Amendments to the Social Security Act providing payment for rural health clinic services, passed in 1977, should do much to increase financing for the services of nurse practitioners and physician's assistants under Medicare and Medicaid.

Many forces discourage a greater concentration of medical resources in rural communities. Medical schools rarely prepare students adequately for rural practice, and frequently undermine their confidence that they can provide quality care without specialized supporting services. Physicians practicing in rural areas frequently resist new entrants to medical practice, recognizing that they can earn an adequate income only by working long hours and caring for a large number of patients at a low charge to each one. Medicaid has done nothing to change this situation because it pays physicians according to prevailing charges or even lower, scaled-down fee schedules. Physicians practicing in traditionally low-income communities continue to be undercompensated for the care they provide.

Transportation is also a significant barrier to medical care in some rural communities. Without special programs to bring patients to medical services or medical services to patients, many rural residents, particularly those with low incomes and the elderly, are unable to get care even if it is provided at little or no cost. This accounts in part for the higher death rates, greater incidence of chronic conditions, and more serious disabling conditions among rural people.

The poor in rural areas are inadequately represented by organizations supporting their interests and usually do not receive their fair share of a wide range of governmental benefits. Ancillary problems that contribute to poor health include insufficient income, poor housing, inadequate diet, impure water, and inadequate sanitation. These intensify the need for medical care of the rural poor but at the same time they limit the effectiveness of medical treatment. Coordination of medical care services with other governmental programs, such as economic development, housing, water supply, and sewage disposal, is therefore crucial.

Through this complex interaction of factors, the rural poor are not receiving assistance from Medicaid commensurate with their health needs. While the poor as a whole have markedly increased their use of physicians' services since the introduction of Medicaid, rural residents have not gained relative to urban residents in the use of medical services, nor has the absolute level of their use of physicians' services risen appreciably. If the benefits of Medicaid are to be more equitably distributed among the poor, supplementary measures must be designed to overcome the non-financial barriers blocking the entry of these disadvantaged groups into the medical care system.

Early and Periodic Screening, Diagnosis, and Treatment

About 70 percent of Medicaid funds go for institutional care in hospitals and nursing homes of the aged, the disabled, and the seriously ill poor. But in 1976, 43 percent of Medicaid recipients (and 49 percent of the poor) were children. Because their health problems are less severe and because the program is oriented toward institutional care, Medicaid payments for services to children account for only 18 percent of Medicaid funds. For a number of reasons, however, it is now believed that poor children should receive greater attention under Medicaid.

First, data indicate that poor children lag well behind middle-income children in the use of physicians' services. In 1973 poor children were 1.6 times more likely not to have seen a physician or a dentist in the past two years than nonpoor children. Fewer than two-thirds had been fully immunized against infectious diseases and fewer than half against polio. The poor in other age groups, by contrast, saw physicians about as frequently as middle-income people did.

Second, there is growing recognition that conditions untreated in childhood take their toll in later years. A study of low-income children in 1967 found that 20 to 40 percent suffered from one or more chronic conditions, but only 40 percent of the conditions were under treatment. Another study of low-income eighteen-year-olds rejected by Selective Service found that 33 percent of the health conditions discovered could have been prevented or corrected if treated before the age of nine, and 62 percent if treated before the age of fifteen.[38]

Third, some believe that long-term cost control of health care expenditures for the poor can best be achieved by reducing their need for health

38. These studies are reported in HEW, Social and Rehabilitation Service, *The Status of EPSD&T: Early Periodic Screening, Diagnosis and Treatment,* (SRS) 75-02052 (HEW, n.d.).

services. This means that greater emphasis on early primary care can reduce future expenditures for Medicaid.

The Social Security Amendments of 1967 provided for the creation of an early and periodic screening, diagnosis, and treatment (EPSDT) program under Medicaid. Its aims were to detect correctable conditions in children at an early stage to ensure that they received appropriate therapy or correction, and to rescreen children periodically to ensure their continued good health.

The rapid rise in Medicaid costs aroused strong resistance to effective implementation of this program. The amendments stipulated that the program be in operation by 1969, but HEW failed to write regulations for it until late in 1971. Congressional dissatisfaction with this slow pace led to the creation of a penalty, effective July 1, 1974, to be assessed against states failing to carry out the program properly. In the first quarter of 1975, the secretary of HEW filed penalties against seven states in an amount equal to 1 percent of Medicaid expenditures for failing to proceed with EPSDT. These penalties, however, were never assessed.

EPSDT is open to all children covered by Medicaid. Unlike other parts of the Medicaid program, states are charged with advising all eligible persons of the availability of benefits and ensuring that all eligible children receive necessary services. Children in need are to be provided with corrective eyeglasses, hearing aids, and dental care regardless of the status of these items in the regular state Medicaid program.

Under considerable pressure from Congress, this program has grown somewhat, but it is still a relatively minor portion of Medicaid activity. Between February 1972 and June 1976, 5 million children were screened out of the 12 million who were eligible.[39] In fiscal 1975 (the year the upturn began) 1.3 million children were screened, more than in the previous two years combined. About 1.7 million children are now being screened annually.[40] The total annual expenditures for the program of approximately $205 million are quite small in relation to the total Medicaid spending for children of $3.1 billion in 1977.

About 45 percent of the children screened are under six (they account for about 45 percent of EPSDT expenditures too). The rest are between the ages of six and twenty. Of those screened, 45 percent have some condi-

39. Health Care Financing Administration, *Data on the Medicaid Program . . . 1966–77*, pp. 49–50, and ibid., *1966–76*, pp. 36–37.
40. Cost and screening data for EPSDT are based on unpublished estimates of March 1978 by the Health Care Financing Administration.

tion requiring referral for further examination or treatment—such as a dental, visual, or hearing deficiency. More conditions are uncovered in older children: 40 percent under six and 75 percent between six and twenty have referrable conditions.

Dental conditions most often require referral for diagnosis and treatment—almost 25 percent of all eligible children have uncorrected dental problems. In southern states such as Alabama, Mississippi, and Tennessee over half the children screened have dental problems. Uncorrected impairments of vision occur in 10 percent of the children screened, and 3 percent have hearing conditions requiring referral for correction.

Each state is required to have EPSDT services for all children eligible under Medicaid, although compliance is not uniform. Each state may determine exactly what types of services will be available and who is eligible to provide them. Some states focus almost exclusively on visual, hearing, and dental conditions. Other states have vigorous screening for lead paint poisoning. Some states offer complete physical examinations by physicians as well as routine screening examinations. Alabama, for example, screens for a wide range of conditions: of those referred in 1973, 54 percent were for dental conditions, 7 percent for anemia, 5 percent for eye conditions, 4 percent for chronic tonsillitis, 4 percent for intestinal parasites, and 4 percent for skin conditions.[41]

Providing all eligible children with EPSDT services has been hindered by various problems. States have been fearful of the cost implications of the program—not primarily because screening is costly, but because the problems uncovered may be widespread and costly to correct. Dental care for children, for example, though restricted to relief of pain, infection, or restoration of teeth, is opposed by many states as potentially costly. Of the almost 2 million children screened annually, most probably need some dental care—although referral rates for corrective treatment are closer to 25 percent. Dental care with increased referral rates could easily exceed the entire cost of the EPSDT program. Even with the relatively low current use, dental costs for children covered by Medicaid in 1975 exceeded $140 million.[42]

41. Department of Public Health (Alabama), Medical Services Administration, *Medicaid Trends in Alabama: A Research Analysis Study, AFY '73* (Montgomery: MSA, 1974), p. 35.
42. HEW, Health Care Financing Administration, *State Tables, Fiscal Year 1975, Medicaid: Recipients, Payments and Services* (HEW, 1978), and unpublished data.

States have also resisted complete implementation of EPSDT on the grounds that turnover in the welfare rolls removes many children from eligibility before corrective services can be completed. Thus the program might discover conditions whose treatment could not be financed once the child was no longer covered by Medicaid. Such arguments reflect the basic unwillingness of the states to provide poor children with adequate services.

Bureaucratic infighting has also delayed carrying out the program.[43] In some states, state and county health departments have gained exclusive responsibility for the administration of the program and children are screened by county health departments. Children with conditions that need correction are then referred to the welfare department, which administers the Medicaid program in some states. Seeing that detected conditions are remedied is frequently neglected. Some county health departments have refused to let private physicians or health centers be reimbursed for conducting screening, and this sometimes leads to duplication of effort. Children are first screened by the county health department programs, and then they are reevaluated by the dentists, physicians, or other health professionals who will treat the conditions. County health departments with limited outreach activities, furthermore, may reach only a limited number of children. Broader participation in EPSDT by physicians and health centers would undoubtedly increase the number of children receiving screening and appropriate correction.

EPSDT is relatively new and may receive greater attention and support in future years. The child health assessment program proposed by HEW in the bill introduced in the House in April 1977 is designed to improve EPSDT and expand it to cover more children. Medicaid would be broader if all low-income children and pregnant women who met state income standards were covered and if the federal financial matching rate for ambulatory care for all children who received health assessments were increased. Debate on the proposed program has focused mainly on its cost and the efficacy of the screening part of the program. (By spring 1978 the bill was still in subcommittee hearings.) Improvement and expansion of the program and a greater awareness of its benefits could make this an important component of Medicaid or national health insurance in the future.

43. See Anne-Marie Foltz, "The Development of Ambiguous Federal Policy: Early and Periodic Screening, Diagnosis and Treatment (EPSDT)," *Milbank Memorial Fund Quarterly: Health and Society,* vol. 53 (Winter 1975), pp. 35–64.

Cutbacks in Medicaid at the State Level

Significant changes in the Medicaid program have been taking place in the last few years at the initiative of state governments. With the fiscal pressure on these governments since 1974, most of the changes they have made have been in the direction of reducing the cost of the program.

Many of these changes exacerbate Medicaid's problems. Rather than addressing the underlying causes of increased cost—such as unemployment, inflation in medical care prices, and high institutional costs—state governments have emphasized three major approaches to curtailing costs: increased limits and restrictions on optional and basic Medicaid services; increased cost-sharing by patients for basic and optional services; and lowered reimbursement-fee levels for services to ambulatory patients. Although choice among these approaches is, to some degree, set by federal law, any one of them would make it more difficult for Medicaid recipients to obtain ambulatory and preventive health care services and would endanger many of the program's achievements.

The following types of changes in Medicaid, made by state governments over the nine-month period from October 1, 1975, to July 1, 1976, illustrate the new barriers Medicaid recipients face.[44]

Reduction in the number of those eligible for Medicaid. Some states have removed unborn children from Medicaid coverage (or, in effect, first-time mothers); others have considered dropping the medically needy.

Limits on basic services for welfare recipients. One of the most typical responses to budgetary pressures has been the reduction of covered hospital days and the number of visits to or by physicians that Medicaid will reimburse.

Copayments for, limits on, or elimination of optional services. A number of states have required Medicaid recipients to pay a portion of prescription drug costs, usually 50 cents a prescription. Adult dental services have been eliminated or curtailed in other states. Optional services such as eyeglasses and hearing aids have been dropped in some instances, or subjected to requirements for patient copayment.

Reduction in reimbursement levels for ambulatory care. Reimburse-

44. Health Care Financing Administration, *Data on the Medicaid Program . . . 1966–77,* pp. 14–18.

ment rates for physicians, dentists, pharmacists, and laboratory services have been a major source of cutbacks.

Reduction in reimbursement levels for hospitals. A few states were granted authority to experiment with different methods of reimbursing hospitals. Some tried freezing hospital reimbursement rates, but the legality of this was successfully challenged.

Reduction in reimbursement to nursing homes. States have typically been reluctant to put serious pressure on these rates, but some have reduced the personal needs allowances of patients in nursing homes.

The experience of Georgia illustrates the types of cutbacks that have been made in a number of states. The state's Medicaid program suffered a blow in 1975 when the state attorney general ruled that it could not use next year's funds to pay for services rendered in the current fiscal year. To meet this deficit, Georgia took a number of actions. It eliminated dental services, dentures, and optical services for adults. It restricted physicians' home and office visits and hospital outpatient visits to one visit a month; physicians' services in hospitals were limited to one visit a day and in nursing homes to one visit a month. Copayments were introduced for prescription drugs, ambulance services, durable medical equipment, and orthodontic-prosthetic services. Prior approval for many physicians' services and related hospital admissions was instituted, along with a requirement that physicians follow a prudent-buyer concept (lowest cost among available alternatives) in prescribing courses of treatment. Physicians were required to sign a provider's agreement to abide by the Medicaid policies and procedures manual. A decision was made in 1975 to settle physicians' claims at slightly less than the full amount.

Actions taken by the state to reduce its high nursing home costs were mild, in response to strong state nursing home lobbies opposed to significant cuts. Personal needs allowances of patients were reduced and Medicaid nursing home payments were lowered to be no higher than under Medicare, a legal requirement in Medicaid.

Georgia also requested a waiver from HEW to permit charging welfare recipients $2 for each visit to a physician or to a hospital outpatient department, and $25 for hospital stays. (The law specifically stipulates that the categorically needy may not be charged a copayment for these services.) This request was initially approved, although the department recommended that the copayment for visits to physicians be only $1 and that the state exempt some types of hospital stays from the $25 copayment. Requiring the copayments was allegedly an experiment to see if they would reduce the use of marginally necessary services. The state, however, made little effort to disguise its request as an experiment. It presented no evidence that overuse existed (in fact, utilization levels in Georgia were well below national and regional averages); it presented no statistical design for separating the effect of the copayments from other changes that were made in its Medicaid program; it presented no evidence that it had the data-processing ability to conduct the experiment (a state report of the previous year called the Georgia Medicaid data system one of the worst in existence); and it made no allowance for Medicaid recipients who would find the copayments difficult to meet with the average monthly cash assistance payment in Georgia of only $32 per person. Because justification for the experiment was lacking and because of the failure to protect beneficiaries from its effects, the district court judge granted a permanent injunction against the copayments in 1976.[45]

Not surprisingly, this proliferation of restrictions and red tape had a dramatic effect on physicians' participation in the Georgia Medicaid program. In many rural counties, Medicaid recipients could not find a physician who would take them as patients. Hospitals that had resisted accepting black Medicaid patients cited the $25 hospital copayment as another barrier to admission. The effect of the changes in Georgia—and of those in other states—has been to diminish the success of Medicaid in assisting many poor people to meet their health care needs.[46]

Directions for Change

The Medicaid program has had a major impact on the health and health care of the poor in the last decade. Its many achievements have gone unheralded and largely unappreciated—obscured by an all-consuming concern with its unexpectedly high cost. But there is little doubt that Medicaid has fallen short of reasonable expectations and should be reformed.

Reform should be sweeping. From the preceding analysis of the inequities, gaps, and other inadequacies in Medicaid coverage, it is clear that the program does not provide the poor with comprehensive protection or ade-

45. *Crane v. Mathews,* Civil Action C75-2317A (N.D. Ga.), Order dated June 16, 1976. See Lawrence Mullen, "Medicaid Cutback Barred by Human Experimentation Regulations" (Los Angeles: National Health Law Program, n.d.; processed).

46. The copayments for physicians' services and outpatient and inpatient hospital services were removed by court order July 30, 1976.

quate financing for their health care needs. Categorical and income restrictions exclude many low-income people from any coverage; benefits vary
widely among states and are unequal for white and minority groups and
for urban and rural groups. Furthermore, the high and rising costs, uneven
quality, and institutional bias of services necessitate a reform agenda that
goes beyond the program's welfare context to tackle fundamental equity,
cost, and quality problems of the whole American health care system.

Although a number of reform proposals have been advanced in recent
years to deal with some of the problems, most stop short of integrating
Medicaid into a national health system. As long as Medicaid remains a
program for poor people only, it is unlikely that it can achieve the dual
social goals of financing adequate health care for the poor and controlling
costs. Unless effectively coordinated with the rest of the health care system, reforms that impose tighter controls on reimbursement policy and on
delivery systems could reduce access to care for beneficiaries. Medicaid,
despite its expected expenditures in 1977 of $16 billion, accounts for only
6 percent of expenditures for physicians' services and 9 percent of expenditures for hospital care—too little to exert control over the costs of those
services. Providers and institutions are reluctant to participate in the program, especially where it restricts them more than do other financing plans.
In fact, many analysts believe that the attempts of some states to control
costs through reimbursement policy have been major contributors to the
growth of "Medicaid mills" and of fraud and abuse. In New York, for
example, despite high medical care prices, Medicaid payments for physicians' services are lower than those of any other state program, yet New
York has not succeeded in controlling costs and recipients get care of uneven quality. Unless the financing of health care for the poor is integrated
with a comprehensive national program for all, such problems as access
and cost control may be impossible to resolve.

Short-run reforms, too, are badly needed. Some program flaws are more
amenable to such reforms, but this would require a renewed federal commitment to comprehensive financing and equal access for poor families in
need. For instance, eligibility reforms that base the extent of coverage on
income rather than other family characteristics, a "basic" benefit package
that precludes arbitrary limits on the amount, scope, or duration of services and improves primary care clinic and preventive coverage, a uniform
federal floor assuring adequate income standards, and a program to cover
the medically indigent would all greatly improve coverage and close serious gaps in the private-public health financing system.

To begin to meet some long-run cost control goals, Medicaid reimbursement policy could be merged with that of Medicare and private insurance plans to improve the influence of both public programs in medical care markets. Merged policy might also facilitate aggressive use of payment mechanisms to encourage practice in rural and underserved areas and to support innovative delivery organizations that serve program beneficiaries. In the past, Medicaid payment policies have merely followed market trends or arbitrarily restricted fees, and they have even discouraged delivery systems that demonstrated an ability to improve the health of low-income people and reach people in poor and rural areas.[47] The extent to which Medicaid reimbursement reforms can influence the supply of services available to the poor will, however, be limited by competition with private financing programs and by the amount of funds available to Medicaid from the federal, state, and local tax base. Recent experience suggests that this base, especially the state and local portions, will restrict aggressive use of reimbursement policy in the future. Also, setting aside a percentage of the Medicaid budget for resource development would help support and encourage a more equitable supply of services to the poor.

Genuine long-term reform of Medicaid will require a broader approach linking the financing of care for the poor with the entire population.[48] This is discussed in chapter 7, which expands on comprehensive reforms that emphasize financing and delivery system issues jointly with the goal of improving the health and health care of the poor. Placing Medicaid in this context and out of the "welfare" system allows a clearer focus on the program as an integral part of the general health care system and the system of public health programs.

47. See chapters 5 and 6 for the failure of Medicaid to support comprehensive health centers in high-poverty areas.

48. For a detailed discussion of the reform of Medicaid, see four studies published in 1977 by the Urban Institute: John Holahan, William Scanlon, and Bruce Spitz, *Restructuring Federal Medicaid Controls and Incentives*, URI 18100; Bruce Spitz and John Holahan, *Modifying Medicaid Eligibility and Benefits*, URI 17700; John Holahan, Bruce Spitz, William Pollack, and Judith Feder, *Altering Medicaid Provider Reimbursement Methods*, URI 17800; and John Holahan and Bruce Stuart, *Controlling Medicaid Utilization Patterns*, URI 17900.

chapter four **Medicare, the Great Society, and the Aged**

Medicare, enacted along with Medicaid in 1965, has enjoyed considerable popular support. It provides hospitalization and medical insurance for those sixty-five and over who are eligible for social security or railroad retirement benefits. Beginning in fiscal 1974 Medicare benefits were also extended to younger persons with chronic renal disease and disabled persons who had been receiving cash benefits for two years or more.

Support for Medicare is related to the political influence of its aged constituency, but the esteem with which it is regarded is largely deserved. It has enabled many elderly people to receive health services in increasing amounts and quality. At least partially as a consequence of the improved access to medical care afforded by Medicare, the health of the aged has improved noticeably since the program began. Perhaps even more important, Medicare has helped protect the elderly and their children from the financial burden of large medical bills. It has also played a role in establishing minimal quality standards for hospitals and nursing homes, and it has enforced nondiscriminatory provision of services in hospitals.

Yet the Medicare program has not been without its shortcomings. In retrospect, one serious mistake of both Medicare and Medicaid was the decision not to initiate reforms of the health care system, to control costs and promote efficiency. Instead, these public programs joined private health insurance in contributing to the spiraling costs of health care.[1]

Medicare has concentrated almost exclusively on assisting the aged and disabled to meet their medical bills. It has neglected the health care needs of those who encounter other barriers—elderly people who live in areas with few health care resources, who cannot travel to available services,

1. Herbert E. Klarman, "Major Public Initiatives in Health Care," *Public Interest,* no. 34 (Winter 1974), pp. 106–23; Karen Davis, "Hospital Costs and the Medicare Program," *Social Security Bulletin,* vol. 36 (August 1973), pp. 18–36.

or who face cultural or educational barriers to care have not received their fair share of Medicare benefits. The program has assumed no responsibility for redressing this imbalance.

Although Medicare has been an important source of financial security for the aged, gaps in the program have made it less than completely successful. It has failed to grapple with the need for long-term care of the elderly who are unable to care for themselves. It has permitted physicians to charge them fees in excess of what the program will pay, and physicians have taken advantage of this with increasing frequency. It does not cover many health care expenses, such as prescription drugs, hearing aids, eyeglasses, and dentures. It has increased the deductible charges for hospital and medical services that must be paid before benefits begin. As a result of these and other features of the program, Medicare in 1976 met only 38 percent of all the health care expenses ($1,521 per capita) and only 26 percent of the physicians' fees incurred by the aged.[2]

These gaps in coverage are particularly burdensome for the elderly poor. Unlike the other Great Society and War on Poverty health programs, Medicare is not solely, or even predominantly, a program for the poor. Yet as an integral part of the overall federal health care effort, it has important implications for the poor.

Although eligibility is not dependent on income, a large portion of Medicare beneficiaries have modest or low incomes. In 1976, 15 percent had incomes below the poverty level ($3,417 for an elderly couple and $2,720 for a single elderly person); 31 percent headed households with incomes below $4,000, and 57 percent headed households with incomes below $7,000.[3] Many of Medicare's disabled beneficiaries under sixty-five also have modest incomes as a result of the loss of earning power.

For some of the poorest elderly people, Medicaid complements Medicare coverage. Medicaid plans in forty-six states purchase Medicare cover-

2. As calculated, Medicare's share does not include the portion financed by premiums paid by the elderly. When these payments are included, Medicare paid 43 percent of all personal health care expenses and 55 percent of physicians' fees. The statistics here and in the text are from Marjorie Smith Mueller, Robert M. Gibson, and Charles R. Fisher, "Age Differences in Health Care Spending, Fiscal Year 1976," *Social Security Bulletin*, vol. 40 (August 1977), with the exception of the percentage of physicians' fees paid by Medicare (excluding premiums), which is estimated from Social Security Administration, *Health Insurance Statistics*, HI Note 78 (September 29, 1977), p. 2.

3. U.S. Bureau of the Census, *Current Population Reports*, series P-60, no. 107, "Money Income and Poverty Status of Families and Persons in the United States: 1976" (Advance Report) (GPO, 1977), tables 13–15.

age for about 13 percent of the elderly, and most state plans supplement Medicare benefits with more extensive coverage for nursing home care, prescription drugs, and other services excluded from Medicare.[4]

Another 50 percent of the elderly have private health insurance to pay all or, more typically, a portion of noncovered expenses. But for over one-third, the expenses excluded from Medicare coverage must be paid entirely from their own limited financial resources.[5] Inadequate Medicare coverage, therefore, falls most heavily on the aged who are ineligible for welfare assistance but unable, for financial or other reasons, to purchase private health insurance.

Medicare Benefits and Coverage

Medicare was enacted after three decades of acrimonious debate over national health insurance.[6] It was propelled forward by the assassination of President John F. Kennedy and the landslide victory of President Lyndon B. Johnson in 1964. Most of its supporters (and opponents) viewed it as the first step toward national health insurance.

Much of the impetus for the Medicare program came from the desire to lighten the burden of heavy medical expenses for the aged. The 1963 Social Security survey of the aged documented that about half of them had no private health insurance.[7] Companies were reluctant to write individual comprehensive policies for the elderly for fear that they would insure an excessive number of poor risks, which could not be screened effectively even with physical examinations. Available policies often limited coverage, exempted preexisting conditions, rarely covered nursing home care in the event of infirmity or senility, and in general offered inadequate protection.

The early pre-Medicare proposals were restricted to hospital benefits,

4. Marian Gornick, "Ten Years of Medicare: Impact on the Covered Population," *Social Security Bulletin,* vol. 39 (July 1976), p. 5.

5. Ibid., p. 18.

6. For more information on the evolution of Medicare, see Peter A. Corning, *The Evolution of Medicare: From Idea to Law,* Social Security Administration (GPO, 1969); Herman M. Somers and Anne R. Somers, *Medicare and the Hospitals: Issues and Prospects* (Brookings Institution, 1967); and Theodore R. Marmor, *The Politics of Medicare* (Aldine, 1973).

7. Ida C. Merriam, testimony in *Blue Cross and Other Private Health Insurance for the Elderly,* Hearings before the Subcommittee on Health of the Elderly of the Senate Special Committee on Aging, 88:2 (GPO, 1964), pt. 1, pp. 3–13.

and these were usually limited to thirty or sixty days. The American Medical Association vigorously opposed any plan that included compulsory insurance of physicians' bills. Congressman Wilbur Mills, then chairman of the House Ways and Means Committee, ingeniously side-stepped this opposition by merging a proposal for mandatory hospitalization benefits with voluntary insurance covering physicians' bills. Medicare was then rapidly adopted.

This led to the creation of a two-part Medicare plan: hospital insurance (HI), known as part A, and voluntary supplementary medical insurance (SMI), or part B. Of the two parts, hospital insurance was the more comprehensive. It provided a broad range of hospital and posthospital services subject to certain deductible and coinsurance provisions.[8] For a given benefit period, beneficiaries must pay a deductible for hospital care set at approximately the cost of one day of hospital care, which increased from $40 in January 1966 to $144 in January 1978. No further charges are paid by patients for covered services for hospital stays of less than sixty days.[9] Between the sixty-first and ninetieth days, they must pay one-quarter of the average daily hospital cost ($36 a day in January 1978); for the next sixty days they must pay one-half the daily cost ($72 a day in January 1978); after that hospital insurance ceases.[10]

To encourage early discharge from hospitals, the Medicare program also covers certain types of posthospital care, such as that in a skilled nursing facility[11] and through home health services. Skilled nursing care is intended for patients who have been hospitalized for the treatment of a medical condition and who, while no longer requiring the full range of hospital services, still need full-time skilled nursing in an institutional set-

8. A deductible is the amount to be paid by the patient before insurance benefits begin. A coinsurance rate is the percentage of the medical bill paid by the patient after meeting the deductible. These patients' charges are sometimes referred to as out-of-pocket costs or as cost-sharing.

9. Patients may, however, be charged for services not covered such as private rooms (except when prescribed by physicians as medically necessary), private duty nurses, television sets, and telephones.

10. Under current law, the last sixty days of coverage constitute a "lifetime reserve." After exhausting the lifetime reserve, subsequent hospitalizations are covered for only the first ninety days. Hospital coverage for the first ninety days, however, is renewed whenever the patient has been out of a hospital or nursing home for sixty days. The deductible and coinsurance payments then begin again under a new benefit period.

11. A skilled nursing facility is an institution, or a distinct part of an institution, that is primarily engaged in providing skilled nursing care or rehabilitation services and that has in effect a transfer agreement with one or more hospitals.

ting. Benefits are payable for persons who have had at least three consecutive days of hospital care and who are admitted to a skilled nursing facility (for treatment of the same condition) within fourteen days from the date of hospital discharge. Beneficiaries are required to pay one-eighth of the average daily hospital cost ($18 a day in January 1978) for the twenty-first through the hundredth day in a skilled nursing care facility, at which point benefits terminate.

The SMI program covers physicians' services, outpatient hospital services, additional home health services, other medical services and supplies, and outpatient physical therapy services furnished by qualified providers. Those sixty-five and over may enroll in the program whether they are eligible for social security retirement benefits or not. Premiums paid by the individual are matched by the federal government from general revenues. Annual premiums charged the elderly have increased from $36 in 1967 to $98.40 in July 1978.

Beneficiaries pay the first $60 of the cost of services covered by SMI incurred during the year.[12] After the deductible is met, the SMI program pays for 80 percent of the allowed charges for covered physicians' services and other medical services. If the physician will not accept the allowable charge as payment in full, the patient must pay all charges in excess of the allowable charge as well as 20 percent of the allowable charge. In 1969 the net assignment rate (the percentage of claims for which physicians agree to handle Medicare billing and accept the allowable charge) was 62 percent. In 1975 only 52 percent of Medicare claims were direct payments to physicians accepting assignment.[13]

The 1965 amendments to the Social Security Act, which authorized Medicaid, provided for the purchase by states of SMI coverage for aged public assistance recipients. Subsequent amendments in 1967 permitted states to purchase SMI coverage for all elderly persons eligible for Medicaid (whether on welfare or medically needy). State election of these provisions is referred to as "buying into" the SMI program. Under a buy-in agreement, a state is responsible for payment of the beneficiary's premium and share of SMI medical expenses—the deductible and coinsurance charges. In 1976, 2.3 million elderly persons were covered by such agreements in forty-six states, the District of Columbia, Guam, and the Virgin Islands.[14]

12. Expenses incurred in the last three months of the previous year may be applied toward the current year's deductible.
13. Gornick, "Ten Years of Medicare," p. 14.
14. Mueller, Gibson, and Fisher, "Age Differences," p. 11.

Medicare Expenditures

Like Medicaid, the Medicare program has experienced tremendous growth in expenditures. Total expenditures increased from $4 billion in fiscal 1967 to $14 billion in fiscal 1975, or 257 percent (see table 4-1). Expenditures for hospital and posthospital care increased slightly faster than expenditures for physicians' and other outpatient services.

About three-quarters of the rise in this period can be traced to inflation in the price of hospital care. The rest of the increase is divided between increases in the number of people eligible (which jumped by 2 million in 1974 when coverage was extended to the disabled and those with chronic kidney disease) and increases in use by those eligible. In constant 1967 dollars hospital expenditures per person eligible grew from $152 in fiscal 1967 to $186 in 1975.[15]

Over two-fifths of the increase in physicians' and other outpatient services (the supplementary medical insurance plan) can be traced to a rise in physicians' fees. Increases in enrollment (both because more people became eligible for Medicare and because a higher fraction elected to enroll in voluntary SMI coverage) accounted for a fifth of the increase in total SMI expenditures. Increases in real physicians' services per person represented over a third of the total rise in expenditures. SMI benefits in constant 1967 dollars increased from $66 per eligible person in 1967 to $104 in 1975.[16]

Some of the increase in hospital and physicians' services may be due to the changing age composition of the elderly and the expansion of Medicare to include the disabled. In 1966 the median age of Medicare enrollees was 72.8 years; in 1975 it was 73.1.[17]

The Medicaid program complements the Medicare program by providing 4 million elderly people with benefits. All states are required to furnish skilled nursing facility services for the elderly covered by Medicaid. Most states provide additional optional services not covered by Medicare, such as prescription drugs and intermediate care facility services.

The combination of Medicare and Medicaid has substantially assisted many elderly people to meet their health care bills. It has been particularly

15. Deflating average hospital and posthospital expenditures by the consumer price index for semiprivate hospital room fees.
16. Deflating average expenditures by the consumer price index for physicians' fees.
17. Gornick, "Ten Years of Medicare," p. 4.

Health and the War on Poverty

Table 4-1. Hospital Insurance and Supplementary Medical Insurance under Medicare, Fiscal Years 1967–75

Year	Expenditures (millions of dollars)	Number of people[a] (millions)	Expenditures per person (dollars)	Related consumer price index[b] (1967 = 100)	Expenditures per person (1967 dollars)
		Hospital insurance			
1967	2,886	19.0	152	100.0	152
1968	3,841	19.4	198	115.9	171
1969	4,641	19.6	236	131.5	179
1970	4,992	19.9	250	148.3	169
1971	5,602	20.3	276	168.0	164
1972	6,161	20.6	299	183.8	163
1973	6,743	20.9	322	193.0	167
1974[c]	8,201	23.1	355	204.6	174
1975[c]	10,471	23.7	442	238.2	186
		Supplementary medical insurance			
1967	1,163	17.8	66	100.0	66
1968	1,490	18.0	83	106.1	78
1969	1,748	18.8	93	112.6	83
1970	1,896	19.3	98	120.7	81
1971	2,072	19.7	105	129.8	81
1972	2,299	20.0	115	136.5	84
1973	2,454	20.4	120	140.0	86
1974[c]	3,256	22.6	144	147.0	98
1975[c]	3,993	23.2	172	165.8	104
Addenda					
Percentage increase, 1967–75					
Hospital insurance	263	25	191	138	22
Supplementary medical insurance	243	30	161	66	58

Sources: Marjorie Smith Mueller and Robert M. Gibson, "National Health Expenditures, Fiscal Year 1975," *Social Security Bulletin*, vol. 39 (February 1976), p. 3; U.S. Comptroller General, *History of the Rising Costs of the Medicare and Medicaid Programs and Attempts to Control These Costs: 1966–1975*, MWD-76-93 (U.S. General Accounting Office, 1976), pp. 5, 6. Figures are rounded.

a. For hospital insurance, number of people eligible; for supplementary medical insurance, number enrolled.

b. For hospital insurance, the consumer price index for charges for semiprivate hospital rooms; for supplementary medical insurance, the consumer price index for physicians' fees.

c. Includes data for the disabled and those with chronic kidney disease.

Table 4-2. Medical Care Expenditures per Capita of People Sixty-five and Older, by Type of Service and Source of Payment, Fiscal Years 1966 and 1975

Expenditures in dollars

Type of expenditure and source of funds	Per capita expenditures		Percentage distribution	
	1966	1975	1966	1975
All medical services	445	1,360	100.0	100.0
Public	133	824	29.9	60.6
Medicare premium	...	68	...	5.0
Private (except Medicare premium)	312	469	70.1	34.5
Hospital care	178	603	100.0	100.0
Public	87	541	48.9	89.7
Private	91	62	51.1	10.3
Physicians' services	90	218	100.0	100.0
Public	5	61	5.6	28.0
Medicare premium	...	68	...	31.2
Private	84	89	93.3	40.8
Nursing home care	68	342	100.0	100.0
Public	29	183	42.6	53.5
Private	40	160	58.8	46.8
Prescription drugs	62	118	100.0	100.0
Public	5	15	8.1	12.7
Private	58	102	93.5	86.4
Other medical services	47	79	100.0	100.0
Public	8	24	17.0	30.4
Private	39	56	83.0	70.9

Sources: Barbara S. Cooper, Nancy L. Worthington, and Mary F. McGee, *Compendium of National Health Expenditures Data*, Social Security Administration (GPO, 1976), p. 102; Marjorie Smith Mueller and Robert M. Gibson, "Age Differences in Health Care Spending, Fiscal Year 1975," *Social Security Bulletin*, vol. 39 (June 1976), p. 20; and Social Security Administration. Figures are rounded.

helpful to the very poor aged and to those with expensive hospital stays. Despite this assistance, however, the average elderly person paid $537 for health care either directly or through insurance premiums in fiscal 1975 (adults under sixty-five made private payments of $330). The elderly also pay more now than they did before Medicare and Medicaid. In 1966 private payments by the elderly were $312 per capita—even when adjusted for general inflation, a slight increase.[18]

The combined contribution of Medicare and Medicaid toward the health care expenditures of the elderly is shown in table 4-2. Per capita

18. From $312 in 1966 to $324 in 1975 (constant 1966 dollars calculated by deflating by the consumer price index, all items).

expenditures for medical care of the elderly increased from $445 in 1966 to $1,360 in 1975, a threefold increase. The share of these expenditures met by public sources increased from 30 percent in 1966 to 61 percent in 1975. Thus in 1975 Medicare, Medicaid, and other minor governmental sources contributed an average of $824 toward the medical care of each elderly person.

Medicare and Medicaid were particularly helpful in protecting the elderly from the cost of hospital care. Private payments (including direct payments and private health insurance premiums) decreased from $91 per person in 1966 to $62 in 1975. Medicare and Medicaid benefits more than kept up with the substantial inflation in hospital costs over this period.

In the case of physicians' services, however, Medicare and Medicaid have been much less helpful to the aged. Private payments increased from $84 per capita in 1966 to $89 in 1975, and the elderly paid an average Medicare premium of $68 in fiscal 1975,[19] making total payments almost twice as high in 1975 as they were in 1966. Medicare, Medicaid, and other government programs contributed only 28 percent of the cost of physicians' services for the aged.

Despite substantial payments by Medicaid and more limited benefits from Medicare, the burden of nursing home expenditures increased. The nursing home industry grew from $1.9 billion gross revenues in 1967 to $9 billion in 1975. Private payments by the elderly increased fourfold, and public payments more than sixfold.

The elderly also face greater expenditures for prescription drugs. Private payments doubled between 1966 and 1975, and the bulk of all expenditures are borne directly by the aged.

Medicare and the Financial Burden of Health Care Expenditures

Remedying the failure of the private market to provide adequate health insurance was one of the chief goals of the Medicare program. Medicare was a major departure from most types of private health insurance coverage available to the elderly. It requires no physical examination for cover-

19. The annual premium for Medicare SMI coverage in 1975 was $80. Premiums for 11 percent of the elderly enrolled in Medicare were met by Medicaid; about 3 percent elected not to enroll in the SMI part of the program. Martin Ruther, "Medicare, Number of Persons Insured, July 1, 1974," Social Security Administration, *Health Insurance Statistics,* HI-73 (April 21, 1976). Thus the average per capita Medicare premium paid by the elderly is somewhat less than $80.

age and does not exclude those with preexisting conditions; it provides a much broader range of benefits than most private plans by including some nursing home and home health benefits; and most people sixty-five and over automatically qualify for participation, regardless of their income.

In some respects, however, Medicare repeated the private insurance approach to coverage. Coverage of physicians' services and other ambulatory services under the SMI program was voluntary, and Medicare beneficiaries electing to enroll were required to pay a premium for coverage (federal general revenues were used to subsidize about half the cost of this coverage). The structure of the SMI plan was similar to that of private plans, and included various charges patients were required to pay. Even the hospital insurance placed limits on the amounts of hospital and nursing home services covered. Other types of services that could be difficult for the elderly with serious chronic conditions to pay—such as prescription drugs, eyeglasses, hearing aids, dental care, private duty nursing— were excluded from coverage. These required payments, and limits on benefits left open the possibility that some elderly people might incur ruinous expenses for health care.

Although Medicare represents a definite improvement over the private health insurance previously available to the elderly, little evaluation has been undertaken to estimate how successful the program has been in reducing the number of the aged that have heavy out-of-pocket outlays for medical care. One obstacle to undertaking such an evaluation is the difficulty of predicting what the situation would have been without Medicare. This is a problem in any evaluation, but it is particularly thorny in the case of Medicare because of the rapid rise in medical care prices since the introduction of the program. Some portion of that inflation was no doubt generated by Medicare; some portion would have occurred without it.

There is a strong logical presumption, however, that the variability of the elderly's out-of-pocket expenditures has been reduced by Medicare, and that fewer are devoting excessively high fractions of their income to medical care than would have been the case without Medicare. Without the program, many elderly people today would be ruined trying to meet their health care bills: even in 1975 the average Medicare hospital stay cost $1,200.[20] On the other hand, had the program never been enacted, it is doubtful that hospital costs would have risen to that level. The theo-

20. U.S. Comptroller General, *History of the Rising Costs of the Medicare and Medicaid Programs and Attempts to Control These Costs: 1966–1975,* MWD-76-93 (U.S. General Accounting Office, 1976), pp. 7, 8.

Table 4-3. Expenditures for Personal Health Services as a Percentage of Family Income, by Income Group and Age of Oldest Member, 1970

Family income group (dollars)	Expenditures as percent of family income	
	Families whose oldest member is 65 or over	Families whose oldest member is under 65
Under 2,000	14.1	15.2
2,000–3,499	11.3	6.9
3,500–4,999	9.4	7.0
5,000–7,499	9.5	5.4
7,500–9,999	5.6	4.5
10,000–14,999	5.0	3.8
15,000 and over	3.8	3.2
All income groups	7.6	4.0
Addenda		
Below near-poverty level[a]	12.9	6.9
Above near-poverty level[a]	6.0	3.8

Source: Ronald Andersen and others, *Expenditures for Personal Health Services: National Trends and Variations, 1953–1970*, DHEW (HRA)74-3105 (HEW, 1973), table 6, p. 13.
a. Near-poverty level is $2,600 annually for a single person, $3,700 for a family of two, and $5,700 for a family of four.

retical work and accumulation of empirical evidence necessary to document this effect have not been undertaken.

A major portion of Medicare funds go for relatively few beneficiaries with large medical bills. In 1969, 10 percent of beneficiaries were reimbursed $2,000 or more by Medicare. This represented 50 percent of all the funds expended.[21] Eighty-six percent of all Medicare funds in 1967 were used to pay for the total cost of illness of hospitalized people who represented only 20 percent of all Medicare beneficiaries.[22]

Despite this protection, many of the elderly, especially those with low incomes, continue to devote large portions of their income to health care. Aged families with incomes below the near-poverty level averaged medical expenditures equal to 13 percent of income in 1970, though younger families with low incomes averaged only 7 percent (see table 4-3).

Continued progress toward the goal of preventing financial hardship for elderly families will require modifications in the Medicare program. Particularly valuable would be to extend program coverage to a wider

21. Social Security Administration, *Medicare: Health Insurance for the Aged, 1969, Section 1: Summary—Utilization and Reimbursement by Person*, DHEW (SSA) 75-11704 (GPO, 1975), pp. 1-11, 1-17.
22. Howard West, "Five Years of Medicare—A Statistical Review," *Social Security Bulletin,* vol. 34 (December 1971), pp. 25, 27.

range of services such as prescription drugs, eyeglasses, and hearing aids, and to introduce limits on the amounts that the elderly would be required to contribute toward their own care.

Use of Medical Services and the Health of the Aged

While the primary objective of Medicare was to protect the aged against the possibility of large medical outlays, the program was also concerned with eliminating the financial barriers that discourage the elderly from seeking "necessary" medical care.

Medicare did result in a quite remarkable increase in hospital care received by the elderly. In 1964 they averaged 190 hospital discharges and 2,300 days of hospital care for every 1,000 people. By 1973 Medicare was providing 350 hospital admissions for every 1,000 people covered and 4,200 days of hospital care. Part of this increase was offset by a reduction in hospital use by the nonelderly, although there was a gradual rise in total hospitalization per capita (from 1,000 days per 1,000 people in 1964 to 1,200 days per 1,000 in 1973). Most of the greater use of hospital care occurred in the early years of the program. After 1968 an increasing proportion of the elderly was hospitalized, but this was offset by a reduction in the average length of stay.

Several factors may account for the steady rise in hospital admissions. Bed capacity has expanded over the period. The very old constitute a growing fraction of the aged: 37 percent of Medicare enrollees were seventy-five or over in 1966 as against 40 percent in 1975. More stringent regulation of nursing home services in the late 1960s may have contributed to greater reliance on hospital care. Nationally, the length of the average hospital stay has declined over this period. Medicare's efforts to review the length of stays may have contributed to the decline.

Medicare accounted for less than 3 percent of the growth in the nursing home industry, where care goes primarily to the aged.[23] Medicaid, on the other hand, paid for more than half of all nursing home expenditures.

Medicare began to apply its requirement that nursing home care be "medically necessary" more stringently in 1969. Claims were increasingly denied, sometimes retroactively, when it was deemed that patients in nursing homes did not require medical services, but merely nursing or domi-

23. Marjorie Smith Mueller and Robert M. Gibson, "National Health Expenditures, Fiscal Year 1975," *Social Security Bulletin,* vol. 39 (February 1976), pp. 4, 8.

ciliary services such as those provided in an intermediate care facility. Days of nursing home care covered by Medicare subsequently dropped from 1,041 per 1,000 people eligible in 1969 to 320 per 1,000 in 1972. Days of nursing home care increased slightly with the addition of the disabled to Medicare; in 1975 Medicare paid for 364 nursing home days per 1,000 people eligible.

Visits to physicians by the ambulatory aged were little changed by Medicare. Perhaps this is not surprising since the cost to the elderly of physicians' services (including the Medicare premium) doubled between 1966 and 1975. The average number of visits to physicians was 6.7 per elderly person in 1964 and 6.6 in 1975. National health expenditure data suggest, however, that real expenditures on physicians' services for the elderly increased over this period. Thus they may have received more care from physicians in institutional settings (in hospitals or nursing homes) and more real services per visit to a physician (laboratory tests, immunizations, minor surgical procedures, and so forth). Again, this may be due in part to the greater health needs of both the disabled and very old Medicare beneficiaries.

Studies confirm that the health of the elderly improved after the introduction of Medicare. Friedman, for example, found that they had fewer days of restricted activity and that this decline was inversely related to the level of personal health care expenditures by the aged.[24] His study revealed that the mortality rates of aged males in 1969 were lower than might have been predicted from previous experience.

Statistics from the Health Interview Survey of the National Center for Health Statistics indicate that the limitation of activity caused by chronic conditions in the aged declined from 1964 to 1973 and that the number of restricted activity days fell by 15 percent over the same period. The statistics for 1973, however, are based on the noninstitutionalized, which biases the comparison.

Income and Medicare Benefits

While Medicare and Medicaid have increased the use of medical care by the elderly as a group, this increase has not occurred equally for dif-

24. Bernard Friedman, "Mortality, Disability, and the Normative Economics of Medicare," in Richard N. Rosett, ed., *The Role of Health Insurance in the Health Services Sector* (Neale Watson Academic Publications for National Bureau of Economic Research, 1976), pp. 365–84.

ferent income groups or for different regions. As one objective of both Medicare and Medicaid was to ensure that elderly people who traditionally used medical services infrequently would not face financial barriers to increased use, such unequal patterns, if not attributable to variations in health needs alone, are cause for concern.

Removing major financial barriers could not be expected to result in equal use by all the elderly since their health status and medical condition vary. It should, however, have increased use by the elderly poor relative to the elderly with higher incomes, as the charges deterred many of the elderly poor from seeking necessary medical care before Medicare. With no financial barriers to obtaining care, the use of medical care services might even be inversely related to income since the poor are typically in poorer health than people with higher incomes.

Several features of the Medicare program, however, offset such an inverse relation and continue to discourage the use of services by the elderly with modest and low incomes. First, Medicare does not eliminate all out-of-pocket costs for medical care, nor does it adjust its cost-sharing requirements to reflect the patient's income. Both the hospital insurance plan and, to a greater extent, the supplementary medical insurance plan require deductible and coinsurance payments by recipients. A $60 deductible and 20 percent coinsurance rate for physicians' services is obviously a greater deterrent to a person with $3,000 income than to one with $15,000 income. It is also easier for those with higher incomes to purchase supplementary private insurance that will pick up all or part of out-of-pocket costs. Only the poor "bought into" Medicare by state Medicaid programs can similarly escape the deductible and coinsurance payments; Medicaid pays these costs.

Supplementary medical insurance coverage for physicians' fees also is only available to the elderly through payment of an annual premium. This premium ($98.40 in July 1978) deters about 460,000 from obtaining SMI.[25] The poor, blacks, and people living in rural areas and the South are disproportionately represented among the excluded.

Several hundred thousand elderly persons receive no Medicare benefits at all as they are ineligible for automatic coverage of hospital benefits. Hospital coverage is available free of charge only to those covered by social security or railroad retirement programs. Although amendments to the Social Security Act in 1972 permitted other elderly people to purchase

25. National Center for Health Statistics, *Health, United States, 1976–1977*, DHEW (HRA) 77-1232 (GPO, 1977), p. 113.

Medicare hospital insurance at a premium-covering cost—approximately $430 in 1975—this provision is of limited benefit to those of the very poor who are excluded from coverage, such as former domestic workers or migrant laborers.[26]

These gaps in coverage, and the costs of Medicare to recipients, reinforce market forces that encourage the use of medical services according to income rather than to health care needs. Variations in the availability of medical resources allow people with high incomes to obtain care more readily than those who are poor. Even if there were no substantial out-of-pocket costs, the time, search, and transportation costs required to obtain medical care can be major barriers for the elderly with modest incomes. As physicians and other health care resources are apt to be concentrated in high-income areas, the aged who can afford to live in them have easier, less costly access to medical care and tend to make use of it more frequently.

The costs and content of medical care services often vary systematically with income. Physicians in high-income areas usually charge higher prices, and the concentration of specialists in these areas leads to a more expensive array of available services. Similarly, hospitals serving communities with high-income patients may have higher costs than hospitals serving poorer patients, as hospitals are likely to respond to high income and extensive insurance coverage by providing more expensive care.[27]

Education, which is positively related to income, may also influence decisions to seek medical care and the type and amount of care obtained. Education can affect the use of medical services in a variety of ways. Educated people are often more aware of the Medicare program and the benefits it provides, and thus more of them than of the less educated may claim benefits for which they are eligible. Educated people may also be more knowledgeable about the potential uses of medical care, more perceptive about symptoms that require medical attention, and more inclined to seek specialized care for specific types of medical problems.

Some patterns of medical care use by the elderly may be traceable to the persistence of habit: people who have not sought medical care for a long time for financial or other reasons may continue not to seek it even with adequate financing.

26. Ruther, "Medicare, Number of Persons Insured, July 1, 1974."
27. Martin S. Feldstein, "Hospital Cost Inflation: A Study of Nonprofit Price Dynamics," *American Economic Review,* vol. 61 (December 1971), pp. 853–72.

Table 4-4. Medicare Payments per Elderly Person, by Family Income, 1970

Incomes and payments in dollars

Family income group	All Medicare services	Hospital services
Under 6,000	326	196
6,000–10,999	449	325
11,000 and over	553	386
All income groups	375	242
Ratio, over 11,000 to under 6,000	1.70	1.97

Source: Estimated from Andersen and others, *Expenditures for Personal Health Services.* The distributions of expenditures and of elderly persons by income for a sample of 1,506 persons sixty-five and over are adjusted to total Medicare expenditures in 1970 of $7,494 million for 20 million elderly people.

The attitudes of physicians and other medical care providers also affect these patterns. To the extent that physicians prefer to treat patients from a socioeconomic class similar to their own, they either consciously or unconsciously discourage lower-income persons from obtaining care. A sign in a physician's office stating that Medicaid patients are not accepted is a blatant example of such discrimination, but more subtle tactics can be equally effective.

All the above factors contribute to the persistence of substantial variations based on income in the use of services and the distribution of Medicare payments. Several studies illustrate this unequal distribution.

The National Opinion Research Center's 1970 survey of medical expenditures reported data on the distribution of Medicare expenditures for three broad income classes of elderly people. Table 4-4 presents estimates of expenditures based on the NORC survey. The survey suggests that per capita Medicare expenditures are about 70 percent higher for the elderly with family incomes above $11,000 than for the elderly with incomes below $6,000. Hospital expenditures per capita are twice as high for the highest income class as for the lowest. Although these estimates were derived from a relatively small sample (only 1,500 elderly people were surveyed), which excluded all those in nursing homes and other facilities, other studies have found similar patterns.

The Current Medicare Survey is a continuing national survey in which information about expenditures on physicians is collected for a large representative sample of elderly beneficiaries; information on the distribution

Table 4-5. Medicare Reimbursements for Covered Services by Physicians under the Supplementary Medical Insurance Program and Number of People Served, by Family Income, 1968

Incomes and reimbursements in dollars

		Reimbursable services		
Family income group	Reimbursement per person enrolled	Number of recipients per 1,000 enrollees	Number of services per recipient	Amount of reimburse- ment per service
Under 5,000	79	432	26	7
Under 2,000	76	438	29	6
2,000–4,999	81	426	23	8
5,000–9,999	104	475	27	8
10,000–14,999	115	527	28	8
15,000 and over	160	552	28	10
All income groups	89	460	27	7
Ratio, over 15,000 to under 5,000	2.04	1.28	1.07	1.48

Source: Calculated from unpublished tabulations from the 1968 Current Medicare Survey, Social Security Administration, Office of Research and Statistics. Figures are rounded.

of hospital expenditures is not collected. Table 4-5 presents findings on the distribution of Medicare reimbursements to physicians by family income. Medicare reimbursements in 1968 for services covered under the supplementary medical insurance plan were $160 per person with family income above $15,000 and $79 per person with income below $5,000—or just over twice as much for the highest income group as for the lowest. This wide difference is partly explained by differences in the amount reimbursed for each service and differences in the use of services by the two income groups. Average Medicare reimbursement per service was $10 for people with family incomes above $15,000 and $6 for those with incomes below $2,000. This difference probably shows the tendency of higher-income people to seek more specialized services.[28]

It is apparent from the table that higher-income elderly people also receive more medical services. Fifty-five percent of Medicare enrollees with family incomes above $15,000 used medical services in excess of the

28. Unpublished data from the 1969 Health Interview Survey, for example, indicated that aged people with incomes below $5,000 received 75 percent of their care from general practitioners and those with family incomes over $15,000 received 65 percent.

$50 deductible (and therefore received some Medicare reimbursement), while only 43 percent of enrollees with family incomes below $5,000 exceeded the deductible. The number of services received by those exceeding the deductible did not vary markedly by income class. However, as poor people are less likely to exceed the deductible, it might be expected that the medical condition of those who do is relatively more serious and that there would be more physicians' visits per poor person than per person with higher income. Under these assumptions, the deductible provision of Medicare, and perhaps the coinsurance payment on medical services, may deter many of the poor from seeking medical care.

In partial support of this hypothesis, table 4-5 shows that the poorest income group (under $2,000) used somewhat more medical services than the next highest income group ($2,000 to $4,999). Medicaid coverage of the very poor would remove deductible and coinsurance payments, but part of the greater use by the very poor may be a consequence of their poorer health status. The survey data unfortunately do not permit the sorting of expenditure levels by eligibility for Medicaid or health status.

There are some data for 1969 that permit an exploration of the effects of Medicaid coverage and supplementary private insurance coverage on the receipt of Medicare benefits. In a study conducted by Peel and Scharff, all elderly people enrolled in the SMI plan were divided into four mutually exclusive groups: those on public medical assistance; those with complementary out-of-hospital insurance coverage; and other enrollees split into two groups on the basis of income and family size.[29] The analysis is restricted to SMI benefits for enrollees who were not admitted to a hospital during the year.

Table 4-6 presents their major findings, recalculated to correspond to the components of reimbursement contained in table 4-5. Public assistance recipients "bought into" the Medicare program by Medicaid used substantially more services than all other groups, receiving out-of-hospital Medicare SMI benefits of $108 per person. Lower-income elderly people without Medicaid coverage received only $42. Peel and Scharff point out that public medical assistance enrollees were older, in poorer health, and less educated, and that a higher percentage were women, persons living alone, and blacks than in other income groups. They therefore hesitated

29. Evelyn Peel and Jack Scharff, "Impact of Cost-Sharing on Use of Ambulatory Services Under Medicare, 1969," *Social Security Bulletin,* vol. 36 (October 1973), pp. 3–24.

Table 4-6. Supplementary Medical Insurance Charges for Enrollees Not Admitted to a Hospital, by Income Group and Coverage, 1969

Coverage and income group	Charge per enrollee (dollars)	Number meeting deductible per 1,000 enrollees[a]	Number of services per person meeting deductible	Charge per service (dollars)
Receiving public medical assistance	108	497	34	6
Lower income[b]	42	318	13	10
Higher income[b]	65	464	13	11
With complementary out-of-hospital coverage	56	386	14	10
All enrollees	55	364	17	9
Ratio, higher income to lower income	1.56	1.46	1.00	1.06

Source: Calculated from Social Security Administration, Office of Research and Statistics, unpublished tabulations from the 1969 Current Medicare Survey. Figures are rounded.

a. Enrollees paid the first $50 (the deductible) of allowed charges for covered benefits received in the calendar year.

b. The dividing point between higher and lower income is $4,000 for a single person, $7,500 for a family of two, $10,000 for a family of three, and $15,000 for a family of four or more. See Evelyn Peel and Jack Scharff, "Impact of Cost-Sharing on Use of Ambulatory Services Under Medicare, 1969," *Social Security Bulletin*, vol. 36 (October 1973), for a description of classifications based on income and insurance.

to draw conclusions about the relation between the relatively greater use of services by public medical assistance recipients and the absence of deductible and coinsurance requirements.

A study by Davis and Reynolds used individual data from the 1969 Health Interview Survey to further investigate patterns of the use of physicians and hospitals among the elderly according to both health status and income class.[30] Using a Tobit regression analysis, they found that the use of medical services by poor people for whom Medicaid pays the premium, deductible, and coinsurance required by Medicare was commensurate with that by middle-income people with similar health needs. Poor people not covered by Medicaid lagged substantially.

These results are summarized in table 4-7. Once physicians' visits are standardized for the health of the elderly person, visits are seen to increase uniformly with income (excluding those on welfare). Among the elderly with an average number of days of disability, the lowest users of physi-

30. Karen Davis and Roger Reynolds, "The Impact of Medicare and Medicaid on Access to Medical Care," in Rosett, *The Role of Health Insurance in the Health Services Sector*, pp. 391–425.

Table 4-7. Average Per Capita Use of Physicians and Hospitals by the Elderly, by Health Status and Family Income, 1969

Family income group (dollars)	Health[a]		
	Good	Average	Poor
Visits to and from physicians			
Under 5,000			
Not receiving aid	2.78	5.64	10.47
Receiving aid[b]	3.86	7.52	13.42
5,000–9,999	3.14	6.60	11.70
10,000–14,999	3.75	7.27	12.98
15,000 and over	5.35	9.53	16.98
Hospital admissions			
Under 5,000	0.114	0.210	0.362
5,000–9,999	0.140	0.250	0.427
10,000–14,999	0.159	0.285	0.472
15,000 and over	0.177	0.312	0.512
Hospital days			
Under 5,000	2.31	4.21	7.21
5,000–9,999	2.78	4.93	8.16
10,000–14,999	2.85	5.02	8.29
15,000 and over	3.52	6.06	9.77

Source: Karen Davis and Roger Reynolds, "The Impact of Medicare and Medicaid on Access to Medical Care," in Richard N. Rosett, ed., *The Role of Health Insurance in the Health Services Sector* (Neale Watson Academic Publications for National Bureau of Economic Research, 1976), pp. 413–14 (Brookings Reprint T-013).

a. Good health is defined as with no chronic conditions, limitation of activity, or restricted activity days. Average and poor health are defined as at the mean and twice the mean levels, respectively, of the three morbidity indicators used.

b. Public assistance recipients.

cians' services were those with incomes below $5,000, who averaged 6.6 visits annually; the highest were people with incomes above $15,000, who visited physicians 9.5 times a year, or 44 percent more frequently. People receiving public assistance saw physicians much more frequently than others in the low-income group and slightly more frequently than the elderly in the $5,000 to $15,000 income range.[31]

Similarly, a comparison of elderly people with comparable health indicated that hospital admissions and average length of stay increased directly with higher family income and that these differences were not totally accounted for by a greater abundance of hospital facilities in higher-income areas or by higher levels of education. High-income people with

31. These rates are based on the assumption that elderly people in each income class have the same amount of education, that medical care is equally available to them, and that they are equally distributed geographically.

average health had 44 percent more hospital days per capita than low-income persons.

These studies, taken together, indicate that substantial income-based differences in the distribution of Medicare benefits and the use of medical services by the elderly do exist and that they are not attributable solely to factors associated with higher incomes such as greater availability of physicians or higher levels of education. They suggest instead that the structure of the Medicare program, with its reliance on uniform cost-sharing provisions for all the elderly irrespective of ability to pay, may be largely responsible for the greater use of medical services by higher-income people.[32]

Equity Implications

Although theoretically the same benefits are available to all enrollees in Medicare, the ability of the elderly to take advantage of these benefits depends not only on income but also on the accessibility of health care. For those who live in areas where health care resources are scarce or who face discriminatory barriers to the receipt of care, actual benefits may be quite limited relative to health care needs.

Differences by Race

Medicare and Medicaid legislation does attempt to remove racial barriers to health care in institutions (not only for the elderly but for all age groups) by requiring that hospitals and nursing homes comply with Title VI of the Civil Rights Act of 1964. This is enforced by on-site examination to certify integration not just for the hospital as a whole but for assignment to semiprivate rooms as well.[33] Although some hospitals, particularly those in the South, initially elected not to serve Medicare patients, within a few years nearly all the hospitals in the country had indicated a

32. One study attempted to isolate the effect of income on the use of medical services. It found no significant income effects, but sufficient data to differentiate between income classes were not available. See Martin S. Feldstein, "An Econometric Model of the Medicare System," *Quarterly Journal of Economics,* vol. 85 (February 1971), pp. 1–20.

33. Robert M. Ball, talk before the Health Staff Seminar, Washington, D.C., October 1973.

willingness to meet Medicare certification requirements. Enforcement of nondiscriminatory provisions for nursing homes was much less rigid, and many abuses still occur.[34]

The advent of Medicare rapidly narrowed differences in hospital care based on race for all age groups. In 1966 whites were hospitalized 27 percent more frequently than blacks and members of other races. Two years later, in 1968, this had fallen to 18 percent. By 1975 the gap had narrowed to 4 percent. For the aged, differences dropped from 70 percent higher hospitalization rates for whites than for other races in 1966 to 25 percent in 1968. In 1975 elderly whites were hospitalized 14 percent more frequently than elderly blacks.[35]

The Social Security Administration early reached the opinion that Medicare had no contractual relation with physicians for the provision of services to Medicare patients. Instead, it viewed itself as making payments to patients who, in turn, purchased services from physicians, and physicians were not required to be in compliance with the Civil Rights Act to participate in Medicare.

Progress in narrowing racial differences in the use of physicians' services has been more moderate. In 1964 elderly whites visited physicians 20 percent more often than elderly blacks and other races; by 1975 elderly whites visited physicians 14 percent more often than other elderly people.[36]

Differences by Location

Medicare benefits have also been unevenly distributed by geographical location. Elderly people in rural areas and in both urban and rural areas of the South have tended to get a smaller than proportionate share of Medicare benefits.

34. *Title VI Enforcement in Medicare and Medicaid Programs,* Hearings before the Subcommittee on Civil Rights and Constitutional Rights of the House Committee on the Judiciary, 93:1 (GPO, 1974).

35. HEW, National Center for Health Statistics, *Persons Hospitalized by Number of Hospital Episodes and Days in a Year, United States, July 1965–June 1966,* and ibid., *1968,* Vital and Health Statistics, series 10, nos. 50 and 64, respectively (GPO, 1969, 1971), pp. 19, 39 and 21, 39; NCHS, *Health, United States, 1976–1977,* p. 291.

36. National Center for Health Statistics, *Volume of Physician Visits by Place of Visit and Type of Service, United States, July 1963–June 1964,* Vital and Health Statistics, series 10, no. 18 (GPO, 1965), pp. 17, 29; and NCHS, *Health, United States, 1976–1977,* p. 265.

Table 4-8. Average Medicare Reimbursement under Hospital and Supplementary Medical Insurance, by Area of Residence, 1975

Reimbursement in dollars

Region	Total	Metropolitan counties		Nonmetro-politan counties	Ratio, counties with a central city to nonmetro-politan counties
		With a central city	With no central city		
Annual hospital insurance reimbursement per person enrolled					
United States	434	484	448	342	1.42
Northeast	502	539	497	379	1.42
North Central	441	505	445	361	1.40
South	364	403	378	316	1.28
West	455	491	448	340	1.44
Annual supplementary medical insurance reimbursement per person enrolled					
United States	169	197	171	121	1.63
Northeast	186	201	186	129	1.56
North Central	143	165	149	112	1.47
South	152	186	153	116	1.60
West	221	240	233	155	1.55

Source: Calculated from Social Security Administration, *Medicare: Health Insurance for the Aged and Disabled, 1974 and 1975, Section 1.1: Reimbursement by State and County* (GPO, 1977), tables 1.1.1, 1.1.6, 1.1.7.

Table 4-8 summarizes the distribution of Medicare reimbursements by metropolitan-nonmetropolitan residence and by region. Medicare payments for hospital and posthospital care per enrollee range from $316 in the nonmetropolitan South to $539 in northeastern metropolitan counties with a central city. Average payments under the supplementary medical insurance plan are twice as high in metropolitan counties of the West as in nonmetropolitan counties of the north central region. For all regions except the South payments for hospital care per enrollee are 40 percent higher in major metropolitan counties than in nonmetropolitan counties and in all regions payments for medical care are 50 to 60 percent higher.

Regional variation in reimbursement for physicians' services corresponds to both the varying proportions of enrollees exceeding the deductible and the average level of reimbursement for those receiving reimbursable services. The proportion of elderly exceeding the deductible is considerably larger in the West than in the North and South. At least part of this variation can be attributed to the varying availability of physicians. The southern and north central regions have fewer physicians per capita (1.34 physicians per 1,000 people) than the Northeast and the West (with 2.00 and 1.83 per 1,000, respectively). Regional patterns in the use of physicians' services are therefore consistent with regional patterns in numbers of physicians per capita.

As regional variation in physicians' charges follows a similar pattern, it further contributes to regional variation in Medicare reimbursement. Average reimbursement levels for physicians' services are lowest in the north central region and highest in the West. For example, the average Medicare payment for an office visit to a general practitioner ranges from a low of $7.50 in the north central region to a high of $9.80 in the West.[37] Even within a region, and controlling for the physician's specialty, Medicare pays significantly different fees for physicians' services in rural and urban areas. In 1975 in the South, office visits to general practitioners ranged from $10 in rural Mississippi to $50 in urban areas of Georgia.[38]

Regional variation in payments for nursing home care is consistent with the proportion of Medicare enrollees exceeding the hospital deductible.[39] The regional pattern in the use of nursing home services, in turn, is linked to the availability of beds in those homes. Where beds are most widely available, the proportion of hospitalized patients transferred to nursing homes is highest. In 1972, for example, in California, which has 4.3 beds per 100 Medicare enrollees, admissions were 5.0 per enrollee. But Mississippi had 0.4 beds per 100 enrollees and 0.8 admissions per enrollee.[40]

The one medical service for which the rate of use does not vary markedly by geographical region—inpatient hospital care—is also the one with the least geographical variation in availability. For instance, 22 percent of Medicare enrollees in the South and 21 percent in the West are hospitalized each year; hospital beds per capita are also virtually the same in the two regions.

Most of the regional variation in hospital reimbursements appears to be explained by the variation in hospital costs. For example, as shown in

37. Social Security Administration, unpublished data for 1975.
38. Ibid.
39. Medicare patients must exceed the hospital deductible before they can receive nursing home reimbursement.
40. Social Security Administration, *Medicare: Health Insurance for the Aged; Selected State Data, Fiscal Years 1968–1972* (GPO, 1974).

Table 4-9. Number of People Receiving Selected Services under Medicare per 1,000 Enrolled and Reimbursement per Person Served, by Geographical Region, 1969

Region	All services[a]	Hospital inpatient services	Physicians' services	Nursing home services
	Number served per 1,000 enrolled			
United States	432	207	418	20
Northeast	443	183	428	19
North Central	406	218	386	17
South	411	217	398	16
West	518	207	510	35
Ratio, West to South	1.26	0.95	1.28	2.19
	Reimbursement per person served (dollars)			
United States	697	955	201	790
Northeast	736	1,167	209	900
North Central	717	935	183	800
South	625	765	196	692
West	702	1,046	219	762
Ratio, West to South	1.12	1.37	1.12	1.10

Source: Social Security Administration, *Medicare: Health Insurance for the Aged, 1969, Section 1: Summary—Utilization and Reimbursement by Person,* DHEW (SSA) 75-11704 (GPO, 1975), pp. 1-4, 1-6.
a. Includes home health services and hospital outpatient services.

table 4-9, approximately the same proportion of enrollees were hospitalized in the South as in other regions, but average reimbursement per person hospitalized was 37 percent higher in the West than in the South. It is quite possible that more expensive hospital technology, broader services, or more amenities contribute to the higher costs in the West and Northeast.[41]

There is some evidence that the gap between the use of physicians' services by the rural aged and use by the urban aged widened in the ten years following the introduction of Medicare. In fiscal 1964 the elderly in metropolitan areas visited physicians an average of 6.8 times per person and those in nonmetropolitan areas 6.5 times, but in 1975 the rates were 6.9 and 6.1, respectively.[42]

Geographical variation in Medicare benefits raises issues somewhat

41. See Martin S. Feldstein, "The Quality of Hospital Services: An Analysis of Geographic Variation and Intertemporal Change," in Mark Perlman, ed., *The Economics of Health and Medical Care* (Wiley, 1974), pp. 402–19.
42. National Center for Health Statistics, *Health Characteristics by Geographic Region, Large Metropolitan Areas, and Other Places of Residence, United States— July 1963–June 1965,* Vital and Health Statistics, series 10, no. 36 (GPO, 1967), p. 31; and NCHS, *Health, United States, 1976–1977,* p. 265.

different from those raised by variations based on income or race. Some geographical variation in the elderly's use of medical services is predictable as medical resources are not uniformly distributed. Were the elderly's use of medical services not sensitive to available supply of hospitals or physicians, younger age groups in scarce resource areas could have even greater difficulty in obtaining adequate medical care.

The unequal distribution of benefits is nevertheless disturbing for two reasons. First, the elderly in rural areas and in the South have a much higher incidence of chronic conditions than the elderly in other areas, which suggests that they should be receiving a more than proportionate share of Medicare funds.[43] Second, the unequal distribution of Medicare benefits (see table 4-8) arises from the method of financing the program. Since a portion of Medicare is financed by premiums paid by the elderly, the unequal distribution of payments means that the aged in rural areas are subsidizing urban residents. In 1972, for example, the elderly in nonmetropolitan areas of West Virginia and Kentucky received average Medicare reimbursements for physicians' services of $56, but the elderly in major metropolitan areas of New York and California received over $160.[44] Since each had to pay an annual premium of $68 for coverage of physicians' services that year, the elderly as a group in some areas of the rural South were paying more than they were getting back.

Such a transfer of funds will occur whenever premium payments do not vary with the costs or use of medical services in an area. This transfer is especially disturbing because areas with higher medical costs and more medical resources also tend to be those with higher-income residents. Medicare's reliance on uniform premiums in effect often transfers funds from the elderly with low incomes to those with higher incomes. The resulting distribution of financing is thus based neither on expected benefits nor on ability to pay.

Medicare further intensifies rural-urban inequities by basing the reimbursement of physicians on the charges prevailing in an area. Medicare pays physicians practicing in low-income rural areas (who consequently charge relatively low prices) less than physicians practicing in high-income urban areas (who generally charge higher prices). This may stimulate demand by elderly rural residents for more medical services, but paying

43. See, for example, Karen Davis and Ray Marshall, "Rural Health Care in the South," preliminary summary report prepared for presentation at the meeting of the Task Force on Southern Rural Development, Atlanta, October 1975, p. 8.
44. Social Security Administration, *Medicare: Health Insurance for the Aged, 1972, Section 1:3, Geographic Index of Reimbursement by State and County,* DHEW (SSA) 76-11709 (SSA, 1975), table 3.

unequal rates for the same services is not likely to attract additional physicians to these areas. Instead, Medicare's policy rewards physicians for practicing in areas where physicians are fairly abundant.

Medicare also hinders rural residents from acting to solve their own problems. Some rural areas are attempting to make up for the scarcity of physicians by establishing health centers staffed by nurse practitioners and physician's assistants, using the part-time services of physicians from larger communities. Before the amendments to the Social Security Act that provide payment for rural health clinic services were passed in 1977, Medicare would not pay for services delivered by these practitioners or certify these centers as eligible for direct reimbursement.[45]

The combination of a standard premium for all and unequal reimbursement rates for urban and rural medical services channels funds away from rural areas. Medicare thus doubly disadvantages people in nonmetropolitan areas, especially in the South and the north central region, where medical resources are relatively scarce: premium payments subsidize the services received by persons in other, wealthier areas, and lower fees and restrictions on the eligibility of potential providers discourage them from locating in rural areas.

Reform

Medicare has without question been an important force in improving the medical care of the elderly and reducing its financial burden. But complacency about the program is unwarranted for several reasons. First, inequities in the distribution of benefits are serious. Second, some portions of the program have been more successful in removing the financial burden of health care than others. Third, inflation in the cost of physicians' services and nursing home services has resulted in even heavier burdens on the elderly than they bore before Medicare and Medicaid. Fourth, noncovered services continue to threaten many elderly people with financial hardship. And finally, variations in expenditures between income classes and between regions persist (and are even encouraged) under Medicare's reimbursement policies despite the program's promise of equal protection to all elderly people.

Reform of Medicare to correct the program's uneven and socially undesirable effects on the delivery of services is crucial. Five areas particu-

45. Amendments to the Social Security Act, enacted December 13, 1977; Public Law 95-210.

larly in need of reexamination are the cost-sharing structure of Medicare; the range of benefits covered and requirements for eligibility; methods of reimbursing providers of services; methods of financing the program; and supplementary measures that need to be taken to improve the access of minority groups and residents of underserved medical areas to adequate care.

Most of the numerous recent reform proposals address only some of these areas, and none adequately address Medicare's failure to protect all the elderly. For instance, a Medicare and Medicaid administrative reimbursement and reform bill introduced in Congress would change methods of reimbursing physicians and hospitals to encourage a tighter control of costs; a comprehensive Medicare reform bill would eliminate the payment of premiums, merge insurance covering the costs of hospitals and physicians into one plan, extend the range of covered services, introduce an income-related payment ceiling, and require all participating providers to accept a predetermined fee schedule as final payment.

Isolating Medicare reforms and policy from national financing policy restricts the latitude policymakers have in improving the equity, quality, and financial protection of the program for the elderly. In particular, cost controls applied to programs covering only one population group tend to hurt rather than help beneficiaries. Thus comprehensive Medicare reform needs a national policy coupling the program with Medicaid and the general population.

Several program-specific reforms of Medicare would lay a foundation for a national financing system. First, a more aggressive use of fee schedules and reimbursement policy to encourage and reward service in underserved areas and enforce nondiscrimination as a condition for the participation of providers would lead to a more equitable distribution of benefits. Elimination of deductibles and a ceiling on out-of-pocket premiums and copayments scaled by income would also improve equity and for the first time guarantee financial protection for covered benefits. Similarly, improving the range of primary and preventive care services to discourage the use of expensive institutionalized care would improve cost performance. Finally, merging Medicare and Medicaid policies would strengthen program performance on behalf of the elderly. To further encourage an adequate supply of services for the poor, a fixed percentage of both programs' budgets could be reserved for resource development in underserved areas.[46]

46. These reforms, in conjunction with recommendations for reforms of other governmental health programs, are further explored in chapter 7.

chapter five **Medical Care for Mothers and Children:**
The Maternal and Child Health Program

Governmental efforts to support the health needs of mothers and children date back to 1912, more than fifty years before the advent of Medicaid and Medicare. Yet relatively little is known about the success or failure of the various public strategies designed to meet the special health care needs of this group. Focus on Medicare and Medicaid has both overshadowed and undermined grants for the maternal and child health (MCH) program; an uncoordinated, piecemeal federal health policy has repeatedly frustrated attempts to integrate or evaluate the activities of the program. As the health problems of mothers and children, particularly those who are poor or otherwise disadvantaged, are far from solved, this neglect is inexcusable.

The maternal and child health and crippled children's programs, as authorized by the Social Security Act, have been the major vehicle for supporting medical care to mothers and children since 1935. Grants for these programs have several major characteristics that differentiate them from other federal health programs. First, they aim funds at mothers and children, especially crippled children. Second, they give funds to those supplying medical services rather than to the recipients. Third, funds are allocated through a formula that gives special priority to rural areas and areas in severe economic distress. Fourth, while concentrating services in needy areas, they make care available free of charge regardless of income; thus the programs are not strictly poverty programs. Fifth, states and local areas must match federal funds. Finally, they are federal-state programs in which states have substantial flexibility to allocate funds and design projects.[1]

This chapter was prepared with the assistance of M. K. Carney.
1. Although state programs must meet general federal guidelines, state plans are not systematically reviewed by the Department of Health, Education, and Welfare before federal funding. Personal communication, C. Arden Miller, March 27, 1975.

MCH funds go to state and local health department programs for maternal, child, and crippled children's services; to special clinics and centers for children and youths and for maternal and infant health care; and to cover training for personnel and research relating to maternal and child health problems. Services provided by the various programs include pre- and postpartum care for mothers, family planning services, counseling for mothers on the proper care of infants, immunizations, well-baby care, care of high-risk infants (particularly those with cardiopulmonary failure or respiratory disease), comprehensive health care for children and youths, school health examinations (particularly tests for vision and hearing), and dental care for children. Special attention is given to crippled children with orthopedic handicaps, epilepsy, hearing impairment, cerebral palsy, cystic fibrosis, heart disease, congenital defects, and mental retardation.

Despite this broad range of services, the MCH program's expenditures and its share of public funds for health care are small relative to those of Medicare and Medicaid. In 1976 it spent only $593 million; Medicare and Medicaid spent $17,777 million and $15,320 million, respectively.[2] To understand and evaluate this great difference in the allocation of resources, it is necessary to look at the history, successes, and failures of the MCH program in its efforts to deliver health services.[3]

Historical Background

With the establishment of the Children's Bureau in 1912, the federal government became involved in the health of women and children. Reformers concerned with the problem of child labor had long pressed for government action, and the creation of the Children's Bureau, with its mandate to investigate and report on the social and economic conditions affecting children, was a limited response to this pressure. Although the powers of the Children's Bureau were restricted to information gathering,

2. Robert M. Gibson and Marjorie Smith Mueller, "National Health Expenditures, Fiscal Year 1976," *Social Security Bulletin*, vol. 40 (April 1977), p. 11.

3. Three sources provided the information for the following section. For the documentary history of federal programs in child health, see Robert H. Bremner, ed., *Children and Youth in America, A Documentary History, Volume 3, 1933–1973, Parts Five through Seven* (Harvard University Press, 1974), pt. 6, pp. 1207–1571. For details on the political and legislative history, see Gilbert Y. Steiner, *The Children's Cause* (Brookings Institution, 1976), pp. 206–39. For a history of the Children's Bureau, see Dorothy E. Bradbury, *Five Decades of Action for Children: A History of the Children's Bureau,* U.S. Department of Health, Education, and Welfare, Children's Bureau (GPO, 1962).

the emphasis on child labor still aroused considerable opposition. To circumvent this, the bureau focused its first studies on the determinants of infant mortality and enlisted support for the studies from employers of children.

The results created a demand for further action. The studies named family income, housing, employment status of the mother, and early care of mothers and infants as crucial factors in determining whether babies and mothers lived or died. In 1913 these were startling facts as it was the first time a study by an official government agency had linked infant mortality to conditions that could be alleviated. The bureau's reports gave ammunition to reformers urging further federal action for children and mothers.

One such action was the adoption in 1921 of an act for the promotion of the welfare and hygiene of mothers and infants,[4] known as the Maternity and Infancy Act. This law, one of the first federal grants-in-aid programs in health, became the administrative responsibility of the Children's Bureau and furnished beginning support for medical services for mothers and children. The program required a state that chose to accept any of the $1.2 million grant money to designate a state administrative agency with responsibility for maternal and infant care and to match federal funds. Forty-five states participated in the program during its eight-year existence. Although the opposition of physicians and the Catholic Church led to its termination in 1929, the program succeeded in laying the groundwork for subsequent federal and state cooperation in the field.

With the onset of the depression and the disappearance of federal support for child health, states found it difficult to provide adequate maternal and child health care. Expenditures by health departments fell to minimal levels. The Children's Bureau issued new reports on the worsening health and welfare of children and recommended a broad federal-state program for children's security. Influenced by these recommendations, the Committee on Economic Security revived the federal-state partnership grant program for the health of women and children in the Social Security Act of 1935. Title V of the act, to be administered by the Children's Bureau, distinguished three programs for children: maternal and child health services, services for crippled children, and child welfare services. The first two were essentially concerned with health while the third was broader, dealing with such matters as adoption procedures and standards for detention homes.

4. 42 Stat. 224.

Title IV of the legislation covered a broad program for cash payments to mothers lacking fathers' support for their children. Responsibility for administering the program was given to the newly created Social Security Board and thus separated from child health money and the Children's Bureau.

Maternal and child health services and crippled children's services were funded separately in the act. For maternal and child health services each state received a flat amount (initially $20,000 for each fiscal year) plus shares of two funds. The share of one fund, which the state was required to match dollar for dollar, was based on the number of live births in the state relative to the number of live births in the whole country. The state's share of the other fund, with no matching requirement, was determined by financial need and the number of live births in the state. The purpose of the latter fund was to encourage and stimulate demonstration and experimental programs for mothers and children. Each state was allotted $20,000 a year from the crippled children's fund; the rest was distributed according to the number of crippled children served and the cost of serving them. Since funding was determined by the number of crippled children served, states had an incentive to locate and help these children; the grant program for maternal and child health services had no such incentive.

Within nine months of enactment, all states were participating in the MCH and crippled children's programs. Although there was considerable variation among states, in the early years the MCH programs focused on preventive health care, the training of health professionals, and the planning of projects; few provided medical or hospital care. This situation changed as the United States entered World War II. Servicemen's wives, often far from home and lacking adequate facilities, needed maternity care. Initially, to provide obstetrical care and hospitalization for these women, the Children's Bureau used unspent monies from the MCH nonmatching fund, but the amount available proved grossly inadequate.

Under increasing pressure to provide pregnancy care for wives as a morale booster for servicemen, Congress in 1943 appropriated funds for emergency maternity and infant care (national defense) for the support of medical, nursing, and hospital maternity care for wives and babies of men in the four lowest pay grades of the armed forces. The program, administered by the Children's Bureau, was promoted as only an emergency extension of the MCH program to circumvent opposition to further federal involvement in the direct delivery of medical care. By the time the program ended in 1949, it had served as a major impetus for hospitalization for maternity care; 1.5 million maternity cases were handled, and 92 percent of the babies were born in a hospital in contrast to 79 percent for the total population.

After the war, the state MCH programs returned to their previous focus on preventive care services; only a small number continued to provide expectant mothers with medical services. The emergency program had established, however, substantial concern about delivering medical services to mothers, rather than just preventive health and educational services.

The crippled children's program also expanded over the years both in the number of children served and the types of handicaps covered. Initially all states had accepted children that needed orthopedic services or plastic surgery.[5] In the 1940s states added the treatment of children with rheumatic heart conditions to their responsibilities. In the 1950s, after advances had been made in the techniques of cardiac surgery, they added the treatment of children with congenital heart disease.

A renewed national commitment to social problems and social protest movements led to major expansions of the MCH programs in 1963 and 1965. Amendments added grants for comprehensive health care projects specifically serving mothers and children in low-income areas.

The 1963 amendments reflected President John F. Kennedy's interest in the problem of mental retardation. They included special grants for maternity and infant care (M&I) projects designed to provide adequate prenatal care, which lowers the risk of mental retardation as well as infant mortality. Both the 1963 and the 1965 amendments, in augmenting formula grants to states, specifically emphasized the prevention and diagnosis of mental retardation, and the 1965 amendments included metabolic disorders. Thus reduction of the incidence of mental retardation became, along with reduction of infant mortality, an explicit goal of the MCH program. The 1963 amendments also authorized funds for research grants and demonstration projects, which, for the first time, could go to private, nonprofit agencies or institutions as well as public agencies.

Presidential preferences also played a part in the 1965 amendments. As an adjunct of President Lyndon B. Johnson's interest in poverty, children and youth (C&Y) projects were added to provide comprehensive health care in poverty-stricken urban areas. The C&Y projects and the M&I projects—initially authorized for five years but later extended—were

5. A large number of states restricted crippled children's services to children "of sound mind," based on the state's definition of an adequate IQ.

both to be demonstrations of comprehensive health care delivery to low-income populations. The federal government, through the Children's Bureau, directly administered these projects. By 1973 federal project grants had created fifty-six M&I projects and fifty-nine C&Y projects. Other federal projects offered intensive care for infants and dental care for children.

Further revision of Title V in 1967 consolidated maternal and child health programs, crippled children's programs, M&I and C&Y projects, research, and training funds for maternal and child health into a single authorization for funds. Out of the resulting federal appropriation, the amendment designated 50 percent as formula grants for maternal and child health and crippled children's programs, 40 percent as funds for project grants, and 10 percent as funds for research and training. The amendment also required that funds from the formula, project, and research grants be made available for the provision of family planning services.[6]

The 1967 revision also stipulated that project grants be phased out in 1972. After 1972 the federal government was to be responsible only for handing out formula grants; the states could then determine what services to fund with this money so long as they included at least one project in each of the following categories: maternity and infant care, care for high-risk infants, dental care, family planning, and child and preschool health care. The phaseout took place on June 30, 1974, after a two-year delay and considerable opposition from children's lobbies.

This increased emphasis on state responsibility for the design and selection of health programs was accompanied by a weakening of the administrative responsibilities of the Children's Bureau. In 1969 administration of Title V health activities was transferred from the bureau to the Public Health Service. It is currently under the Division for Maternal and Child Health of the Bureau of Community Health Services, which is also in charge of other programs offering health care to low-income populations, such as neighborhood health centers, migrant workers' projects, and family planning projects.

The Maternal and Child Health Program in General

The various amendments to the Social Security Act left a loose federal-state partnership with no cohesive public policy toward the MCH program

6. See *Welfare in Review*, vol. 6 (May–June 1968), pp. 1–34, for a legislative history and summary of the provisions of the 1967 Social Security Amendments.

and no strong agency taking responsibility for policy leadership. Each state now designs its own program with little evaluation or guidance. As receipt of federal funds is not contingent on demonstrated efficacy, efficiency, or equity, accountability for public funds is virtually nonexistent. States have not even been required to spend the funds on services; they can, if they choose, devote all federal support to the administration of the program.[7]

There is little coordination between maternal and child health activities and other federal programs affecting children—particularly Medicaid. Nor has the research on child health and development conducted by the National Institute of Child Health and Human Development been linked with service delivery programs.

Evaluation of the performance of the program has been hampered by inadequate statistical reporting. Many of the achievements of the program have been obscured by the lack of systematic evidence as reports present primarily anecdotal descriptions of isolated projects.

Goals

The primary emphasis of the MCH program has always been on promoting the health of mothers and children. Objectives such as providing general high-quality medical care, making it more readily available to the poor, and reducing its financial burden have never been major objectives per se. Unlike Medicare and Medicaid, which are immediately concerned with financing medical care for the poor and the elderly, the MCH program has selected a more difficult goal: actually bringing about tangible changes in health status.

Reducing infant and maternal mortality is the major focus of the program's effort to improve health. Other objectives are reduction of the incidence of mental retardation, reduction of the incidence of conditions leading to crippling, reduction of unwanted pregnancies through improved family planning services, immunization against disease, identification and early treatment of hearing and vision problems, and reduction of dental

7. For a detailed analysis of the MCH program in one state, with emphasis on how states and local governments use federal funds, see George Silver, "The Hands of Esau: Reflections on Federalism and Child Health Services in the USA," paper presented to the Sun Valley Forum on National Health, Sun Valley, Idaho, August 1975. Silver found that a major portion of federal funds are spent on administration while state and local funds are allocated to services. The analysis in this chapter is concerned with all funds spent under the program, regardless of source.

disease. Many program activities, such as counseling and the treatment of medical conditions, may lead to improvements in less measurable aspects of children's developmental and learning capacity.

The Social Security Act gives priority to serving specific groups of mothers and children, namely, those living "in rural areas and in areas suffering from severe economic distress."[8] While the MCH program does not define areas of severe economic distress, the 1963 and 1965 amendments to the Social Security Act did stress the importance of reaching mothers and children in urban areas of poverty as well as continuing the traditional focus on rural areas. Consequently, most of the projects funded by the program are located either in rural areas or in low-income central city areas.

The apportionment of part of the funds under the maternal and child health and crippled children's formula grants-in-aid programs, in keeping with the statutory emphasis on rural areas, counts a rural child twice for each urban child. Rural states thus receive a proportionately larger share of federal funds and have a more favorable matching requirement than urban states.[9] This favoritism, however, does not guarantee that funds are spent on rural residents.

Major Trends

Though special medical care programs for mothers and children do not approach the scale of the Medicare and Medicaid programs, they do represent a large portion of the funds spent by the federal government for the delivery of specific health services. Over one-third of all federal expenditures for community health services go to the MCH program.

The program grew from a total of $29 million in federal, state, and local expenditures in 1950 to a total of $443 million in 1973. Most of this growth occurred after the expansion of the program in 1963. In the ten-year period before 1963, MCH expenditures increased by $100 million. In the ten years following the 1963 amendments to the program, expenditures increased by about $250 million (see table 5-1).

After 1963 the federal government assumed an increasing share of financial responsibility for the MCH program because of the addition of

8. 49 Stat. (pt. 1) 629, sec. 501.
9. See Arthur P. Lesser and Eleanor P. Hunt, "Maternal and Child Health Programs and Rural Areas," in *Rural Poverty in the United States,* A Report by the President's National Advisory Commission on Rural Poverty (GPO, 1968), pp. 333–55, for a discussion of special problems in rural areas.

Table 5-1. Federal, State, and Local Expenditures for Maternal and Child Health and Crippled Children's Services, by Formula and Project Grants, Selected Fiscal Years, 1950–73

Type of expenditure and services	1950	1954	1963	1967	1970	1973
	Amount (millions of dollars)[a]					
Federal, total	19.4	23.4	50.4	135.2	186.7	209.1
Maternal and child						
health	11.6	12.3	25.1	88.6	129.0	150.2
Formula	11.6	12.3	25.1	47.7	49.8	59.2
Project	...	...	...	40.9	79.3[b]	91.0[b]
Crippled children	7.8	11.1	25.3	46.7	57.7	58.9
State and local, total	9.7	66.0	138.7	170.9	235.3	234.3
Maternal and child						
health	5.8	41.0	81.2	103.4	140.1	131.3
Formula	5.8	41.0	81.2	93.1	113.6	101.0
Project	...	...	...	10.2	26.4[b]	30.3[b]
Crippled children	3.9	25.1	57.5	67.6	95.2	103.0
Federal, state, and local	29.1	89.4	189.2	306.1	422.1	443.4
	Percentage distribution[a]					
Federal, total	66.7	26.2	26.6	44.2	44.2	47.2
Maternal and child						
health	39.9	13.8	13.3	28.9	30.6	33.9
Formula	39.9	13.8	13.3	15.6	11.8	13.4
Project	...	...	...	13.4	18.8[b]	20.5[b]
Crippled children	26.8	12.4	13.4	15.2	13.7	13.3
State and local, total	33.3	73.8	73.3	55.8	55.8	52.8
Maternal and child						
health	19.9	45.9	42.9	33.8	33.2	29.6
Formula	19.9	45.9	42.9	30.4	26.9	22.8
Project	...	...	...	3.3	6.3[b]	6.8[b]
Crippled children	13.4	28.1	30.4	22.1	22.6	23.2
Federal, state, and local	100.0	100.0	100.0	100.0	100.0	100.0

Sources: Ida C. Merriam and Alfred M. Skolnik, *Social Welfare Expenditures Under Public Programs in the United States, 1929–66*, Research Report 25, U.S. Department of Health, Education, and Welfare, Social Security Administration (GPO, 1968), p. 219; and unpublished data from HEW, Maternal and Child Health Services. Figures are rounded.

a. State and local amounts and percentages include administrative expenses.

b. Excludes family planning projects.

project grants. Between 1954 and 1963 the federal share remained slightly more than a quarter of the total, but after the expansion the federal share increased to almost half. In 1973 federal, state, and local expenditures for specific projects accounted for 25 percent of all funds.

Unfortunately, little information is available on the amounts of money spent on specific health care services. Funds are only broken down by program category. In 1973, 36 percent of the combined federal, state, and local funds went for the care of crippled children, another 30 percent went for state and local health department services to mothers and children, and the remaining 34 percent was spent by the federal government for M&I and C&Y projects and services.

Federal MCH funds have been heavily concentrated on specific project grants—42 percent in fiscal 1974. The estimated distribution of federal obligations was 25 percent for crippled children's services, 23 percent for state and local health department services to mothers and children, 17 percent for M&I projects, 18 percent for C&Y projects, 7 percent for family planning projects, 8 percent for research and training, and relatively small amounts for dental health and intensive care of infants.

Expenditures for Title V have not kept up with inflation. Federal obligations were $262 million in 1972 and $259 million in 1974.[10] This freeze on total expenditures during a period of rapidly rising medical costs has undoubtedly made it difficult for the program to maintain a constant level of real services. There is no detailed service information, however, to show which services and which people have suffered.

Services for Children: State and Local Health Department Programs

The formula grant funds for child health services are used primarily to provide immunizations, health examinations in schools for vision and hearing abnormalities, and preventive care. Health departments conduct well-child conferences with a physician present, which periodically assess child development, screen for abnormal conditions, and arrange for immunization against infectious diseases.[11] Health departments' general pediatric clinic services furnish consultation, diagnosis, treatment, and follow-up care for sick children; special clinics provide similar services for children with such conditions as rheumatic fever or hearing impairment. Some states spend part of their federal formula grant funds on nursing services to children in their homes, hospital care for premature and, in some cases, full-term infants, and corrective dental services.

10. *National Health Insurance Resource Book,* prepared by the staff of the House Committee on Ways and Means (GPO, 1974), p. 507.
11. Treatment of detected conditions, however, may be financed from other sources, such as the Medicaid program.

Each state has considerable discretion to allocate formula grant funds between services for mothers and services for children. Unfortunately, no information is available on the proportion of federal-state-local formula funds spent on children as a group or on specific services for children. Detailed data are only collected on the number of children that receive various types of services, not on how many receive more than one service or how many receive at least one service.

The state and local health department programs have concentrated on immunizing and screening a limited number of children. While unduplicative counts of children receiving services are not available, it seems unlikely that more than 10 million—less than 15 percent of all those under eighteen in the United States—are served by the program. In fiscal 1972 almost 9 million children received visual examinations, 6 million received audiometer tests, and 3.5 million received tetanus, diphtheria, and polio immunizations. Few children received diagnostic or treatment services; only 1.5 million, 80 percent of whom were under five, received some care from a physician in well-child conferences, and 2.8 million received some nursing services.[12] Thus many children received only a vision and hearing test in school, and when a deficiency was discovered, the program took no responsibility for ensuring that it was corrected by eyeglasses or a hearing aid. Similarly, it had no procedure for updating immunizations.

During the 1960s and early 1970s, although formula funds to state and local health department programs grew, the number of children served hardly grew at all. Expenditures for MCH formula grants increased almost 25 percent between fiscal years 1963 and 1973 (see table 5-1), but the number of children receiving visual screening only increased by 12 percent, the number receiving care at well-child conferences, nursing services, or general pediatric services remained almost constant, and the number receiving dental and physical examinations declined slightly.[13] Apparently, most of the growth in expenditures under the formula grant portion of the legislation went to meet the rising cost of providing services rather than to extending services to a greater number of children or providing more comprehensive care. By 1973 average expenditures were roughly only $8 per child receiving services.[14]

12. HEW, Health Services Administration, *Maternal and Child Health Services of State and Local Health Departments, Fiscal Year 1972,* DHEW (HSA) 74-5801 (HSA, 1973), tables 7, 8, 10, 11.
13. Ibid., tables 2, 3.
14. Based on the assumption that states allocated half their formula funds to children and served a total of 10 million children.

With little growth in expenditures, there was some indication of a decline in child health services between fiscal years 1971 and 1972. The number of children aged one to seventeen reached by well-child conferences fell from 994,000 in 1971 to 950,000 in 1972. In thirty-one states the number receiving nursing services decreased though nursing services to children across the nation increased by almost 8 percent. Screening through school health programs declined nationwide. Smallpox vaccinations fell by almost 50 percent.[15]

Services for Children: Children and Youth Project Grants

Unlike the formula grants to the states for child health services, the C&Y grant funds are specifically designated for the comprehensive health care of children in high-need communities.[16] In 1972 there were fifty-nine C&Y projects in 170 sites in twenty-eight states, the District of Columbia, the Virgin Islands, and Puerto Rico, serving about 500,000 children at an annual cost of $62 million in 1971, or about $125 a registered child (approximately the same as health care expenditures for all U.S. children). From 1968 to 1972 centers doubled the number of children served but reduced the average annual cost per child by about 35 percent (from $200 to $130).[17]

Each project serves a specific low-income area, ranging in size from 0.1 to 6,300 square miles; the median is about 6 square miles. A total of 3.5 million children live in these areas. Two-thirds of the projects, and nearly 90 percent of the children enrolled, are in the inner cities. The median enrollment of the projects is 4,500, the smallest project having fewer than 1,000 children and the largest 40,000. Approximately equal numbers of health departments, teaching hospitals, and medical schools operate the projects.[18] The children and youth health centers offer comprehensive

15. HEW, Maternal and Child Health Service, *Promoting the Health of Mothers and Children, Fiscal Year 1973,* DHEW (HSA) 74-5002 (MCHS, 1973), p. 25.

16. Much of the information on the C&Y projects in this section is from Maternal and Child Health Service, *The Children and Youth Projects: Comprehensive Health Care in Low-income Areas* (GPO, 1972); and *National Health Insurance Resource Book,* pt. 4, pp. 496–518.

17. Some services, such as hospital care, may be paid for with Medicaid funds, however.

18. For a discussion of the effect of sponsorship, see Willy De Geyndt and Linda M. Sprague, "Differential Patterns in Comprehensive Health Care Delivery for Children and Youth: Health Department, Medical School, Teaching Hospital," *American Journal of Public Health,* vol. 60 (August 1970), pp. 1402–20.

health care to registrants and engage in active outreach programs to register patients, to follow up on broken appointments, and to attempt to keep patients in the health care system. Once a child is registered, usually because he or she needs episodic care, the project staff attempts to carry out a health assessment; once discovered conditions have been treated, the projects provide health supervision with periodic follow-up care. Patients are classified as registered only, in the assessment process, or under health supervision. By the end of the fourth quarter of 1972, more than 70 percent of all registered children were under health supervision.[19]

The C&Y centers' comprehensive services emphasize preventive measures including medical, dental, nutritional, and social services. After screening or diagnosis, children receive any necessary treatment, including items such as eyeglasses and hearing aids. Some projects dispense prescription drugs, obtain food from supplemental feeding programs, and provide counseling and classes for parents as well as children. Projects engage in special activities dictated by the needs of the children they serve such as detection of lead paint poisoning, screening for sickle cell anemia, rat eradication, counseling for families in child abuse cases, and even efforts to obtain better heating in housing projects. In these activities, they frequently recruit the assistance of community organizations and supporting agencies. Most projects emphasize dental services, particularly for young school age children. Nearly all projects that serve wide areas provide transportation for children.

The screening program has uncovered a high incidence of correctable defects. For the year ending June 30, 1971, of the 71,000 children screened for visual impairment, 14 percent failed the test, and of the 77,000 children who took hearing tests, 7.6 percent failed. A cooperative effort between the Chicago Board of Health, the Illinois state health department, the Office of Economic Opportunity, and the C&Y program screened 116,261 children for lead poisoning over a three-year period in the Chicago area; of these, over 10,000 had abnormally high lead levels indicating excessive exposure. A C&Y project in New York City found 60 percent of 435 blood samples had elevated lead levels. The New York City Health Department also screened 30,000 children and found 57 percent had elevated lead levels.

Discovery of such high incidence rates can be and is followed up with

19. Minnesota Systems Research, Inc., Systems Development Project, "Report Series: Quarterly Summary Report," no. 20 (October–December 1972) (Minneapolis: MSRI, n.d.; processed), p. 7.

corrective actions in C&Y projects, which in 1970 provided 240,000 immunizations, 215,000 dental fillings, and 6,100 pairs of eyeglasses. Such follow-up affects health status substantially. In comparisons of the diagnoses of children made at the initial examination with follow-up examinations, the proportion of children diagnosed "well child" has consistently increased 25 percent. At recall examinations for dental services, dental caries decreased by over 50 percent. Since the beginning of the program, 50 percent fewer children served by the projects have needed hospitalization. Average hospital days per 1,000 registrants declined from 101 in the fourth quarter of 1968 to 42 in the fourth quarter of 1972.[20] Such evidence, taken as a whole, indicates that the comprehensive scope of the projects has been effective.

Projects make available a professional team that includes physicians, dentists, nurses, social workers, and nutritionists. Most projects also have psychological and speech and hearing specialists. Several have broadened the clinical responsibilities of members of their nursing staffs to include well-child supervision, and some are affiliated with training programs for pediatric nurse practitioners. Assistants, aides, and volunteers complement the professional staff.[21]

The projects also involve parents in the planning and implementation of services. In 1972, 43 percent of the projects had developed community advisory boards, although this is not required by law.

Children and youth projects received high marks for the quality of the care they provide in a study conducted by Mildred Morehead. The study compared the quality of pediatric care in outpatient departments affiliated with medical schools, neighborhood health centers, group practices, health department well-baby clinics, and C&Y projects, and gave the C&Y projects the highest scores.[22] The dimensions of service considered in the study included history and physical examinations, routine measurements, hemoglobin count and urinalysis, immunizations, screening for tuberculosis,

20. Ibid., p. 14, and MSRI, "Quarterly Summary Report," no. 18 (April–June 1972), p. 15.

21. Neighborhood people are often employed in such staff positions as laboratory aide, X-ray aide, visual screening aide, pharmacist's aide, physician's aide, dental aide, nurse's aide, community health worker, nutrition aide, home management aide, social work assistant, family health aide, physical therapy aide, occupational therapy aide, recreation aide, and playroom worker.

22. Mildred A. Morehead, Rose S. Donaldson, and Mary R. Seravalli, "Comparisons between OEO Neighborhood Health Centers and Other Health Care Providers of Ratings of the Quality of Health Care," *American Journal of Public Health,* vol. 61 (July 1971), p. 1302.

time between first visit and completed assessment, and frequency of visits. The overall score for C&Y projects was 160, much higher than the standard of 100 for outpatient departments affiliated with medical schools. Because of the lengthy procedure required for assessing quality, however, the study surveyed only four C&Y projects; these particular projects may not have been representative.

All in all, the C&Y projects have demonstrated their ability to provide high-quality, comprehensive health care, concentrating not only on providing medical services but also on improving many factors that influence health.

Services for Crippled Children

Over one-third of all funds for the maternal and child health program have gone for the diagnosis and continuing care of crippled children. Expenditures increased from $12 million in 1950 to $162 million in 1973 (see table 5-2). In this period the number of crippled children served more than doubled—from 214,000 children in 1950 to 513,000 in 1973.

Expenditures per child have increased markedly—both because medical care costs have risen and because the severity and complexity of conditions treated by the program have increased. The original emphasis of

Table 5-2. Expenditures and Number of Children Served, Crippled Children's Program, Selected Fiscal Years, 1950–73

Year	Expenditures (millions of dollars)	Number of children served[a] (thousands)	Expenditures per child served (dollars)
1950	11.6	214	54
1955	39.9	278	144
1960	62.3	355	175
1963	82.8	396	209
1967	114.2	476	240
1970	152.9	492	311
1972	168.7	513	329
1973	161.9	513	316

Sources: Merriam and Skolnik, *Social Welfare Expenditures, 1929–66*, p. 219; HEW, Health Services Administration, *Children Who Received Physicians' Services under the Crippled Children's Program, Fiscal Year 1972*, MCH statistical series 8, DHEW (HSA) 74-5008 (HSA, 1974), table 1; HSA, *Children Who Received Physicians' Services, Fiscal Year 1973*, MCH statistical series 10, DHEW (HSA) 77-5731 (HSA, 1977), table 1; and data from the Maternal and Child Health Service.
a. Data through 1963 are for calendar years.

the crippled children's program was on congenital malformations and diseases of the bones and organs of movement, but the program was expanded to include a wide range of crippling conditions. About one-fourth of the diagnoses were diseases of the nervous system and sense organs (for instance, cerebral palsy and epilepsy), another one-fourth were diseases of the bones and organs of movement, and one-fifth were congenital malformations (including heart defects, cleft palate, and dislocation of the hip).[23]

Coverage under the program, however, varies from state to state, so that a child with a particular problem may receive extensive benefits in one state but not in another, and children with serious but noncrippling diseases may receive no benefits in any state. Virginia and Ohio have extensive hemophilia programs, California covers hyaline membrane disease, and North Dakota now covers children with refractive difficulties and dental caries; but other states continue to emphasize congenital malformations and orthopedic handicaps and provide few services for children with other types of crippling conditions.[24]

The definition of a crippled child has changed as states have added conditions to their eligibility requirements. But there is some indication that the incidence of various types of crippling conditions has also changed. Children born with some impairment make up the largest single group, their number having grown from about 44,000 in 1950 to more than 125,000 in 1970,[25] or from 1 percent to 3 percent of all children born in these years. Many crippled children's agencies are providing follow-up care for the large number of children handicapped as a result of the worst rubella (German measles) epidemic in U.S. history (1963–65). Some, thought to be mildly affected at first, exhibited signs of brain damage and developed learning problems when they reached school age. The number of children with severe hearing defects has also increased.

A complex case load contributes to a higher cost per child. In Idaho, for example, the case load is increasingly composed of children with severe disabling conditions, such as scoliosis (curvature of the spine). The average total cost, including surgery and hospital care, for such cases was $3,125. The average cost to the crippled children's program (after

23. HEW, Health Services Administration, *Children Who Received Physicians' Services under the Crippled Children's Program, Fiscal Year 1973,* MCH statistical series 10, DHEW (HSA) 77-5731 (HSA, 1977), table 12.

24. HEW, Maternal and Child Health Service, *Promoting the Health of Mothers and Children, Fiscal Year 1972,* DHEW (HSM) 73-5002 (GPO, 1972), pp. 29–32.

25. *National Health Insurance Resource Book,* p. 498.

other sources of insurance payment) was $2,450. The parents of children covered by the program, whose average income was $5,200, could pay little of this cost.[26]

The costs of treating various types of crippling conditions may be high, but therapy often leads to successful rehabilitation and enables children to become self-supporting adults. The Missouri crippled children's program, for example, reported:

For the 235 patients with meningomyelocele [a disease affecting the spinal cord and spinal column], the average cost of treatment was $1,128. One patient, whose care before he was 21 years of age cost $16,000, has been rehabilitated and is now self-supporting.

To treat paraplegia and similar conditions due to accidents costs an average of $1,215 per patient. There were 123 patients with such conditions. Many of these individuals can be rehabilitated and before they are 21 can be placed in training programs to become financially self-sustaining.

The Missouri program cared for 86 patients with acute burns at an average cost of $1,400. Most of these individuals will recover, but may require extensive plastic surgery later.[27]

In some cases, the crippled children's program has also been effective in reducing the costs of treatment. In Oregon the program tried training parents to treat hemophiliac children at home; this reduced hospitalization costs by 50 percent.[28] In a study of forty-five hemophiliacs, Levine found that home therapy with infusions of Factor VIII or IX cut health care costs by 44.5 percent and reduced the average annual days of illness at home from 26.3 to 6.8.[29]

Since the allocation of federal funds is based on the number of crippled children served, the states have had an incentive to conduct effective outreach programs to find eligible children. Procedures include screening in hospitals' newborn nurseries, follow-up nursing visits to the homes of newborns, and checking birth certificates for any congenital malformations reported. Efforts to find young children who need help include screening in well-baby clinics, day care centers, nursery schools, Head Start centers, and school health programs.

26. Maternal and Child Health Service, *Promoting the Health of Mothers and Children, Fiscal Year 1972*, p. 31.

27. Maternal and Child Health Service, *Promoting the Health of Mothers and Children, Fiscal Year 1973*, p. 2.

28. Ibid., p. 28.

29. Paper presented at the American Academy of Pediatrics, Spring 1973, by Peter Levine, director of the Blood Coagulation Laboratory, Tufts-New England Medical Center, reported in ibid.

Most care occurs in clinics offering diagnostic treatment and rehabilitation. Almost three-fourths of the children served in fiscal 1973 were treated by physicians in such clinics.[30] Eighty-two thousand, or 16 percent, of the children received hospital inpatient care; but since twenty-one states did not cover it, fewer than 5,000 children received convalescent-home care.

The crippled children's program grew between 1950 and 1970, and it made extensive efforts to locate handicapped children, to provide diagnostic services, and to see that each child got the care he or she needed. Because the problems of the children they serve are complex, the average cost per child has been relatively high—more than $300 a year in 1970–73. But the greatest drawbacks are the substantial differences in coverage between states.

Services for Mothers: State and Local Health Department Programs

As with children, services for mothers and infants are provided both through state and local health department programs and through specific project grants. The state and local programs deliver three major types of services to pregnant women and newborn infants: maternity services in clinics; nursing visits to the homes of newborn infants; and classes for expectant parents.

In 1972, 335,000 women received maternity services in clinics; this represented about 9 percent of all live births in that year (see table 5-3). Little information is available about the comprehensiveness of the care rendered these women or at what stage of pregnancy they began to receive prenatal care. States vary in the services offered pregnant women. In 1972 fifteen states had no physicians in their maternity clinics; in some of the other states physicians were available only in clinics in metropolitan areas. The maternity nursing services reached more women: 624,000 (17 percent of all live births) in 1972. All but two states reported the provision of nursing services, which consisted primarily of visits by nurses to the homes of newborn infants for initial counseling and guidance of mothers.

30. Health Services Administration, *Children Who Received Physicians' Services, Fiscal Year 1973*, table 7.

In the three states that do not cover physicians' services either in the home or in the doctor's office, the clinics are the only source of such services. Physicians' services are donated in some of the crippled children's programs.

Table 5-3. Trends in Selected Services of State and Local Health Departments Received by Expectant Parents, Selected Years, 1959–72ª

Year or periodᵇ	Maternity medical clinic services	Maternity nursing services	Classes for expectant parents
Number enrolled (thousands)			
1959	236	530	57
1960	254	525	64
1963	271	534	83
1967	366	480	75
1970	331	529	88
1972	335	624	101
Percentage change			
1959–72	42.3	17.9	77.5
1963–72	23.7	16.9	21.2
As percent of live births			
1959	5.4	12.2	1.3
1960	5.9	12.1	1.5
1963	6.5	12.8	2.0
1967	9.8	12.7	2.0
1970	8.9	14.2	2.4
1972	9.2	17.1	2.7

Source: Health Services Administration, *Maternal and Child Health Services of State and Local Health Departments, Fiscal Year 1972*, DHEW (HSA) 74-5801 (HSA, 1973), table 1. Figures are rounded.
a. In the United States and its territories.
b. Calendar years, 1959–63; fiscal years, 1967–72.

Most states also held classes for expectant parents, 100,000 of whom enrolled in 1972.

Unlike state and local programs for children, the programs for pregnant women have served an increasing number of women since 1963. Realistic estimates of the cost per woman served are difficult to make as there is no information on total costs and services delivered. A rough estimate, which assumes that about half of state and local health department Title V funds were allocated to pregnant women and that some 700,000 women were served, is an average expenditure per woman of $114 in 1973. If it is assumed that most Title V funds go for clinic services instead of nursing services, the average 1973 expenditure per woman increases to $240.[31] These two estimates represent upper and lower bounds on program costs per women served.

31. Only about 335,000 women received clinic services. For eligible women, some additional expenses may have been paid by the Medicaid program.

Services for Mothers: Maternity and Infant Care Project Grants

Amendments to the Social Security Act in 1963 authorized maternity and infant care projects to provide comprehensive medical care to pregnant women. In 1972 these projects served 141,000 women, most of whom lived in urban areas with high infant mortality rates, low income levels, crowded public health facilities, and shortages of physicians in private practice.

Unlike state and local health department programs, the M&I projects render a broad range of services to patients, including dental, nutrition, educational, and social services as well as prenatal care, hospital delivery, and postpartum care. The projects engage in outreach programs designed to attract women early in pregnancy and to maintain continuity of care through the postnatal period.

The emphasis on comprehensive care is reflected in the cost of the program. As shown in table 5-4, the M&I projects spent more than $500 per maternity admission in 1972, almost twice the estimated average expenditure of less than $250 in the state and local health department maternity clinic programs.

The M&I projects have served many unmarried women who would otherwise have received little or no care. In 1972, 45 percent of all women

Table 5-4. Expenditures and Number of Women Served, Maternity and Infant Care Projects, Fiscal Years 1965–72

Year	Expenditures[a] (thousands of dollars)	Maternity admissions (thousands)	Expenditures per maternity admission (dollars)
1965	5,167	57.3	90
1966	15,659	83.1	188
1967	35,445	103.8	341
1968	37,490	118.3	317
1969	52,508	116.4	451
1970	46,554[b]	128.7	362
1971	46,036	141.5	325
1972	73,616	141.0	522

Sources: Expenditures, Maternity and Child Health Service, unpublished data; admissions, MCHS, "New Maternity and Infant Care Projects Reported Statistics, FY 1964 to 1972," tabulation (1973; processed). Figures are rounded.
a. Beginning with fiscal 1969, family planning projects are excluded.
b. Includes federal administrative expenses.

admitted to the projects for maternity care were pregnant out of wedlock. This high percentage is the result both of the high incidence of pregnancy among low-income single women and of the concentrated efforts of many projects to reach this group through neighborhood canvassing and through formal referral arrangements with schools and other community agencies.

As the M&I projects serve a large proportion of women who have had little previous medical care—because of financial, social, or emotional barriers or limited education—significant numbers enter the projects late in the course of pregnancy. Outreach programs, however, have been successful in increasing the proportion of women entering in the first trimester of pregnancy (this proportion doubled between 1967 and 1972) and in reducing the proportion receiving care for the first time at delivery (from 10 to 5 percent between 1967 and 1972).[32] In individual projects, the change is even more striking. For example, the Baltimore M&I project was able to increase the number of women beginning care in the first trimester from fewer than 10 percent in 1964 to more than 50 percent in 1972. The Greenville, South Carolina, project estimates that the number of project women admitted to the hospital for delivery with no prenatal care dropped from 25 percent in 1966 to fewer than 2 percent in 1972.[33]

The M&I projects also received high marks on the quality of care in the Morehead study. A comparison of the quality of obstetrical care in M&I projects with that of a number of other health providers indicated that the M&I projects provided care of higher quality than other types of providers, including outpatient departments affiliated with medical schools, neighborhood health centers, and group practices.[34] The only low mark received by the M&I projects was in the percentage of patients beginning prenatal care in the first trimester of pregnancy. As with the C&Y projects, however, the assessment was based on a limited number (six) of the M&I projects, whose experience may not be broadly representative of all projects.

Family Planning Services

The maternal and child health program has also made an effort to provide postpartum care and family planning for women in the maternity pro-

32. Maternal and Child Health Service, "New Maternity and Infant Care Projects Reported Statistics, FY 1964 to 1972," tabulation (1973; processed).

33. Maternal and Child Health Service, *Promoting the Health of Mothers and Children, Fiscal Year 1973*, pp. 30–31.

34. See Morehead and others, "Comparisons between OEO Neighborhood Health Centers and Other Health Care Providers," p. 1300.

gram. Federally subsidized family planning for low-income women is a recent development. Congress explicitly called for such services in the amendments to the Social Security Act in 1967, which ordered some family planning services; the Family Planning Services and Population Research Act of 1970, which provided for family planning projects; and amendments to the Social Security Act in 1972, which gave further support to family planning efforts.

Data collected from all programs with organized family planning projects—maternity and infant care projects, state maternal and child health programs, neighborhood health centers, family planning projects, and federally supported planned parenthood programs—and estimates for organized programs outside the reporting system indicate a threefold increase in users from 1968 to 1972. In 1973 an estimated 3.2 million women received services under organized family planning programs, including privately funded programs. Nearly all the women in the M&I projects received family planning services after pregnancy (126,000 out of 140,000 women in 1972). These services were usually introductory; follow-through was frequently switched to family planning projects under the 1970 Family Planning Services Act.

Family planning clinics are an important source not only of contraceptive services,[35] but also of other medical procedures, usually preventive, such as breast and pelvic examinations, Pap smears, and testing for venereal disease. Of all visits to a family planning clinic, 95 percent include at least one medical service besides family planning.[36]

Evaluation of the Maternal and Child Health Program

All the projects and services encompassed by the MCH program are aimed at improving the health of mothers and children, especially in rural, urban poverty, and economically distressed areas. Two types of evaluation of programs' effectiveness are therefore appropriate. Did the program benefit those it was intended for? Did it improve the health of mothers and children?

35. Although various contraceptive methods are available through the organized programs, 85 percent of the women enrolled use either oral contraceptives or an intrauterine device.

36. Center for Family Planning Program Development, "Data and Analyses for 1974 Revision of DHEW Five-Year Plan for Family Planning Services" (New York: CFPPD, Technical Assistance Division of Planned Parenthood–World Population, n.d.; processed), pp. 57, 64.

Table 5-5. Percentage of Recipients of Maternal and Child Health Services Living in Nonmetropolitan Areas, by Region, Fiscal Year 1972

| Region | State and local health department services | | Federal maternal and child health projects | | |
	Well-child conferences	Medical clinics	Children and youth	Maternity and infant care[a]	Services for crippled children
United States	25	43	10	7	48
Northeast	13	2	n.a.	1	35
North Central	21	10	n.a.	0	60
South	39	62	n.a.	15	56
West	22	12	n.a.	11	34

Source: Derived from data from Health Services Administration.
n.a. Not available.
a. Data are for the first half of fiscal 1970.

Urban-Rural Distribution of Benefits

Although it is explicitly directed to concentrate on rural areas and areas of severe economic distress, the program maintains limited information on the geographical location of recipients and no systematic information at all on the incomes of recipients or on the distribution of program expenditures between rural and urban areas. The data that are available suggest that the program has not concentrated on the health problems of women and children in rural areas. Table 5-5 summarizes the collected data on the distribution of the recipients of various MCH services between metropolitan and nonmetropolitan areas.[37] Over half the recipients of each type

37. The terms "nonmetropolitan" and "rural" do not encompass the same population. In general, "metropolitan" or "standard metropolitan statistical area" refers to a county or a group of counties with at least one city with a population of 50,000 or more; nonmetropolitan includes all other areas. The Bureau of the Census generally defines as "rural" those people living in places with populations under 2,500, while the Department of Labor defines as "rural" counties where a *majority of the people* live in places with populations under 2,500. "Nonmetropolitan" is usually applied to a population larger than the rural population, but the rural population is not strictly a subset of the nonmetropolitan population. Under the Census Bureau's definition of rural, some of the rural population reside in metropolitan areas (that is, in places with population under 2,500 but located in counties with more than 50,000 population). For a discussion of these as well as other definitions of rural, see Ray Marshall, *Rural Workers in Rural Labor Markets* (Olympus, 1974), pp. 14–19.

The only available data on the residence of recipients of maternal and child health services are divided according to the Census Bureau's definitions of metropolitan and nonmetropolitan.

of service reside in metropolitan areas; 90 percent or more of the registrants in M&I and C&Y projects are in large cities.[38]

The crippled children's program has a relatively high proportion of rural recipients. In fiscal 1972, 48 percent of all crippled children served by the program were from nonmetropolitan areas (32 percent of all children in the country under the age of fifteen live in nonmetropolitan areas). As there is no evidence indicating that the incidence of crippling conditions among children is significantly higher in rural areas than in urban areas,[39] this high proportion of nonmetropolitan recipients is probably due to a deliberate policy focusing attention on and giving priority to the needs of crippled children in rural areas.

Although data on the distribution of all recipients are not available, two of the most costly services—well-child conferences and maternity services in medical clinics—do report data by residence. Approximately 25 percent of all well-child conferences and 45 percent of maternity services in clinics are received by mothers and children in nonmetropolitan areas. Other types of services, such as maternity nursing services and school health services, may also be focused more specifically on rural areas, but they probably account for a fairly small portion of all state and local health department expenditures.

The specific projects funded under the 1963 and 1965 amendments benefit urban areas almost exclusively. Of the fifty-nine C&Y projects in operation in 1972, two-thirds (and 90 percent of the registrants) were in central city areas.[40] Of the women admitted to M&I projects in the first half of fiscal 1970, over 90 percent were from metropolitan areas.[41]

Receipt of MCH services by nonmetropolitan residents other than crippled children is almost nonexistent outside the South. Mothers and children in nonmetropolitan areas outside the South received only 10 percent of well-child conference services and less than 5 percent of maternity services in medical clinics in 1972.

38. For a discussion of the few projects serving rural areas, see Lesser and Hunt, "Maternal and Child Health Programs and Rural Areas."

39. While the incidence of crippling conditions is not known, the National Center for Health Statistics reports that the percentage of noninstitutionalized children under seventeen with some limitation of activity resulting from chronic conditions is 2.7 percent in both metropolitan and nonmetropolitan areas. NCHS, *Limitation of Activity Due to Chronic Conditions, United States, 1969 and 1970,* Vital and Health Statistics, series 10, no. 80, DHEW (HSM) 73-1506 (GPO, 1973), p. 30.

40. Maternal and Child Health Service, *The Children and Youth Projects,* p. 6.

41. Calculated from Maternal and Child Health Service, "Statistical Summary of Patients Served under Maternity and Infant Care Projects, First Two Quarters, Fiscal Year 1970" (MCHS, n.d.; processed), table 1.

Some data are also available on the distribution of services. Total expenditures in nonmetropolitan areas can be roughly estimated if it is assumed that the average expenditure per recipient is the same in metropolitan and nonmetropolitan areas. This being the case, the proportion of nonmetropolitan expenditures would of course be the same as the proportion of recipients residing in nonmetropolitan areas.

This assumption, however, undoubtedly overstates rural expenditures for a number of reasons. First, the costs of services (including the wages of the personnel providing the services) tend to be higher in urban areas than in rural areas, making the average cost per user higher in urban areas even if the same services are provided in all areas. Second, the greater availability of specialists and sophisticated medical services in urban areas suggests that urban recipients receive care that is more comprehensive, specialized, and of higher quality. For example, urban children with crippling conditions are more likely to receive extensive physical therapy than their rural counterparts are. Third, most rural mothers and children served by the program live in the South, where medical costs are lower and medical resources more limited. The average cost of care received by those in the rural South could be expected to be considerably lower than the average costs of the care urban residents receive. Partially offsetting these factors, however, is the possibility that services received by users for whom residence is unknown—such as maternity nursing services and school health examinations—may be more extensively provided in rural areas.

Any estimate of the distribution of expenditures is therefore tenuous, but distributing expenditures between metropolitan and nonmetropolitan areas according to the number of recipients in each area should provide an upper limit on expenditures in nonmetropolitan areas. These estimates indicate that nonmetropolitan areas received about $140 million from the MCH program in fiscal 1973, or 32 percent of all program funds. If the crippled children's program is excluded, nonmetropolitan areas received less than 23 percent of all funds. Since 32 percent of all children live in nonmetropolitan areas, it is clear that the MCH program, originally aimed at rural areas, allocates a less than proportionate share of money to rural areas.

Benefits to Low-Income Mothers and Children

The MCH program was also intended to concentrate on low-income mothers and children. Lack of data on the income of recipients makes any direct assessment of the distribution of benefits by income impossible. In the case of services for schoolchildren—such as school health examinations and immunizations—nonpoor children as well as poor children benefit. No income test is applied, and all children of a given age in selected schools are eligible for services. Whether most states deliberately·give higher priority to school districts with heavy concentrations of low-income children in the allocation of MCH funds is unknown.

Most maternity and infant care and children and youth projects are located in central city areas with large numbers of poor people. While lower-, middle-, and upper-income families residing in the areas served by the projects are eligible for care, data from the family planning program indicate that clinics are used predominantly by the poor.

The Planned Parenthood–World Population organization has made some estimates of the income distribution of women receiving family planning services from organized programs, some of which include M&I projects. Their estimates indicate that about half the recipients of family planning services have incomes below the poverty level, and about three-fourths have near-poverty incomes (less than 150 percent of the poverty level). Whether these estimates are representative of all women served by the M&I projects is unknown.[42]

Though most maternal and child health projects are in low-income neighborhoods, there is no evidence that they are selectively located in areas of greatest economic distress. The Tuskegee, Alabama, M&I project is in a county 37 percent of whose population are at or below the poverty level and more than half of whose population live in rural areas. The University of Nebraska M&I project in Omaha, on the other hand, serves a county with a 7 percent poverty population and few rural residents.

The C&Y and M&I projects do reach large numbers of minority women and children. The racial-ethnic composition of children registered at C&Y projects is 57 percent black, 18 percent Hispanic, and 25 percent other white children.[43] Sixty percent of the women admitted to M&I projects are black.[44]

The maternal and child health program has attempted to allocate more funds to states with low incomes. Formula funds are specifically tied both

42. Center for Family Planning Program Development, "Data and Analyses for 1974 Revision of DHEW Five-Year Plan," p. 42.

43. Minnesota Systems Research, "Quarterly Summary Report," no. 20, p. 4.

44. Maternal and Child Health Service, "New Maternity and Infant Care Projects Reported Statistics, FY 1964 to 1972."

Health and the War on Poverty

Table 5-6. Maternal and Child Health Expenditures and Number of Poor Children, by Region and State, 1969[a]

Region and state	Expenditures (thousands of dollars)	Number of poor children (thousands)	Expenditures per poor child (dollars)	Percentage distribution Expenditures	Percentage distribution Poor children
United States	387,417	12,614	31	100.0	100.0
Northeast	76,524	2,121	36	19.8	16.8
Maine	3,631	59	62	0.9	0.5
New Hampshire	1,899	26	73	0.5	0.2
Vermont	2,114	22	96	0.5	0.2
Massachusetts	7,874	210	37	2.0	1.7
Rhode Island	3,520	44	80	0.9	0.3
Connecticut	3,898	96	41	1.0	0.8
New York	15,460	893	17	4.0	7.1
New Jersey	9,856	256	38	2.5	2.0
Pennsylvania	28,272	515	55	7.3	4.1
North Central	95,486	2,588	37	24.6	20.5
Ohio	15,132	455	33	3.9	3.6
Indiana	7,311	212	34	1.9	1.7
Illinois	18,060	498	36	4.7	3.9
Michigan	19,768	378	52	5.1	3.0
Wisconsin	4,971	182	27	1.3	1.4
Minnesota	8,864	169	52	2.3	1.3
Iowa	5,011	125	40	1.3	1.0
Missouri	7,716	276	28	2.0	2.2
North Dakota	1,585	44	36	0.4	0.3
South Dakota	1,858	55	34	0.5	0.4
Nebraska	2,292	78	29	0.6	0.6
Kansas	2,918	116	25	0.8	0.9
South	145,238	5,972	24	37.5	47.3
Delaware	1,234	29	43	0.3	0.2
Maryland	9,186	189	49	2.4	1.5
District of Columbia	8,840	64	138	2.3	0.5
Virginia	13,651	337	41	3.5	2.7
West Virginia	4,868	166	29	1.3	1.3
North Carolina	12,389	484	26	3.2	3.8
South Carolina	7,151	313	23	1.8	2.5
Georgia	7,677	457	17	2.0	3.6
Florida	15,370	476	32	4.0	3.8
Kentucky	9,615	326	29	2.5	2.6
Tennessee	10,170	378	27	2.6	3.0
Alabama	7,168	417	17	1.9	3.3
Mississippi	5,860	398	15	1.5	3.2

Table 5-6 (*continued*)

Region and state	Expenditures (thousands of dollars)	Number of poor children (thousands)	Expenditures per poor child (dollars)	Percentage distribution Expenditures	Poor children
Arkansas	5,669	236	24	1.5	1.9
Louisiana	5,978	481	12	1.5	3.8
Oklahoma	4,579	198	23	1.2	1.6
Texas	15,833	1,023	15	4.1	8.1
West	70,169	1,935	36	18.1	15.3
Montana	1,786	42	43	0.5	0.3
Idaho	1,833	42	44	0.5	0.3
Wyoming	2,361	18	131	0.6	0.1
Colorado	5,712	130	44	1.5	1.0
New Mexico	2,311	126	18	0.6	1.0
Arizona	4,838	138	35	1.2	1.1
Utah	2,231	61	37	0.6	0.5
Nevada	2,527	19	133	0.7	0.2
Washington	6,755	149	45	1.7	1.2
Oregon	4,009	101	40	1.0	0.8
California	29,300	1,053	28	7.6	8.3
Hawaii	2,997	35	86	0.8	0.3
Alaska	3,509	21	167	0.9	0.2

Sources: Barbara S. Cooper and Nancy L. Worthington, *Personal Health Care Expenditures by State*, vol. 1: *Public Funds, 1966 and 1969*, Social Security Administration, DHEW (SSA) 73-11906 (GPO, 1973), table 32; U.S. Bureau of the Census, *Census of Population, 1970, Detailed Characteristics*, Final Report PC(1)-D (GPO, 1972), individual state reports, tables 207, 215, 216. Figures are rounded.

a. Expenditures are for fiscal 1969. The number of poor children is determined by family income for calendar year 1969 and consists of those in families classified by the Census Bureau as below the poverty level.

to the number of live births in the state and to per capita income. Yet allocating funds by per capita income has not resulted in a distribution of funds roughly proportionate to the incidence of poverty. In 1969, as shown in table 5-6, states in the South spent only 38 percent of all MCH funds though 47 percent of poor children live in the South, and the variation in expenditure per poor child in that region ranged from $12 in Louisiana to $138 in the District of Columbia. Sparsely populated areas in the Northwest and Northeast, such as Wyoming, Nevada, Alaska, Vermont, and Rhode Island, had the highest expenditures in relation to poverty. Southern states with high incidence of poverty and large rural populations, such as Mississippi, Louisiana, Texas, and Georgia, received one-fourth to one-tenth the average expenditure per poor child of these northern states.

Health Effects: Infant and Maternal Mortality

The primary focus of the maternal and child health program has been on improving the health of mothers and children, with special emphasis on reducing infant mortality, a goal that was explicitly included in the 1963 amendments to the program. Better health is particularly difficult to achieve. Many factors beyond the control of the program—low incomes, inadequate diets, environmental hazards, limited education, poor sanitation—can be expected to impede progress. Even where there is a marked improvement in a given health status indicator, it is difficult to attribute it to a particular program.

Reductions in infant mortality in the last decade have been striking. Infant mortality rates fell rapidly from 1935 to 1950, leveled off somewhat from 1950 to 1965, and then plummeted between 1965 and 1975, from 24.7 deaths per 1,000 live births to 16.1, a 35 percent decline, or 3.5 percent a year (see table 5-7). Maternal mortality, though much rarer, has also declined markedly. Between 1966 and 1975 the maternal death rate fell more than 50 percent.

Table 5-7. Infant and Maternal Death Rates, by Race, Selected Years, 1961–75

Category	Rate per 1,000 live births			Annual percentage decline	
	1961	1966	1975[a]	1961–66	1966–75
All infants	25.3	23.7	16.1	1.3	3.6
White	22.4	20.6	14.2	1.6	3.5
Other	40.7	38.8	24.2	0.9	4.2
Neonatal infants	18.4	17.2	11.6	1.3	3.6
White	16.9	15.6	10.4	1.5	3.7
Other	26.2	24.8	16.8	1.1	3.6
Postneonatal infants	6.9	6.5	4.5	1.2	3.4
White	5.5	5.0	3.8	1.8	2.7
Other	14.5	13.9	7.4	0.8	5.2
Mothers	0.369	0.291	0.128	4.2	6.2
White	0.249	0.202	0.091	3.7	6.1
Other	1.013	0.724	0.290	5.7	6.7

Sources: HEW, National Center for Health Statistics, *Vital Statistics of the United States: 1970*, vol. 2: *Mortality*, pt. A (GPO, 1974), tables 1-16, 2-1; NCHS, *Monthly Vital Statistics Report, Provisional Statistics: Annual Summary for the United States, 1975*, vol. 24 (June 30, 1976), p. 8; and NCHS, *Monthly Vital Statistics Report, Final Mortality Statistics, 1975*, vol. 25, supplement (February 11, 1977), pp. 3, 6.
a. Provisional.

Table 5-8. Infant Mortality Rates, Selected Countries, 1962, 1967, and 1971

Country	Rate per 1,000 live births			Annual percentage decline	
	1962	1967	1971	1962–67	1967–71
Sweden	15.4	12.9	11.1	3.2	3.5
Netherlands	17.0	13.4	11.1	4.2	4.3
Norway	17.7	12.8	12.8	5.5	0.0
Denmark	20.1	15.8	13.5	4.3	3.7
New Zealand	20.4	18.0	16.6	2.4	1.9
Australia	20.4	18.3	17.3	2.1	1.4
Finland	20.5	14.2	11.8	6.1	4.2
Switzerland	21.2	17.5	14.4	3.5	4.4
United Kingdom	22.4	18.3	17.9	3.7	0.5
Czechoslovakia	22.8	22.9	21.6	a	1.4
United States	25.3	22.1	19.2	2.5	3.3
France	25.7	20.7	14.4	3.9	7.6
Japan	26.4	15.0	12.4	8.6	4.3
Belgium	27.5	22.9	19.8	3.3	3.4
Canada	27.6	22.0	17.6	4.1	5.0
Ireland	29.1	24.4	18.0	3.2	6.6
West Germany	29.2	22.8	23.1	4.4	a
East Germany	31.6	21.2	18.0	6.6	3.8
Hong Kong	36.9	25.6	18.4	6.1	7.0

Sources: Myron E. Wegman, "Annual Summary of Vital Statistics—1972, with Some Observations on China," *Pediatrics*, vol. 52 (December 1973), p. 879; and Wegman, "Annual Summary of Vital Statistics—1968," *Pediatrics*, vol. 44 (December 1969), p. 1034.
a. Negligible increase.

It is not clear how much of the credit for this dramatic reduction goes to the MCH program. Improved diets, higher incomes, better education, and growing awareness of the importance of early care in pregnancy all affect the likelihood that a baby will live and be healthy. Part of the decline may also be attributable to other programs that have improved the access of the poor to medical care, such as Medicaid; to changes in medical technology in the care of premature or low-birth-weight babies; and to more widely available birth control measures and abortions, reducing the number of unwanted babies. The similar experience of other countries with infant mortality rates suggests that these broader factors may be at play. Declines were sharper in many other countries than in the United States in both periods covered in table 5-8.

Furthermore, as the MCH program is modest, providing care in only about 10 percent of all live births, its effect could not be expected to be adequately detected by an examination of nationwide or global trends.

Only comparisons of small areas will reveal effects that can reasonably be attributed to the program.

The MCH program does report on smaller geographical areas. It cites a number of specific maternity and infant care projects that have greatly reduced infant mortality—declines that have not occurred for other residents of the same city or county or for other low-income families in the area. For instance,

In Providence, R.I., the inner city served by the M&I Project at St. Joseph's Hospital showed a reduction in infant mortality from 47.4 per 1,000 live births in 1966 to 25.2 per 1,000 in 1970, while in more affluent census tracts the rate increased from 20.1 per 1,000 live births in 1966 to 21.4 in 1970. . . .

In the Minneapolis, Minn., M&I Project, the infant death rate decreased well below the national average—to 10.5 per 1,000 live births in 1971, although project patients come from areas with the highest percentage of risk factors. . . . In the Albuquerque, New Mex., M&I Project, infant mortality decreased from 22.7 per 1,000 live births in 1967 to 12.2 in 1971.[45]

And

In the Dade County, Fla., M&I Project the infant mortality rate dropped from 20.7 per 1,000 live births in 1968 to 10.9 in 1972, while for the county as a whole the 1968 rate was 21.5, and for 1972, 15.9. . . . In Broward County, Fla., infant mortality statistics for the period from 1967 through 1972 show that patients cared for under the M&I Project produced infants with a 70 percent lower average mortality rate than Broward County indigent patients not cared for in M&I clinics.[46]

Detailed studies of individual projects have verified these differences. One study, for example, demonstrated that care given 4,878 medically indigent mothers by an M&I project during a two-and-one-quarter-year period reduced maternal morbidity, stillbirth rates, the number of premature infants, neonatal morbidity, and infant mortality.[47] Another study found a drop in infant mortality following the establishment of a Care-by-Parent unit at the University of Kentucky Medical Center high risk infancy nursery.[48]

Although these studies suggest that the M&I projects do affect infant

45. Maternal and Child Health Service, *Promoting the Health of Mothers and Children, Fiscal Year 1972*, p. 6.

46. Ibid., *Fiscal Year 1973*, pp. 4–5.

47. Betty J. Vaughn, "Maternity and Infant Care Project: Results in Dade County, Florida," *Southern Medical Journal*, vol. 61 (June 1968), pp. 641–45.

48. Vernon L. James and Melvin J. Lerner, "The Care-by-Parent Unit for Hospitalization of Children," in Maternal and Child Health Service, *The Maternal and Child Health Services Reports on Research to Improve Health Services for Mothers and Children*, DHEW (HSM) 73-5116 (GPO, 1973), pp. 1–4.

Table 5-9. Rates of Infant and Maternal Mortality and Low Birth Weight, and Characteristics of Women Admitted to Maternal and Infant Care Projects, by Region, First Half of Fiscal Year 1970[a]

Description	United States	North-east	North Central	South	West
Number of live births	40,583	7,775	10,923	18,605	3,280
Neonatal deaths per 1,000 live births	15.4	13.5	10.0	18.2	21.6
Number weighing under 2,500 grams per 1,000 live births	133	122	131	143	104
Fetal deaths per 1,000 births	42	37	25	51	59
Number of maternal deaths	17	2	3	12	0
New maternity patients	57,068	12,711	15,080	24,499	4,778
Status (percent)					
Unmarried	40	46	25	47	41
Under 16	6	6	7	6	4
35 and over	4	5	5	5	3
Black	62	54	77	76	25
Initiating care after					
First trimester	84	79	84	87	76
Second trimester	28	17	29	32	28

Source: Maternal and Child Health Service, "Statistical Summary of Patients Served under Maternity and Infant Care Projects, First Two Quarters, Fiscal Year 1970" (MCHS, n.d.; processed), tables 1, 2, 5.
a. Based on fifty-one projects reporting data.

mortality, they could be selective, isolated instances that are not generally representative. The M&I program, however, has collected data on neonatal infant deaths (deaths in the first month after birth) for the first half of fiscal year 1970 for fifty-one projects (table 5-9).[49]

The fifty-one M&I projects reporting data for July–December 1969 accounted for 40,600 live births. The average neonatal mortality rate was 15.4 deaths per 1,000 live births; in the same period the neonatal death rate for all live births in the United States was 15.5. That the M&I projects could achieve the same average neonatal death rate as the United States as a whole is remarkable when one takes into account that the women served by the program are higher risk. Since the projects tend to be in low-income areas, a large proportion of the women have below-poverty in-

49. Because of the short time covered, infant mortality rates for specific projects may not be representative of longer periods. Unusually low or high death rates in individual projects, however, should be averaged in the regional and national totals to obtain reasonably accurate estimates of typical experience.

comes and limited educations and are unmarried or black. Most did not come for care until after the first trimester of pregnancy; 28 percent not until after the pregnancy was more than six months advanced. All these characteristics typically increase the probability of complications and infant mortality.[50]

If the experience of M&I projects were compared to that of a similar group of women not covered by the program, much greater differences would be observed. For example, during the same period the estimated neonatal death rate for blacks was 21.6 per 1,000 live births, and for low-income blacks, 24.3.[51] Thus if a group of infants with the same racial composition and low income as those in the projects were drawn at random from the population, its neonatal death rate could be expected to have been 21.7 per 1,000 live births in the first half of fiscal 1970. This suggests that the M&I projects were successful in reducing the neonatal death rate from 21.7 per 1,000 live births to 15.4, or by 29 percent. Additional adjustment for the high rate of unmarried women and late entry into the program should show that the program had an even greater effect.

Projects in some areas of the country have many risk factors to overcome. For example, of the women admitted to twenty-two M&I projects in the South, 47 percent were unmarried, 76 percent were black, and 32 percent were more than six months pregnant at the time of entry. The nine M&I projects in the north central region—mostly inner city projects in large cities such as Chicago—which served similar groups of women, achieved a neonatal death rate of 10.0 deaths per 1,000 live births—well below the national neonatal death rate even before adjustment for income, race, and other risk factors.

The M&I projects do not appear to have been as successful in reducing the incidence of low-birth-weight babies (those weighing less than 2,500 grams at birth). As shown in table 5-9, the projects averaged 133 low-

50. For documentation of high risk factors, see David M. Kessner, project director, *Infant Death: An Analysis by Maternal Risk and Health Care* (National Academy of Sciences, 1973).

51. The black neonatal mortality rate for July–December 1969 is based on the average rate for calendar years 1969 and 1970. The low-income neonatal mortality rate is estimated by assuming that the low-income black neonatal rate is 1.57 times the average neonatal rate and the low-income white neonatal rate is 1.12 times the average neonatal rate (as they were in 1964–66). See National Center for Health Statistics, *Infant Mortality Rates: Socioeconomic Factors, United States,* Vital and Health Statistics, series 22, no. 14, DHEW (HSM) 72-1045 (GPO, 1972), p. 33; and Myron E. Wegman, "Annual Summary of Vital Statistics—1972, with Some Observations on China," *Pediatrics,* vol. 52 (December 1973), p. 878.

birth-weight babies for each 1,000 live births. This is at the high end of the scale for babies in low-income families. In 1969–71 black families living in poverty areas averaged 151 low-birth-weight babies and white families in poverty areas averaged 93. In view of the high proportion (62 percent) of black women admitted to the M&I program, a rate of about 114 in each 1,000 would prevail (without controlling for source of care).[52]

Although the projects continue to have high rates of women who are admitted late in pregnancy and a large proportion of low-birth-weight babies, noticeable progress has been made. As noted earlier, between 1967 and 1972 the proportion of expectant mothers receiving care in the first trimester of pregnancy doubled and the proportion receiving care for the first time at delivery fell from 10 to 5 percent. The MCH program noted progress at several projects in the early delivery of care and fewer low-birth-weight babies:

In 1972, only 12.8 percent of the babies delivered by the Denver, Colo., project weighed between 500 and 2,500 grams, compared with 18.9 percent in 1965, the year the project started. . . .

Region IV has 15 Maternity and Infant Care Projects, some serving predominantly urban populations, such as Atlanta, some with mostly rural populations, and some with a mixed urban-rural clientele. While each project operates in response to local conditions, all report decreased infant and maternal mortality, decreased prematurity and incidence of low birth weight, a decrease in the number of patients receiving no prenatal care, and increases in the rate of postpartum return, the number of patients accepting family planning services, and the number of patients seeking care during the first and second trimesters of pregnancy.[53]

Health Effects: Young Children

Evaluating the effect of the maternal and child health program on the health of young children is somewhat more difficult than evaluating its effect on infants because a single summary measurement like mortality rates is not as readily available. The program's success in meeting health needs is therefore best assessed by the emphases of the various MCH programs: for state and local health department programs, immunization

52. Calculated from HEW, National Center for Health Statistics, *Selected Vital and Health Statistics in Poverty and Nonpoverty Areas of 19 Large Cities, United States, 1969–71*, Vital and Health Statistics, series 21, no. 26, DHEW (HRA) 76-1904 (GPO, 1975), p. 11.

53. Maternal and Child Health Service, *Promoting the Health of Mothers and Children, Fiscal Year 1973*, pp. 29–30.

against communicable diseases and screening for hearing and visual defects; for the crippled children's program, reduction in the incidence and severity of crippling conditions and the rehabilitation of as many children as possible; for the comprehensive children and youth projects, prevention and early treatment of children's diseases to reduce hospitalization, high costs of care, future illness, and absence from school because of illness.

Regardless of which indicator is chosen, evidence on national changes in the health of children and youths is not encouraging. Although the death rates of young children declined somewhat more rapidly in the late 1960s and early 1970s after the creation of the C&Y projects than in the early 1960s, the death rates for older children and young adults (fifteen to twenty-four) have increased in recent years.

Reports of the incidence among children of chronic conditions that cause some limitation of activity suggest that, if anything, the incidence has increased, not declined. From 1965 to 1967, 1.9 percent of all children under seventeen had some limitation of activity caused by chronic conditions. By 1969–70 this had increased slightly, to 2.7 percent.[54] It is conceivable, of course, that these rates might have increased even more rapidly had there been no maternal and child health program.

Nor are the trends in immunizations against infectious diseases encouraging. From 1967 to 1973 the percentage of children between one and four immunized against diphtheria, whooping cough, and tetanus (DPT) fell slightly, from 78 to 73. Declines in protection against polio and measles were more marked. In 1964, 88 percent of all children one to four were immunized against polio, but by 1973 the percentage was only 60. More than a third of young children had not been immunized against rubella or measles (see table 5-10). In 1974 and 1975 the percentages for each kind of immunization increased slightly.

Gaps in immunization protection are particularly alarming for certain segments of the child population. Rates of immunization for black children in central cities are much lower than for other children for DPT, polio, and measles. Children in nonmetropolitan areas are less likely to have been vaccinated for polio and German measles.

These findings confirm evidence of deficiencies in immunization di-

54. National Center for Health Statistics, *Limitation of Activity Due to Chronic Conditions, United States, 1969 and 1970*, p. 5. These statistics are based on the noninstitutionalized population.

Table 5-10. Percentage of Children Aged One to Four Immunized against Selected Diseases, 1960–75

Year	DPT vaccine (3 or more doses)	Polio vaccine (3 or more doses)	Measles vaccine	Rubella vaccine
1960	n.a.	72.2	n.a.	...
1961	n.a.	74.3	n.a.	...
1962	67.8	78.4	n.a.	...
1963	72.9	84.1	n.a.	...
1964	76.0	87.6	24.0	...
1965	73.9	73.9	33.2	...
1966	74.5	70.2	45.4	...
1967	77.9	70.9	56.4	...
1968	76.5	68.3	58.8	...
1969	77.4	67.7	61.4	...
1970	76.1	65.9	57.2	37.2
1971	78.7	67.3	61.0	51.2
1972	75.6	62.9	62.2	56.9
1973	72.6	60.4	61.2	55.6
1974	73.9	63.1	64.5	59.8
1975	75.2	64.8	65.5	61.9

Sources: HEW, Public Health Service, Center for Disease Control, *United States Immunization Survey, 1971*, DHEW (HSM) 72-8094 (Center for Disease Control, 1971), p. 6, and *United States Immunization Survey, 1975*, HEW (CDC) 76-8221 (CDC, 1976), p. 4.
n.a. Not available (data were not collected).

rectly available from the maternal and child health program. Although funds for the program grew, the proportion of children immunized was virtually constant throughout the 1960s and declined for some types of immunizations in the early 1970s. Recent cutbacks in real funds for the program may therefore have contributed to some of the national reduction in immunization.

The C&Y clinics have apparently been much more successful in meeting the needs of the children they serve. Various studies show the clinics have reduced the incidence of serious illnesses, decreased the need for hospitalization, improved school attendance, discovered and treated a high incidence of correctable defects, and lowered the long-run cost of providing medical care to children. Days of hospitalization declined from 101 per 1,000 registrants in the fourth quarter of 1968 to 42 in the fourth quarter of 1972 (table 5-11). In the same period registrants judged to have no conditions currently requiring medical treatment increased from 46 percent of all registrants to 71 percent. This decline in hospitalization

Table 5-11. Performance of Children and Youth Projects, Fourth Quarter, 1968–72

Year (fourth quarter)	Days in hospital per 1,000 registrants	Percent of registrants under medical supervision[a]	Average annual cost per registrant (dollars)
1968	101	46	201
1969	60	53	162
1970	45	60	140
1971	56	66	126
1972	42	71	131

Source: Minnesota Systems Research, Inc., Systems Development Project, "Report Series: Quarterly Summary Report," no. 18 (April–June 1972), p. 15, and no. 20 (October–December 1972), p. 14.
a. No conditions currently requiring treatment.

and increased healthiness of the children registered at the projects also helped reduce the cost per registrant: in spite of the rapid rise in medical care costs, the average annual cost per registrant fell from $201 in the fourth quarter of 1968 to $131 in the fourth quarter of 1972.

Carefully controlled studies of the effect of C&Y projects on the incidence of serious health problems are rare. One notable exception is a study of the incidence of rheumatic fever in Baltimore by Gordis.[55] He examined the annual incidence of hospitalized first attacks of rheumatic fever for black children aged five to fourteen living in census tracts that had three C&Y clinics and one OEO neighborhood health center in 1968. Their rates of hospitalization were compared both with rates for a similar group of children living in the area in 1960–64 before the establishment of the centers and with rates for a comparable group of children ineligible for care at the centers in 1968–70.

Gordis found that the rate of rheumatic fever for tracts with comprehensive care centers in 1968–70 was about one-third lower than for the rest of Baltimore. From 1960–64 to 1968–70 rheumatic fever decreased 60 percent in tracts with comprehensive care centers but was unchanged in the rest of the city. Furthermore, the declining incidence in Baltimore was traced to a reduction in preventable cases—cases preceded by clinical respiratory infections. The prompt identification and treatment of streptococcal infections, emphasized by the comprehensive care centers, led directly to a reduction of first attacks of rheumatic fever requiring hos-

55. Leon Gordis, "Effectiveness of Comprehensive-Care Programs in Preventing Rheumatic Fever," *New England Journal of Medicine,* vol. 289 (August 16, 1973), pp. 331–35.

pitalization. Gordis concluded that comprehensive care programs were critical in reducing the incidence of rheumatic fever in the inner city.[56]

A somewhat less conclusive study by Kaplan and others investigated the impact on school attendance of a C&Y project in Pittsburgh.[57] Attendance at two elementary schools serving two public housing projects, one with a health project and the other without, was measured. A four-way classification of pupils was made: those living in the first housing project and enrolled in the health project; those living in the first housing project but not enrolled in the health project; children living in the second housing project; and children living elsewhere in the city. Using multivariate regression analysis, the study estimated school absences as a function of sex, age, residence in public housing, enrollment in health project, and various interaction terms. It concluded that school attendance rates are determined by many complex underlying factors: "A comprehensive care project does produce an improvement in attendance, but the effect is small compared to other variables, such as the proximity of the school, race, sex, and socioeconomic conditions."[58]

Alpert found that in Boston low-income families treated by a comprehensive family-focused pediatric health care team had fewer operations, hospitalizations, and physicians' visits for illness, and more physicians' visits for preventive health care, than a control group of similar low-income families.[59] Klein and others found that hospital days for children in the Rochester, New York, area served by a comprehensive health center were reduced by 50 percent.[60]

Other types of benefits yielded by the maternal and child health program are reported, though unsystematically, by the programs themselves. The C&Y projects have found that high incidences of correctable defects —particularly dental caries and hearing and visual defects—have been reduced by the projects. The crippled children's program reports cases of

56. Ibid., p. 331.

57. Robert S. Kaplan, Lester B. Lave, and Samuel Leinhardt, "The Efficacy of a Comprehensive Health Care Project: An Empirical Analysis," *American Journal of Public Health,* vol. 62 (July 1972), pp. 924–30.

58. Ibid., p. 929.

59. Joel J. Alpert and others, "Effective Use of Comprehensive Pediatric Care: Utilization of Health Resources," *American Journal of Diseases of Children,* vol. 116 (November 1968), pp. 529–33.

60. Michael Klein and others, "The Impact of the Rochester Neighborhood Health Center on Hospitalization of Children, 1968 to 1970," *Pediatrics,* vol. 51 (May 1973), pp. 833–39.

the alleviation of various crippling conditions that has permitted children to develop into self-supporting adults.

Appraisal and Recommendations

The MCH program, especially the comprehensive health projects, has been able to meet the health care needs of many of the poor. It has specifically aimed funds at high-risk population groups, and it has focused on services—particularly prenatal care for women and immunization and preventive care for infants and young children—that have demonstrably improved health. It has had sufficient flexibility to offer a wide range of services, including environmental, nutritional, and social services as well as medical care. The one significant failure of the program is its neglect of rural areas despite the special priority given these areas in the authorizing legislation.

Unfortunately, some of the advantages and strengths of the program can only be suspected, not proved, because of the lack of systematic statistical reporting and documentation of results. It is disturbing that so little is known about who benefits and where the money goes in a program that has been in existence since 1935. Medicare and Medicaid—newcomers by comparison—provide far more evidence on the distribution of benefits and expenditures. The MCH program should make a serious effort to move from isolated, episodic accounts of success to full statistical reports detailing the services provided, the allocation of funds among the various parts of the program, and the distribution of benefits among various geographical and socioeconomic groups. Attempts should be made to determine whether the services provided have a lasting impact on the health of the mothers and children receiving them.

Even though the available data are limited, some weaknesses in the program are apparent. First, benefits are inequitably distributed: some mothers and children receive high-quality comprehensive care while equally needy women and children receive none. The C&Y projects provide half a million children with a full range of health services at an annual cost of $125 a child, but the state and local health department programs provide approximately 10 million children with only limited immunization and health screening examinations in schools, at an average annual cost of about $8 a child, and many low-income children in rural and central city areas receive no benefits at all from the MCH program. There are similar disparities in prenatal care for women.

This uneven distribution of benefits might be justified if it could be demonstrated that all projects were located in the areas of greatest need (those with high poverty rates, limited benefits under other public programs such as Medicaid, crowded or nonexistent private health facilities) and that in the allocation of funds each project gave highest priority to those least able to obtain care without assistance. Although most of the areas currently selected for projects appear to be deserving, there is no evidence of attempts to reach other, equally deserving areas. Statistics allowing comparisons between areas with projects and other areas are not available for poverty rates, infant mortality rates or incidence of preventable illness in children, service by other public programs, or the availability of private health resources to the poor.

A second disadvantage of the MCH program is that its delivery of health services may not be responsive to the needs or desires of the community it serves. Most projects are sponsored by medical schools or health departments rather than community groups. Only 43 percent of the C&Y projects have voluntarily established community advisory boards to make suggestions and criticize.

The state and local health department programs have been remarkably stagnant, treating virtually the same number of children and only a moderately increased number of women during a period (1963–73) in which expenditures have grown by 60 percent. Since formula funds are based on the number of births and the per capita income in the state, rather than on its performance in reaching target groups or in providing high-quality services, perhaps it is not surprising that the states have had little incentive to carry out aggressive outreach and expansion policies.

Two measures would make the program more responsive to community needs. First, funds should be allocated according to services provided rather than independent measures such as per capita income and number of children or births in the area. It makes little sense to give states with large rural populations a larger share of federal funds without requiring that those funds be used to serve rural women and children (or low-income urban women and children).

Second, the categorical grant approach of the MCH program tends to tie benefits to specified conditions. The crippled children's program has become a complex maze, which must be puzzling to any parent seeking assistance. Each state has wide leeway to define the range of conditions covered. Some adhere to the traditional emphasis on congenital malformations; others cover everything. A parent with a hemophiliac child may be eligible for expensive services in one state but not in another. Children with equally serious but noncrippling conditions receive no benefits in any state. Most states restrict benefits to special facilities for the care of crippled children so that parents have a limited choice of physicians. The MCH program would be improved if the definitions of crippling conditions were made broader and uniform throughout the nation and if there were stronger administration at the national level. Beneficiaries should also be permitted greater freedom in selecting the locus of care and in seeking care from private physicians (with compensation by the program) as well as from crippled children's facilities.

In 1974 specific project grants were eliminated and states now receive one formula grant. They can allocate the funds as they wish, subject to the requirement that every state have at least one of each of the following projects: maternity and infant care, health care for high-risk infants, dental care, family planning, and child and preschool health care. This requirement is unlikely to move the states toward locating specific projects according to the greatest need if they are not already doing so. A state such as Mississippi, with numerous pockets of concentrated poverty, a high infant mortality rate, and limited assistance from public and private health programs, could choose to have only one maternity and infant care project while a higher-income state with a low infant mortality rate would also have one. And the requirement that each state have a center for the care of high-risk infants could consume most of any additional funds flowing to the program since few states currently have such programs.

There is ample reason for worry that greater state discretion in the use of funds will reduce the effectiveness of the program rather than enhance it. The programs over which the states had the greatest control in the past —their health departments' programs—have been the least successful in providing high-quality, comprehensive care.

Recommendations for improving or expanding the program must therefore take into account its experience since 1974 as well as its whole history. Careful monitoring and complete, accurate statistical reporting are essential.

Finally, the concept of separate programs for children and pregnant women should be reexamined. It may well be that resources could be more efficiently used in supporting health centers serving entire communities— not just the poor or just one age or population group.

chapter six **A New Approach to Health Care Delivery**

The neighborhood health center program, started as a pilot program by the Office of Economic Opportunity in 1965, embodied many of the dreams and concepts of the War on Poverty. The program went further than Medicare and Medicaid and the various maternal and child health programs, to a multifaceted attack on poverty and health that directly addressed both the financial and the nonfinancial obstacles standing in the way of improved health in poor neighborhoods.

Based on the belief that significant improvements in health could only be obtained by attention to the nonmedical influences on health as well as to the delivery of quality medical care, the centers sought to improve the health of the poor by giving residents of impoverished neighborhoods access to comprehensive health care services in local facilities and participation in running those facilities. The program established several principles defining its concept of a multidimensional neighborhood center. First, the center must be located in an area with a high concentration of poverty. Second, it should integrate and coordinate its services with existing health and other community facilities. Third, it should provide personal, high-quality health care. Fourth, it should involve members of the community through their participation on boards of directors or advisory boards. Fifth, it should provide employment opportunities and training for community residents.[1]

Delivery of medical care was thus not the sole or, perhaps, even the main concern of the neighborhood health center program. Although the

This chapter was prepared with the assistance of Roger A. Reynolds.

1. See, for example, Thomas E. Bryant, "Goals and Potential of Neighborhood Health Centers," *Medical Care,* vol. 8 (March–April 1970), pp. 93–94; and Lisbeth Bamberger Schorr and Joseph T. English, "Background, Context and Significant Issues in Neighborhood Health Center Programs," *Milbank Memorial Fund Quarterly,* vol. 46 (July 1968), pt. 1, pp. 289–96.

centers did concentrate on the delivery of health care, the OEO saw them as potential tools for the development of human resources and economic well-being in poor communities. Each center's health activities could provide members of the community with employment, training in job skills, the opportunity to develop stable work histories, and experience in managerial positions.

Underlying much of the motivation of those involved in the program was a desire to use the centers as an organizing device and a means of increasing the political power of the poor through community participation in the governance and operation of the centers. Leaders capable of making the needs of the poor more widely known could be developed. Experience with voting, serving on boards, and organizing for health care at the community level could raise the political consciousness and effectiveness of members of minority groups and the disadvantaged. Removing discriminatory barriers faced by blacks and other minority groups became a major goal of many of the projects' efforts.

The experience of the health centers has been valuable to less poor communities as well. As a pilot demonstration program, the centers could experiment with innovations in health care delivery—these have reached beyond the centers to the mainstream delivery of medical care. One such innovation is the use of a team of health professionals to deliver health care rather than reliance on a single practitioner, which has demonstrated the ability of a range of health practitioners other than physicians to deliver quality medical care.

Any complete appraisal of the effectiveness and social value of the program should therefore go well beyond looking at the use or cost of medical services in the centers or even the effect of the centers on the health of the poor. But to evaluate the program's total effect on the social conditions influencing poverty and health in poor neighborhoods or its indirect effect on the practice of medicine is extremely difficult. Many potential achievements, such as the breaking down of racial barriers or the development of leaders, do not lend themselves to quantitative measurement and are difficult to attribute directly. Furthermore, as it will take longer than a decade for many of the program's effects to become apparent, no final evaluation can yet be made.

A comprehensive appraisal of the program is in any event beyond the scope of this study. The discussion that follows therefore excludes any evaluation of the nonhealth achievements of the program and concentrates on the success of the centers in delivering health care. It uses available quantitative and descriptive evidence to document this success.

History

Federal support for the neighborhood health centers began with eight centers, which were funded by the community action program of the OEO in 1965 under its research and development authority. The health center concept gathered wide support because it offered features attractive to the poor and those who worked with them, people in the civil rights movement, health professionals, and cities and rural areas uneasy about the growing unrest in poverty-stricken areas. Thus in 1966 specific legislative authority for a program to support the "development and implementation of comprehensive health services programs focused upon the needs of persons residing in urban or rural areas having high concentrations of poverty and a marked inadequacy of health services" was enacted in amendments to the Economic Opportunity Act.[2]

The Department of Health, Education, and Welfare published in 1967 a comprehensive report, which, after summarizing the health problems of the poor, estimated the number of comprehensive health care projects that would be required to help improve the health of the poor and carefully calculated the benefits of an extensive health care delivery program. From these estimates, a detailed plan was presented for establishing 1,000 health centers to serve 25 million low-income people by 1973 at a total cost of $3.35 billion.[3]

The Partnership for Health Amendments of 1967 provided additional funds for comprehensive community health projects to be administered by HEW. These projects, however, placed less emphasis on the nonmedical services included in the OEO projects.[4] Thus the responsibility for

2. 80 Stat. 1463.
3. U.S. Department of Health, Education, and Welfare, Office of the Assistant Secretary (Planning and Evaluation), *Delivery of Health Services for the Poor* (GPO, 1967), pp. 5a, 52.
4. For more information on the projects funded under the Health Amendments, see Walter Merten and Sylvia Nothman, "Implications of the Neighborhood Health Center Experience for Future Investment of Federal Funds in Delivery of Health Services," paper presented at the American Public Health Association Annual Meeting, Atlantic City, New Jersey, November 15, 1972.

demonstration health centers that combined medical care services with active community participation fell mainly on the OEO program.[5]

At first the health centers served all residents of the surrounding area regardless of income. It was expected that, because of the high level of poverty in these areas, most users would be poor and that the centers' dependence on patients with low incomes would be financially feasible since the OEO anticipated that Medicare and Medicaid would be major sources of financial support for ongoing operations—estimates went as high as 80 percent. An agreement of mutual support to this effect was signed by the director of the OEO and the secretary of HEW in May 1967.[6]

Those who feared competition from the centers as a free source of health care, however, were not content to allow such a loose definition of eligibility as "neighborhood." Strong opposition to the "open-door" policy from private practitioners and other providers of health care in the private sector led Congress in 1967 to limit free care to patients from low-income families. The law, as interpreted in 1969, also limited paying or partially paying registrants to 20 percent of all registrants, classifying neighborhood health centers as "poor people's" medicine.[7] These restrictions guaranteed the almost total dependence of the neighborhood health center program on public funds.

The program's financial independence was further circumscribed because support of the magnitude anticipated from Medicaid and Medicare never materialized. By 1975 funds from Medicare and Medicaid covered only 10 to 20 percent of the operating costs of most centers. Consequently, the program had to rely on annual appropriations and federal grants for its continued survival.

For the duration of the 1960s the neighborhood center concept received the necessary federal support. OEO planners argued persuasively that only

5. The Department of Housing and Urban Development also helped finance health centers under its model cities program, but few accounts of the experience of these centers are available. For case studies of attempts by three cities to start centers, see Lawrence D. Brown, "Coordination of Federal Urban Policy: Organizational Politics in Three Model Cities" (Ph.D. dissertation, Harvard University, 1973), chap. 5.

6. "Coordinated Funding of Health Services," A Joint Statement of the Department of Health, Education, and Welfare and the Office of Economic Opportunity (May 1967; processed).

7. Daniel I. Zwick, "Some Accomplishments and Findings of Neighborhood Health Centers," *Milbank Memorial Fund Quarterly,* vol. 50 (October 1972), pt. 1, p. 410.

a health center, as opposed to health insurance, could, in addition to financing services, simultaneously treat a variety of the causes of deficient medical care common to poverty areas such as the scarcity of physicians and health facilities; inadequate transportation to areas with more abundant resources; crowded facilities with long waits and care that was frequently impersonal or minimal; physicians who, pressed for time, seldom undertook extensive workups, provided counseling, or explained fully the nature and importance of a prescribed treatment; and discriminatory practices that restricted the access of minority groups to sources of care open to whites.[8]

As an integral part of the OEO's War on Poverty, the centers were directed to treat a wide range of debilitating social and environmental conditions besides scarcity of medical care. Guidelines for acceptable services published by the OEO in 1968 included prevention, screening, diagnosis, and treatment; arrangements for institutional care, prescription drugs, home health care, and finding cases and other outreach services; rehabilitation, dental care, family planning, mental health, patient and community health education, and social work; services aimed at the prevention and treatment of alcoholism and narcotic addiction; transportation; environmental health services; training of personnel; and administrative functions, including planning, reporting, and evaluation.[9] The guideline flexibility allowed the services offered by a particular health center to vary with the

8. For further discussion of the various influences on health and health care patterns among low-income families, see Robert E. Anderson and Susan Morgan, *Comprehensive Health Care: A Southern View* (Atlanta: Southern Regional Council, 1973); Ronald Andersen and others, *Health Service Use: National Trends and Variations, 1953–1971,* DHEW (HSM) 73-3004 (HEW, Health Services and Mental Health Administration, 1972); Karen Davis and Roger Reynolds, "The Impact of Medicare and Medicaid on Access to Health Care," in Richard N. Rosett, ed., *The Role of Health Insurance in the Health Services Sector* (Neale Watson Academic Publications for National Bureau of Economic Research, 1976), pp. 391–435 (Brookings Reprint T-013); Joseph L. Dorsey, "Physician Distribution in Boston and Brookline, 1940 and 1961," *Medical Care,* vol. 7 (November–December 1969), pp. 429–40; J. Romm, *Initial Analyses of Baseline Surveys for Neighborhood Health Centers* (Bethesda, Md.: System Sciences, Inc., 1971; available from National Technical Information Service); and *Economic Opportunity Amendments of 1969,* Hearings before the Subcommittee on Employment, Manpower, and Poverty of the Senate Committee on Labor and Public Welfare, 91:1 (GPO, 1969).

9. Office of Economic Opportunity, *The Comprehensive Neighborhood Health Services Program: Guidelines* (GPO, March 1968).

health needs of the neighborhood population.[10] Many centers obtained additional funding from other programs for nutrition, day care, and child development. In some areas, particularly rural ones, the activities of the centers were extended to trying to deal with inadequate sewage disposal, sanitation, and housing and water problems.

Household surveys of several low-income neighborhoods, where health centers were subsequently set up, gave a glimpse of the pressing need for such comprehensive care. In nine urban areas surveyed, the children were 52 percent more likely to be limited in activity by chronic conditions than the average child living in an urban area in the United States.[11] In the Roxbury section of Boston and the Bedford Stuyvesant section of Brooklyn, 30 percent of the population with family incomes under $3,000, adjusted for age, suffered from chronic conditions, although the national average was 20 percent.[12]

Table 6-1 shows the lack of medical care utilization in these communities. The average number of physicians' visits for rural residents in the United States was more than 50 percent greater in all age groups than for residents of the surveyed high-poverty rural areas. For those between the ages of fifteen and forty-four, it was 85 percent greater. In urban areas surveyed the disparities were most apparent among children—children in metropolitan areas across the nation visited physicians 50 percent more often than those in urban poverty areas and 35 percent more were admitted to hospitals.

Dental care was particularly deficient in both urban and rural areas surveyed, lagging at least 22 percent behind national levels in all cases and 100 percent behind national levels for the elderly, urban children, and urban adults between forty-five and sixty-four. The surveys also found that an average 20 percent of poor residents never received dental care;

10. See H. Jack Geiger, "Community Control—or Community Conflict?" National Tuberculosis and Respiratory Disease Association, *Bulletin* (November 1969), pp. 4–10, for a description of the impact of particular neighborhoods on the services offered by their centers.

11. Data are for children under fifteen. System Sciences, *Appendices to Further Baseline Survey Analyses for Neighborhood Health Centers* (System Sciences, 1973), p. D-15; National Center for Health Statistics, *Limitation of Activity Due to Chronic Conditions, United States, 1969 and 1970,* Vital and Health Statistics, series 10, no. 80, DHEW (HSM) 73-1506 (GPO, 1973), p. 29.

12. Gerald Sparer and Louise M. Okada, "Chronic Conditions and Physician Use Patterns in Ten Urban Poverty Areas," *Medical Care,* vol. 12 (July 1974), table 4, p. 553.

Table 6-1. Use of Health Care Services in Poverty Areas Compared with That in the United States, by Age Group, 1969–71 Surveys[a]

Age group	Urban			Rural		
	United States	Poverty areas	Ratio	United States	Poverty areas	Ratio
Physicians' visits per person per year						
Under 15[b]	4.0	2.7	1.48	3.3	2.1	1.57
15–44[c]	4.5	3.9	1.15	4.1	2.2	1.86
45–64	5.1	5.0	1.02	4.6	3.0	1.53
65 and over	6.3	6.3	1.00	6.0	3.6	1.67
Dental visits per person per year						
Under 15[b]	1.6	0.8	2.00	1.1	0.9	1.22
15–44[c]	1.8	1.3	1.38	1.4	1.1	1.27
45–64	1.8	0.9	2.00	1.1	0.8	1.38
65 and over	1.2	0.6	2.00	0.8	0.4	2.00
Hospital admissions per 1,000 persons per year						
Under 15[b]	68	50	1.36	66	67	0.99
15–44[c]	148	143	1.03	165	100	1.65
45–64	142	137	1.04	159	168	0.95
65 and over	214	168	1.27	275	289	0.95

Source: Roger A. Reynolds, "Improving Access to Health Care Among the Poor—The Neighborhood Health Center Experience," *Milbank Memorial Fund Quarterly: Health and Society*, vol. 54 (Winter 1976), p. 49.

a. The survey for the United States was conducted during 1969 and 1970; the survey of the poverty areas from July 1, 1970, to June 30, 1971.

b. Under seventeen for U.S. averages.

c. Seventeen to forty-four for U.S. averages.

the level was as high as 35 percent in a low-income neighborhood in Charleston, South Carolina.[13]

To receive funds for a health center, each poor neighborhood had to have a sponsor for the project. At first, most communities chose medical schools, hospitals, local health departments, or other nearby groups providing health services that already had managerial experience, experience in recovering third-party reimbursement, medical expertise, and specialized backup medical resources.[14] Such groups sponsored 63 percent of all OEO projects at the time of original funding and 65 percent of the projects

13. System Sciences, *Appendices to Further Baseline Survey Analyses.*

14. See, for example, Anthony R. Kovner and others, "Relating a Neighborhood Health Center to a General Hospital: A Case History," *Medical Care*, vol. 7 (March–April 1969), pp. 118–23.

administered by HEW under the Partnership for Health Amendments of 1967.[15]

Conflicts between local residents' perceptions of broad community health needs and the expectations and medical focus of professional groups, however, subsequently led to the transfer of a number of projects to community control. The OEO encouraged such consumer sponsorship by giving preferential treatment to new nonprofit health corporations governed and administered by community residents. Planners judged that local sponsors would promote the employment and training of community residents and be sensitive to local health care needs.

Most community centers were established as free-standing clinics— clinics not attached to medical schools, hospitals, or other institutions— with salaried health professionals. This, rather than contracts with hospital outpatient departments, physicians in group practice, or prepayment plans, permitted local control.

As the health centers gained community support, they were also useful in obtaining other benefits for local residents. Personnel at health centers frequently helped applicants work through the maze of requirements for eligibility for welfare, food stamps, social security, and other public benefits. As the personnel became skilled at "federal grantsmanship," they turned their attention to proposals for improvements in housing, nutrition, water and sanitation development, and other environmental activities. Other examples are a legal services program attached to a health center and the preferential location of the bank accounts of health centers in financial institutions willing to make loans to community residents.

Since the centers were usually located in areas with high concentrations of minority groups, the personnel were generally concerned with advancing the position of such groups. Toward this end, the centers constituted a mechanism for developing leaders among black and other minority residents—either by having them serve on health center boards or as administrators, or by attracting minority health professionals to the community. These leaders could then perform functions in the community besides their duties at the health centers. The centers also encouraged participation of the poor in voting for board members or serving on boards in an attempt to raise the political consciousness and effectiveness of members of minority groups and the disadvantaged. By organizing around health care issues,

15. See Zwick, "Some Accomplishments and Findings of Neighborhood Health Centers," p. 393.

community leaders were often able to bypass or overcome local resistance to the mobilization and economic progress of blacks and other groups suffering from local discrimination.[16]

Not surprisingly, the centers' broad range of activities and definition of health care threatened many representatives of more traditional health care and local institutions. Local medical societies sometimes fought the establishment of centers, refused to supply patient records, and worked to restrict hospital staff privileges for health center physicians. In some cases, local interests pressured county judges, who were required to sign a waiver legalizing the OEO's presence in rural counties, and governors to close down nascent centers. Medical schools' attempts to use the centers for training medical students and conducting research frequently clashed with community demands for dignified, personal, and humane health care with strong community control.[17] Furthermore, the focus of many health professionals on narrower medical objectives created friction between them and center employees concerned with outreach, environmental health, or other nonmedical activities. In areas with a concentration of minority residents, racially biased local people often fought the centers' efforts to include minorities in mainstream economic activity.

Some centers fell to this opposition.[18] For those that survived it, striving to achieve such a wide range of often conflicting objectives was a slow, arduous process. Working with inexperienced management led to many frustrations: paychecks were late, bills were not submitted or remitted promptly, and supplies were not kept in stock.[19] Lack of experience in dealing with private insurance companies and government financing programs and lack of cooperation from third-party payers impeded the finan-

16. The Mound Bayou health center in Mississippi, for instance, successfully organized a farm cooperative and food processing plant for the black community as part of its effort to combat malnutrition. Geiger, "Community Control—or Community Conflict?"

17. See, for example, Milton S. Davis and Robert E. Tranquada, "A Sociological Evaluation of the Watts Neighborhood Health Center," *Medical Care,* vol. 7 (March–April 1969), pp. 105–17.

18. For the history of an Appalachian health center in Floyd County, Kentucky, that was not successful in countering the opposition it faced, see Richard A. Couto, *Poverty, Politics, and Health Care: An Appalachian Experience* (Praeger, 1975).

19. Interviews by Karen Davis with the staffs of several neighborhood health centers in the rural South. See also Paul R. Torrens, "Administrative Problems of Neighborhood Health Centers," *Medical Care,* vol. 9 (November–December 1971), pp. 487–97.

cial stability and independence of most centers.[20] And working with un-
trained, inexperienced local consumer boards and advisory groups was
often frustrating.[21]

Most of the neighborhood health centers, however, did survive, flourish,
and become stable sources of accessible health services. They achieved
much success in delivering quality health care and providing a tool for
community development.[22]

Despite generally favorable evaluations, after 1970 the neighborhood
health center program began to take on a different character and shape
from that of the original design. From 1970 to 1973, jurisdiction over
OEO centers was shifted in stages to the Department of Health, Education, and Welfare. To lay to rest fears about what would happen to the
centers under HEW, the director of the OEO and the secretary of HEW
signed an agreement guaranteeing their future.[23]

The spirit of that agreement did not hold and the neighborhood health
center program stagnated. For several years the Nixon and Ford administrations requested substantial cutbacks in the number of centers supported and the level of funding. Congressional opposition prevented such
cutbacks, but the program was held at a constant level of funding despite
the rapid increase in health care costs.

Instead of the 1,000 centers serving 25 million low-income people en-
visioned in early HEW planning documents, the program serves about 1.5
million people in roughly 125 centers.[24] Instead of funding at the originally
planned level of $3.35 billion, the 1976 budget provided for approxi-

20. Many of these problems also affected centers sponsored by medical schools.
See, for example, Robert J. Blendon and Clifton R. Gaus, "Problems in Developing
Health Services in Poverty Areas: The Johns Hopkins Experience," *Journal of Medi-
cal Education*, vol. 46 (June 1971), pp. 477–84.

21. See, for example, Gerald Sparer, George B. Dines, and Daniel Smith, "Consumer Participation in OEO-Assisted Neighborhood Health Centers," *American
Journal of Public Health*, vol. 60 (June 1970), pp. 1091–1102.

22. For a brief review of the literature, see James C. Stewart and Lottie Lee
Crafton, *Delivery of Health Care Services to the Poor: Findings from a Review of
the Current Periodical Literature, With a Key to 47 Reports of Innovative Projects*
(University of Texas at Austin, Center for Social Work Research, 1975).

23. "Comprehensive Health Service Projects (Neighborhood Health Centers):
Memorandum of Understanding," agreement signed by Elliot Richardson, Secretary,
Health, Education, and Welfare, and Donald R. Rumsfeld, Director, Office of Eco-
nomic Opportunity, November 2, 1970.

24. In 1976 neighborhood health centers, family health centers (smaller medical
centers), and networks of various health providers were all classified by HEW as
"community health centers."

mately $197 million in federal grants. The Ford administration recommended cutting funds to $155 million for 1977 and eliminating twenty centers. The Carter administration reversed this trend, requesting $301 million in the 1979 budget.

Other program changes have gradually shaped the character of the program. After the switch to HEW, funds for training personnel were no longer allowed, and support for environmental and other nonmedical activities was curtailed. Under the Nixon and Ford administrations, HEW placed, instead, much more emphasis on the traditional narrow medical approach to care.

Amendments to the program encouraged the centers to admit patients who were not poor, to charge a sliding fee schedule based on patients' incomes, and to recoup, where possible, revenues from third parties. Pressure on the centers to become, or at least to behave like, financially self-supporting medical practices intensified.[25]

The health centers found it difficult to respond to these changed directives. Resentment and misunderstanding followed attempts to institute charges where care was once free. Also, most centers were unable to obtain adequate reimbursement from Medicaid and other third-party payers, as insurers tend to cover only physicians' services, not a broad range of clinic services. An amendment to Medicaid to require state coverage of clinic services with 95 percent federal funding was defeated in 1972. Medicare has been similarly hesitant to compensate health centers adequately for all services provided—especially for those rendered by health professionals such as nurse practitioners and physician's assistants.

The Nixon and Ford administrations downplayed the neighborhood health center model and supported less comprehensive approaches such as the rural health initiatives projects, which use National Health Service Corps personnel and are usually sponsored by county governments, and family health centers, which emphasize a more traditional range of medical services for family health care. In part, these programs were added to reduce the OEO centers' original emphasis on urban poverty and relative

25. Complete self-sufficiency is impossible for centers situated in high poverty areas, since Medicaid does not adequately cover poor and medically needy families. For instance, one study showed that 48 percent of the users of outpatient facilities in poor areas of Buffalo and Cleveland were medically needy and receiving neither Medicaid nor Medicare, and their costs had to be paid out of grants and charity funds. *Outpatient Health Care in Inner Cities: Its Users, Services, and Problems,* Report to the Congress by the Comptroller General of the United States (General Accounting Office, 1975), p. 5.

neglect of rural health problems; the new projects, being smaller, are better able to survive in areas of low population density. The major effect of the policy shift so far, however, has been to redirect the neighborhood health center program toward a narrower, purely medical approach to care for the poor and disadvantaged.

Increasing pressure has been applied to the neighborhood health centers to pursue good management practices. They are instructed to hire only trained personnel, already qualified for the tasks they are to perform. Each center receives guidelines for meeting certain fixed goals—the number of patients seen by physicians and other health professionals per hour, the ratio of nonmedical staff to medical staff, the proportion of costs allocated to direct health care, the number of health professionals per registrant.[26] These guidelines are based on standards prevalent in medical practices serving the nonpoor and thus do not take into account the effectiveness of nonmedical activities, the need for patient education and counseling and outreach services, or the greater complexity of the health problems of the poor. Nor are the standards adjusted for the location of centers (urban, rural), the length of time they have been operating, the health problems of the community served, or the difficulties of both obtaining and retaining staff. As yearly funding decisions can depend on the centers' success in meeting these "efficiency" criteria, performance is often crucial to survival.

President Ford made several unsuccessful attempts to transfer decisions for funding the comprehensive health centers to state governors. Such action, if unaccompanied by a mechanism through which individual projects could appeal adverse decisions to some nonstate agency, would have exacerbated the projects' vulnerability to local political pressure.

The narrowly defined efficiency criteria and the uncertainty of continued funding have created great difficulties for the neighborhood centers still in operation. They find it difficult to recruit physicians and other health professionals when they can be assured of only one year's funding at a time. The morale of staff is frequently low, as their inability to communicate the special needs of their own projects continues.

Yet even without strong federal support some centers have become so firmly entrenched locally that they have achieved organizational stability. The formation of the National Association of Community Health

26. For program examples of efficiency guidelines, see HEW, Bureau of Community Health Services, "Rural Health Initiative: Program Guidance Material for RHI/HURA Grants" (BCHS, 1976; processed), app. F.

Centers and state associations has given them a way to express their concern at national and state levels and to gain information on proposed policy changes.

Achievement of Multiple Objectives— the Lee County Cooperative Clinic

Perhaps the best way to begin a systematic examination of the neighborhood health center program is with a case study of a single project. One that has lived up to the many ideals of the original OEO model is the Lee County Cooperative Clinic (LCCC).[27]

Lee County is located in the rural Mississippi delta region of eastern Arkansas. Marianna, the county seat and home of the clinic, is sixty miles from Memphis. Of the county's total population of 18,000, 44 percent fall below the poverty level, 58 percent are black, and 28 percent have had less than five years' education. Lee County also embodies many of the other characteristics associated with a rural, extremely poor, predominantly black county in the South—limited employment opportunities, high proportions of substandard housing, and inadequate plumbing. Half of the homes in the county have no telephone, and a third of the families have no automobile.

In the mid-1960s the Ku Klux Klan maintained a strong influence over the social and economic conditions of blacks in the Mississippi delta region surrounding Lee County; racial discrimination denied black people employment opportunities, housing, and education. For health care services, local blacks with serious problems were given a one-way bus ticket to Memphis and a map of the city indicating the charity hospital.

In 1968 the civil rights movement, which had come earlier to other parts of the South, gained momentum in eastern Arkansas. A march on the office of Governor Winthrop Rockefeller in Little Rock prompted him

27. The information contained in this section was obtained by Davis through interviews with Lee County Cooperative Clinic personnel as part of a study of rural health care in the South. For more information on this study, see Karen Davis and Ray Marshall, "Rural Health Care in the South," preliminary summary report prepared for presentation at the meeting of the Task Force on Southern Rural Development, Atlanta, October 1975. For a look at other comprehensive health centers in the South, see Anderson and Morgan, *Comprehensive Health Care: A Southern View.* A collection of articles documenting the experiences of individual health projects is contained in Robert M. Hollister, Bernard M. Kramer, and Seymour S. Bellin, eds., *Neighborhood Health Centers* (Heath, 1974).

to seek some solution to many of the problems plaguing the area. Arrangements were made with VISTA for a community organizer, a nurse, and a physician to come to Lee County in 1969. Through local contributions of time and money, the group rented and renovated a black undertaker's house as a health clinic and opened its doors in March 1970. In April they received a small grant from the OEO; this was followed by larger grants over the next two years. In 1972 the OEO awarded the clinic a grant of $1.2 million to support eighteen months of operation and the construction of a new facility.

From the start the project encountered considerable opposition from the white community of Lee County. In each case, however, the clinic devised successful strategies to overcome the opposition. Three of the four practicing physicians in Lee County voted to deny LCCC physicians staff privileges at Lee Memorial Hospital in Marianna. The LCCC responded by filing a court suit against the hospital. When it became apparent that the hospital would lose the suit, it settled out of court and paid the LCCC's legal fees out of the county treasury. Now the clinic has a cooperative relationship with the hospital that includes the sharing of resources, joint purchasing, and other mutually desirable arrangements.

Another example of opposition encountered in the early stages of the project was the refusal of the county judge to sign the waiver making the OEO's role in the county legal. When a black opposition candidate vigorously campaigned for the judge's seat in 1970, the incumbent relented and shortly before election time signed the waiver. The changed attitude of the community since then is shown by the recent decision of the county to pave the street leading to the clinic.

But when the LCCC announced in 1972 its intention of building a new, permanent facility, white opposition crystallized. Local whites approached Governor Dale Bumpers and insisted that he close the clinic. Bumpers declined but urged the clinic to include some local white representation on its board. The clinic responded by adding two appointed members to the fourteen board members elected by patients registered at the clinic. This action, plus the economic effect of the clinic's local bank accounts, countered the white opposition.

Much of the credit for the survival of the clinic through this turbulent period belongs to a gifted administrator, Olly Neal, Jr. Neal grew up in Marianna and was hired away from a nutrition program in Memphis when the clinic started. He succeeded in attracting highly qualified and capable people to assist him; his recruitment efforts have maintained a full staff of health professionals, a large majority of whom are black. His enthusiasm about what could be accomplished inspired a number of employees to seek further training; several, with moral and financial support from the clinic, passed high school equivalency tests and went on to finish college. The resulting esprit de corps has contributed to the dedication of the staff (90 percent of whom are black, many of whom are local residents), who are willing to work overtime without compensation and are rarely absent.·

To ensure community participation in the direction of health care policy, the clinic has developed the skills of community board members. The chairman takes an active interest in the clinic and follows its daily activities. The board meets monthly and has become quite knowledgeable about health care.

As a result of its strong ties to the community, the clinic has supported activities other than the delivery of health care. A vegetable growers' cooperative operates next to the clinic. A proposal developed by clinic personnel led to a $2 million grant for a national demonstration water project to develop a water and sewage project for a multicounty area in eastern Arkansas.

The LCCC provides a wide variety of health-related activities. Its four full-time physicians, three health professionals (physician's assistant, medex, and nurse practitioner), and nursing staff provide primary medical care to 8,000 registered patients, 20 percent of whom are white, including some affluent whites. Dental care is provided by two dentists and three dental assistants. Visiting nurses change dressings at home, monitor the use of medications for housebound patients, and administer "de-worming" medication to families with positive tests. The pharmacy dispenses about 20,000 prescriptions annually. The laboratory is staffed by a bacteriologist and other personnel, who provide accurate, prompt tests for the many bacterial infections encountered. The nutrition division designs diets for patients with special health problems and sponsors a garden club, a weight-watchers' club, and an infant feeding program with Department of Agriculture funds authorized in 1973 to make special foods available to women, infants, and children (the WIC program). Professional child development services are available, and parents are instructed in methods of promoting children's learning skills. The environmental health program supplies residents with window and door screens, sprays mosquito-infested areas, engages in rodent eradication, drains standing puddles, and helps build pit privies. Transportation to the Little Rock medical center for specialized services is also furnished by the clinic.

Most of these services are paid for from HEW grants. Only 3 percent of revenues come from Medicare though Medicare patients make up 7 percent of active registrants. Similarly, only 9 percent of revenues come from Medicaid though 22 percent of active registrants are under Medicaid. Both programs fail to cover the costs of the services provided by the clinic.

Few studies have been conducted to determine the clinic's effect on the health of community residents. Given the severity of the health problems before the clinic opened, however, there can be little doubt that it has contributed substantially. The most readily documented result is the decline in infant mortality in Lee County. The infant mortality rate for blacks was cut in half between 1970 and 1974, from 36 deaths per 1,000 live births to 18 per 1,000, and remains considerably below the state average for blacks of 22 per 1,000. This is a remarkable achievement considering that the county has the lowest educational level of any county in the state and one of the highest poverty rates.

One study of the child development efforts of the LCCC was conducted. The clinic supplied the parents of all the children who had low scores on the Denver Developmental Screening Test with special instructions for teaching at home. An evaluation of this program indicated that the performance of 70 percent of the children whose parents received this assistance improved on subsequent testing.

Impressionistic evidence from health professionals at the LCCC also suggests some tangible improvements in health. One serious problem of county residents is the high incidence of impetigo caused by insect bites and bacterial infection. In the early days, the clinic encountered children whose skin abcesses had developed into severe deep muscle and joint inflammations that required expensive hospitalization. Now, though the clinic continues to see a fair amount of impetigo, it treats patients in much earlier stages so that hospitalization and crippling do not take place.

Another serious problem in which health professionals have observed major changes is diarrhea in infants. In the past, improper sterilization of bottles and the addition of impure water to formula meant that babies were exposed to harmful bacteria, which often resulted in severe dehydration, hospitalization, and at times death. The clinic participates in a WIC infant feeding program that furnishes mothers with prepared formula. This eliminates a number of hazards involved in the proper preparation of formula. As a result of this program, the clinic sees fewer cases of dehydration, and these are more frequently caught before they advance to the stage requiring hospitalization.

Access to health care for the poor in Lee County today is light years removed from the situation of a few years ago when blacks were provided only cursory care in segregated physicians' offices or, if seriously ill, shunted off to Memphis for charity care. The Lee County Cooperative Clinic has demonstrated that comprehensive health care, including dental care, home health care, nutrition, child development, and environmental health services, can be made available in a poor, black, rural community and that poor patients will assist in upgrading their health with the benefit of education and counseling.

But perhaps the most striking achievements of the clinic have been the nonhealth aspects. In overcoming the opposition of local physicians, the county judge, white citizens, county health departments, and pharmacists, the black community has developed a sense of strength and participation in the political process. Outstanding leaders and spokespeople for the black community have emerged. Illiterate residents who had never held jobs before have been trained and placed in useful jobs. A substantial number of poor community residents have undertaken additional education and training.

In short, much of the potential of the neighborhood health center as an instrument for social, economic, and political change has been realized. While not all the centers funded by the OEO succeeded in overcoming the obstacles they faced and many fell short of reaching their multiple objectives, there are a sufficient number of success stories like that of Lee County to argue for continued support of such centers. They have warranted the faith of Thomas E. Bryant, who was director of the OEO's Office of Health Affairs when the Lee County Cooperative Clinic was funded. Dr. Bryant stated: "It has been suggested that the Neighborhood Health Center tries to do too much. This criticism may well be appropriate. But in view of the long history of neglect, dare we try less?"[28]

Evaluations

The neighborhood health center program requires all centers to provide detailed data on the persons served and the use of services.[29] Standard reports indicate that the centers have successfully provided a wide range of services to low-income people. In calendar year 1974 an estimated 1.4

28. Bryant, "Goals and Potential of Neighborhood Health Centers," p. 94.

29. OEO, "Reporting Requirements for OEO Comprehensive Health Services Projects," OEO Manual 6128-2 (OEO, 1971; processed). The data are reported in HEW, Health Services Administration, Bureau of Community Health Services, "Neighborhood Health Centers, Summary of Project Data," and BCHS, *Comprehensive Health Services Projects: Data Base Report,* both issued quarterly. Data on registrants and use in this section are taken from various issues.

million people were registered at 105 neighborhood health centers—an average of 13,330 at each.

Of these 1.4 million registrants 36 percent were children below the age of fifteen. Children and adults between fifteen and forty-four made up another 45 percent. The elderly represented only 6 percent, considerably less than their 14 percent representation in the poor population. About 56 percent of all registrants were female, with women between fifteen and forty-four greatly outnumbering men in the same age group.

More than 50 percent of all neighborhood health center registrants are black; another 20 percent are Hispanic. This means that three-fourths of those served are members of minority groups.

Most neighborhood health centers offer a full range of outpatient services. A financial audit of a sample of sixty centers in 1973 showed that all offered medical care and laboratory services, 96 percent provided dental care, 90 percent had X-ray equipment, and 94 percent had pharmacies.[30]

Besides the basic services, there is wide variation in special services offered at centers. The emphasis on and inclusion of these services vary according to sociodemographic characteristics and consequent health needs of the population served. The majority of centers, for instance, have home health care programs but only a limited number offer physical or speech therapy or family planning programs:[31]

	Centers offering service (percent)
Direct health activities	
Mental health care	76
Home health care	83
Physical or speech therapy	26
Optometry	37
Sickle cell anemia treatment	40
Lead poisoning testing and treatment	31
Family planning	26
Supporting health activities	
Social and community services	94
Transportation	93
Training of personnel	81
Community organization	53
Environmental activities	29
Research and evaluation	67

30. *Health Revenue Sharing and Health Services Act of 1974,* H.R. 93-1161, 93:2 (GPO, 1974), p. 60.
    31. Ibid.

Budgetary constraints prohibit many centers from offering a full range of supplementary services; cutbacks in the mid-1970s forced the discontinuation of some services.

Patients registered at neighborhood health centers had approximately 6.5 million "encounters" during 1974, or about 4.6 encounters per registrant.[32] These included visits by patients to physicians and other medical personnel, dentists, pharmacists, and other primary providers in the center. Medical encounters represented 66 percent of all encounters. The average number of medical encounters per registrant was 3.1 in 1974—somewhat lower than the 1973 average of 5.6 physicians' visits for all low-income persons and 4.9 visits for the higher-income population.[33] The fear of many that free health care would lead to overuse of the centers thus appears unwarranted.

Several factors may contribute to the somewhat lower use in neighborhood health centers. First, less frequent use is one of the goals of neighborhood health centers—it means that the centers are effective in improving the health of registered patients. When registrants seek preventive attention regularly, illness or disease may be detected at an earlier stage and more easily treated. Thirty percent of all medical encounters in neigh-

32. An encounter is the basic unit of utilization in neighborhood health center reporting systems. The OEO defines an encounter as: "A face-to-face meeting between a patient and a health care provider in which significant health care is given to the *patient*. This meeting may be in the center or a part of the project's outreach program. However, the provider of care in an encounter must be acting independently and not just assisting another provider. For example, if a nurse assists a doctor during a physical examination by taking a history or drawing a blood sample, the nurse *is not* credited with a separate encounter. The nurse is simply participating in an encounter in which a doctor is conducting an examination. On the other hand, if a patient comes in every week for some medication that a nurse administers on a standing order of the doctor (but without the doctor's actually seeing the patient each time), then these visits should be counted as an encounter in which the nurse is the provider. Although this is not always an easy distinction to make, the most senior professional present should usually be shown as the provider." OEO, "Reporting Requirements for OEO Comprehensive Health Services Projects," p. 31.

Thus a single encounter may involve not only contact between a patient and a number of health professionals—physician, nurse, laboratory technician, pharmacist —but also the receipt by the patient of a number of services—physical examination, laboratory tests, immunizations, prescriptions. Repeat visits to have a prescription refilled or to have physical symptoms monitored by a nurse are also counted as encounters. When a patient sees a physician and a dentist on the same visit to the center, this is counted as two encounters, since the physician and the dentist provide health care independently of each other.

33. HEW, National Center for Health Statistics, *Health, United States, 1975,* DHEW (HRA) 76-1232 (NCHS, 1976), p. 289.

borhood health centers are for preventive and long-term maintenance care, as against 25 percent for the whole population.[34] And as the enrollment at a center rises, the average number of medical encounters per registrant decreases. This is because the larger the center, the longer it has probably been in operation and the longer it has had to treat the same patients. As the size of a center increases, the probability that a registrant will use the center in any three-month period drops sharply. In the first six months, new registrants must undergo the required complete health assessment and the treatment of conditions identified by the assessment. Strauss and Sparer have shown that frequency of use declines at least 20 percent six months after registration.[35]

A second explanation is that registrants may continue to rely on outside sources for some portion of their health care. Many complex cases may be treated by specialists, and the poor may turn to hospitals in the evening, when the centers are closed.[36] Other patients may continue to see private physicians to maintain the relationship in case the health center closes or employs health professionals the patient finds unacceptable.

Third, the mobility of the poverty population suggests that the typical registrant does not reside in one community for a full year. Utilization figures may thus reflect less than an entire year's use of the health center.[37] And even when patients do continue to live in the community, registration records may not be kept up to date and may overstate the population base used in calculating rates of use. In support of this possibility, rates for those with at least one encounter at the center were comparable with national rates of users.[38]

Studies of the experience of individual health centers have indicated that their utilization rates are, in fact, comparable to rates for the nonpoor.

34. Roger A. Reynolds, "Improving Access to Health Care Among the Poor—the Neighborhood Health Center Experience," *Milbank Memorial Fund Quarterly: Health and Society,* vol. 54 (Winter 1976), pp. 57, 59.

35. Mark A. Strauss and Gerald Sparer, "Basic Utilization Experience of OEO Comprehensive Health Services Projects," *Inquiry,* vol. 8 (December 1971), pp. 36–49.

36. See, for example, Gordon T. Moore, Roberta Bernstein, and Rosemary A. Bonanno, "Effect of a Neighborhood Health Center on Hospital Emergency Room Use," *Medical Care,* vol. 10 (May–June 1972), pp. 240–47.

37. See Jacob J. Feldman, Eva J. Salber, and Helen Johnson, "The Effect of Residential Mobility on Registration Rates of a Population Served by a Neighborhood Health Center," *HSMHA Health Reports,* vol. 86 (September 1971), pp. 803–09.

38. See Reynolds, "Improving Access to Health Care Among the Poor," p. 58.

Sparer and Anderson, for example, examined the use of services by OEO-covered patients enrolled in four prepaid group-practice plans.[39] They found the rates of the OEO enrollees below national averages, though comparable to those of regular nonpoor members of the prepaid group plans.

Bellin and Geiger examined utilization rates at the Tufts–Columbia Point Health Center in Boston after its third year of operation.[40] They found that the average number of encounters with physicians in 1968 was 4.6 for all Columbia Point residents. For people who used the facility one or more times, average encounters with physicians were 6.1. These rates were comparable with national averages. Bellin and Geiger also found that the health center was the central source of care for five out of six residents; previously residents had relied on hospital emergency rooms and outpatient departments.

Salber and others found that children averaged 3.4 pediatric encounters at the Martha M. Eliot Family Health Center in Boston in 1968. For those children with at least one encounter, the average was 4.8. These rates are roughly comparable with the average of 4.2 visits to physicians for all children in the population and of 3.9 visits for low-income children in 1974.[41]

One fairly well-documented accomplishment of the neighborhood health centers is the reduction of inpatient hospitalization among their patients. Most centers do not provide hospitalization services, so this reduction is not a direct cost saving to the centers and they have no financial interest in it. The reduction therefore undoubtedly results from improved health and better access to primary care.

Alpert found that low-income children treated by a comprehensive, family-focused pediatric health care team had fewer operations, hospitalizations, and visits to physicians for illness, and more visits to physicians for preventive health care, than a control group of similar low-income

39. Gerald Sparer and Arne Anderson, "Utilization and Cost Experience of Low-Income Families in Four Prepaid Group-Practice Plans," *New England Journal of Medicine*, vol. 289 (July 12, 1973), pp. 67–72.

40. Seymour S. Bellin and H. Jack Geiger, "Actual Public Acceptance of the Neighborhood Health Center by the Urban Poor," *Journal of the American Medical Association*, vol. 214 (December 21, 1970), pp. 2147–53.

41. Eva J. Salber and others, "Utilization of Services at a Neighborhood Health Center," *Pediatrics*, vol. 47 (February 1971), pp. 415–23; National Center for Health Statistics, *Health, United States, 1975*, p. 405. Low income is defined here as under $5,000.

children in Boston.[42] Klein and others found that the number of hospital days for children in the Rochester, New York, area served by a comprehensive health center was reduced by 50 percent.[43] An HEW study indicated that hospital days per 1,000 people averaged 742 for persons treated in comprehensive health centers, 34 percent below the national average.[44]

A study of the Mile Square Health Center in Chicago reported similar rates of hospitalization. The annual rate of inpatient days for patients served by that center was reduced from 1,000 days per 1,000 people to about 750 days over three years.[45] Even lower rates of inpatient care were reported for OEO patients treated in a prepaid comprehensive group practice.[46]

Moore and others investigated the effect of a Charlestown, Massachusetts, neighborhood health center on the use of the emergency room at Massachusetts General Hospital.[47] Although they found that the existence of the center had not changed the number of emergency room visits (which may have been an improvement over what would have occurred without the center since rates of emergency room use increased in other poverty neighborhoods), patients registered at the center tended to use the emergency room in different ways after the center opened—they were more likely to be referred to the emergency room by a primary physician and to use it in the evening when the center was closed.

Despite such success in reaching the poor and improving their patterns of medical care use, neighborhood health centers have been criticized for promoting two-class health care because they treat mainly the poor. Although this is true, the centers' patients are primarily those with low incomes because of both the centers' location and congressional restrictions

42. Joel J. Alpert and others, "Effective Use of Comprehensive Pediatric Care: Utilization of Health Resources," *American Journal of Diseases of Children,* vol. 116 (November 1968), pp. 529–33.

43. Michael Klein and others, "The Impact of the Rochester Neighborhood Health Center on Hospitalization of Children, 1968 to 1970," *Pediatrics,* vol. 51 (May 1973), pp. 833–39.

44. HEW, Bureau of Community Health Services, "Community Health Centers: Program Status and Management Plan" (BCHS, October 1975; processed), p. 19.

45. Reported in Zwick, "Some Accomplishments and Findings of Neighborhood Health Centers," p. 403.

46. Theodore J. Colombo, Ernest W. Saward, and Merwyn R. Greenlick, "The Integration of an OEO Health Program into a Prepaid Comprehensive Group Practice Plan," *American Journal of Public Health,* vol. 59 (April 1969), pp. 641–50.

47. Moore and others, "Effect of a Neighborhood Health Center on Hospital Emergency Room Use."

on their use by nonpoor patients, not because they choose to exclude non-poor community residents. Far from promoting different standards of care for the poor, the centers promote standards more like those of care for the nonpoor.

The few studies that have been made of the quality of care delivered by the centers indicate that they often score higher than traditional sources of care do—particularly other sources of care for low-income people.[48] Morehead conducted a study of three types of care offered by neighbor-hood health centers—adult health assessments, pediatric care of infants, and obstetrical care—for which there are generally accepted procedural standards.[49] The study audited a sample of the medical records of people registered at thirty-five centers. It was limited to patients who had made at least three visits to the center in a period of at least four months. The auditors scored each of the three types of care—adult, child, and preg-nancy—according to a list of standard procedures.

By comparing the scores generated by these audits with scores for hos-pital clinics affiliated with medical schools, private group practices, chil-dren and youth projects, and health department clinics, Morehead con-cluded that the quality of care at neighborhood health centers was equal to or better than that offered by these other sources of care. For adult assessments, the centers had higher average scores in all components au-dited than either the clinics affiliated with medical schools or group prac-tices. Health center performance was notable for the completeness of routine laboratory studies and chest X-rays. All three types of providers had similar scores for obstetrical programs, although the health centers had a smaller proportion of women who had registered during the first trimester of pregnancy, for family planning counseling, and for post-partum visits. The scores for pediatric care were also generally compar-

48. There is little agreement among health professionals over what constitutes an adequate indication of the quality of health care. Ideally, the quality of a service would be directly indicated by whether it produced a desired health outcome. Quality assessment studies in general, however, have examined services rendered per patient encounter and compared actual services to some predetermined activity criteria, on the assumption that following these criteria is likely to produce the best results.

49. Mildred A. Morehead, Rose S. Donaldson, and Mary R. Seravalli, "Compari-sons between OEO Neighborhood Health Centers and Other Health Care Providers of Ratings of the Quality of Health Care," *American Journal of Public Health,* vol. 61 (July 1971), pp. 1294–1306. See also Morehead, "Evaluating Quality of Medical Care in the Neighborhood Health Center Program of the Office of Economic Oppor-tunity," *Medical Care,* vol. 8 (March–April 1970), pp. 118–31.

able with those of other providers except the children and youth projects; these scored 60 percent higher than the centers. Neighborhood centers showed some deficiency in the completeness of appropriate immunizations when compared with group practices, health department well-baby clinics, and children and youth projects.[50]

Another approach to gauging the quality of medical care at neighborhood health centers was used by Sparer and Johnson.[51] They listed the components of an ideal center, among which were availability of major medical specialists to health center patients, formal relations with backup hospitals, emphasis on physician-patient continuity, and innovative, productive use of community residents to complement the range of services handled by other employees. They found that most health centers funded by the OEO scored high on each of these criteria.

Ultimately the efficacy of the comprehensive care approach is judged by its ability to improve health. But many difficulties are encountered in trying to make such an assessment—the lack of routine reporting of health outcomes even for such readily measurable ones as infant mortality, as well as the lack of any suitable way of measuring other health outcomes, the long-term nature of certain types of improvements in health, and interaction among different types of health outcomes and between health and medical care. Sample sizes inadequate for detecting changes in the incidence of some types of health problems among the people served by the centers constitute a particularly troublesome obstacle. Dealing with small samples often makes it impossible to isolate the causes of reduced mortality rates, especially where information on pre-center health care patterns is unavailable.

The studies that do exist, however, suggest that the neighborhood health centers have had a positive effect on the health of the patients they serve. Anderson and Morgan found that infant mortality rates had been lowered in communities served by several southern centers.[52] For instance, the infant mortality rate in Lowndes County, Alabama, had been reduced from 46.9 deaths per 1,000 live births in 1967 to 28.3 in 1971, a period during

50. Although the health centers scored well in this type of review, the study rated the quality of only a small part of the services offered. Morehead also cautioned that, as there was wide variation in any one group of providers, any one score might depend more on an individual provider's commitment and performance than on organizational techniques.

51. Gerald Sparer and Joyce Johnson, "Evaluation of OEO Neighborhood Health Centers," *American Journal of Public Health,* vol. 61 (May 1971), pp. 931–42.

52. Anderson and Morgan, *Comprehensive Health Care.*

which a neighborhood health center served the county. Over the same period infant mortality rates in neighboring counties hardly changed. Similarly, in Bolivar County, Mississippi, the infant mortality rate dropped from 48.5 per 1,000 to 31.0 in the four years after the introduction of a neighborhood health center. For blacks, which nearly all the patients served at the Bolivar center were, the rate for infants fell from 57.2 to 35.7 while the rate for the whites in the county rose slightly, from 13.5 to 13.7.

Other types of health improvement have also been documented. A carefully controlled study of the incidence of first attacks of rheumatic fever requiring hospitalization in Baltimore found a 60 percent reduction over a ten-year period in census tracts with centers but an unchanged rate in the rest of the city.[53] The study concluded that the prompt identification and treatment of streptococcal infections emphasized by the centers had reduced first attacks of rheumatic fever needing hospitalization.

Kent and Smith found that using community residents in outreach activities substantially increased the early registration of pregnant women.[54] Women seen in their first or second trimester of pregnancy rose from 32 to 50 percent.

More conclusive evidence on the full range of health effects of neighborhood health centers will have to await future studies. The neighborhood health center program, however, has already been the subject of more evaluations than most other health programs. These evaluations suggest that the program has been successful in achieving its goals of improving the access of the poor to quality health care and indicate that some health improvements resulted from this improved access.

The Distribution of Neighborhood Health Center Benefits

The requirements for federal assistance to a neighborhood health center under OEO include a large number of poor people in the area and the lack of readily available alternative sources of services for ambulatory patients. Federal support was designed to be a "last dollar" source of funding, reserved for communities which could prove that without such support many would be deprived of adequate medical care.

53. Leon Gordis, "Effectiveness of Comprehensive-Care Programs in Preventing Rheumatic Fever," *New England Journal of Medicine,* vol. 289 (August 16, 1973), pp. 331–35.
54. James A. Kent and C. Harvey Smith, "Involving the Urban Poor in Health Services through Accommodation—The Employment of Neighborhood Representatives," *American Journal of Public Health,* vol. 57 (June 1967), pp. 997–1003.

There have always been many more communities able to meet these criteria than could be financially supported. To carry out the demonstration purposes of the program, funds were distributed to as wide a variety of geographical areas as possible. But although 40 percent of the poor lived in nonmetropolitan areas, three-quarters of neighborhood health centers were located in urban areas. All regions were represented among the centers funded, although the South, with 45 percent of the poor, received only 30 percent of the funds.

Most of the communities in which centers are located are dominated by one ethnic group, usually black, although a special effort was made to include minorities other than blacks. A center in King City, California, serves a population about evenly divided between low-income permanent residents and migratory farm workers.[55] In Red Lake, Minnesota, a center was established to supplement an attempt by a Public Health Service hospital to provide comprehensive coverage for the Chippewa Indian reservation.[56] Centers in communities with strong racial or ethnic characteristics are nevertheless meant to serve all community residents.

Because of the desire to test the validity of the neighborhood health center approach in a wide range of settings, centers have not always been placed in areas with comparable standards of need. Among the rural centers, for instance, county poverty rates range from 8 percent for the Wilkes-Barre center in Pennsylvania to 67 percent for the Medgar Evers center in Mississippi.[57] The center in Denver covers nearly all the poor, but centers in large urban areas, such as New York, can reach only a small fraction of them.

Care at neighborhood health centers is not restricted to people below the poverty level; patients who are better off, however, must pay, though the charge is often reduced for near-poor patients. A 1971 household interview survey of twenty-one OEO center target areas showed that the users of the centers in these areas were generally those who most needed a local health center. Relative to the eligible population, users had lower incomes and were members of larger families than nonusers; they were younger and more of them were black. There were no significant differences in education or length of residence in the community, but they were

55. "King City: Care in a Rural Setting," *Journal of the American Medical Association,* vol. 211 (March 23, 1970), p. 1951.
56. OEO, *The Tide of Progress,* Third Annual Report (OEO, 1968), pp. 47–48.
57. Reynolds, "Improving Access to Health Care Among the Poor," p. 53.

Table 6-2. Services per Person per Year Delivered by Neighborhood Health Centers, by Selected Characteristics of the Centers, Year Ending September 1973

Characteristic	Medical care	X-rays	Laboratory tests	Prescriptions	Dental care
All centers	2.6	0.30	1.8	2.5	0.59
Location					
Urban	2.6	0.32	1.9	2.5	0.59
Rural	2.4	0.24	1.5	2.2	0.57
Ratio, urban to rural	1.09	1.32	1.28	1.14	1.03
Region					
Northeast	3.1	0.25	1.7	1.8	0.68
North Central	2.3	0.28	1.9	2.4	0.44
South	2.8	0.32	2.0	3.3	0.70
West	2.2	0.36	1.7	2.4	0.51
Ratio, West to South	0.80	1.11	0.84	0.72	0.72
Predominant ethnic group served[a]					
White	3.2	0.26	1.5	1.9	0.63
Black and other	2.7	0.30	1.9	2.8	0.64
Ratio, white to black and other	1.19	0.87	0.79	0.68	0.98

Sources: Based on four quarters beginning October 1972; data from Office of Economic Opportunity, "Comprehensive Health Services Projects: Summary Report, Fourth Quarter 1972" (June 1973; processed); and Department of Health, Education, and Welfare, Bureau of Community Health Services, "Comprehensive Health Services Projects: Data Base Report, Third Quarter 1973," report 4 (March 1974; processed); and reports 1, 2, 3. Figures are rounded.

a. Represents the ethnic group of the majority of registrants. Some centers where no group predominated are not included in this categorization. Centers with predominantly Hispanic registrants are included with black and other.

more likely to have been confined to bed by an illness in the twelve months before the survey.[58]

Despite extreme variation in the social, economic, and demographic characteristics of the areas where the centers were located—from dense urban ghettos in New York and Chicago to rural towns such as Fayette, Mississippi, and Red Lake, Minnesota—service delivery patterns across regional, urban-rural, and ethnic lines were remarkably consistent (see table 6-2). The regional differences in services per registrant, however,

58. Joann H. Langston and others, *Study to Evaluate the OEO Neighborhood Health Center Program at Selected Centers,* Final Report for Office of Economic Opportunity (Rockville, Md.: Geomet, Inc., 1972; available from National Technical Information Service, PB-217 955).

Table 6-3. Annual Use of Medical Care per Person Served by Neighborhood Health Centers, by Selected Characteristics, Year Ending September 1973, and Related Data for the United States, 1969

Characteristic	Medical encounters per neighborhood health center registrant during year		Annual number of visits to physicians per person, United States[a]	Percent of visits for diagnosis and treatment		Number of visits to physicians per person with at least one visit	
	With physicians	Total		Health centers	United States	Per quarter, health centers	Per quarter, United States
Average	1.8	2.6	4.3	70.0	75.0	2.3	1.6
Place of residence							
Urban	1.9	2.6	4.4	71.7	74.8	2.3	1.6
Rural	1.5	2.4	3.9	57.7	75.4	2.3	1.3
Ratio, urban to rural	1.27	1.09	1.13	1.24	0.99	0.98	1.23
Region							
Northeast	2.2	3.1	4.4	71.0	77.1	2.5	1.6
North Central	1.7	2.3	4.0	63.2	74.2	2.3	1.5
South	1.8	2.8	4.1	75.8	74.3	2.3	1.5
West	1.7	2.2	4.6	67.0	74.2	2.2	1.6
Ratio, West to South	0.94	0.81	1.12	0.88	1.00	0.97	1.07
Predominant ethnic group served[b]							
White	2.2	3.2	4.4	75.9	74.6	2.9	1.6
Black and other	1.9	2.7	3.5	68.8	78.5	2.2	1.4
Ratio, white to black and other	1.16	1.19	1.26	1.10	0.95	1.31	1.14

Sources: Same as table 6-2, and HEW, National Center for Health Statistics, *Physician Visits: Volume and Interval Since Last Visit, United States—1969*, Vital and Health Statistics, series 10, no. 75, DHEW (HSM) 72-1064 (GPO, 1972). Figures are rounded.
a. Includes those who did not see a physician during the year.
b. See table 6-2, note a.

were surprising; services in the South, where they were traditionally the lowest, exceeded national levels for most activities.[59]

Blacks and rural registrants continued to use the medical services at centers somewhat less than whites and urban residents (table 6-3). And

59. This, however, may be because the poor in the South tend to derive all their ambulatory care from health centers, while the poor in other regions supplement health center services with care from other providers.

there is only a small difference between registrants at urban centers and those at rural centers in the likelihood that they will use a center. Furthermore, though people living in urban areas averaged only 13 percent more visits to physicians than rural residents nationally, the difference was 27 percent at health centers. When care by other medical providers, such as nurse practitioners, was taken into account, the difference was only 9 percent.

Use of paramedical personnel also contributed to the relatively high rates of services per person in southern centers, increasing the annual number of medical encounters per person from 1.8 to 2.8. This is a major contribution to health care delivery. Health centers have demonstrated that the provision of medical care can be markedly improved where there are few physicians if they are supplemented with professional assistants. Subsequent studies have praised the ability of these practitioners to furnish high-quality care, to reach and to be accepted by patients.[60] The centers, with their emphasis on innovation and their flexibility in attempting to meet specific health needs, must be credited for much of the acceptance and increased use of paramedics in the health care system.

Costs

Despite the manifest ability of the centers to reach and serve people in disadvantaged areas, the program has received few rave reviews—instead, an image of costliness and inefficiency has plagued it. Numerous media accounts have unfavorably compared the costs of services at the centers with the costs of care from private physicians.[61]

This image is largely undeserved. A careful examination of the available data indicates that medical care is no more expensive when rendered in a neighborhood health center than elsewhere. Furthermore, the total costs of health care may be substantially lower than in traditional settings

60. For studies on new health practitioners, see Eva D. Cohen and others, "An Evaluation of Policy Related Research on New and Expanded Roles of Health Workers," and "An Evaluation . . . Annotated Bibliography" (both Yale University School of Medicine, Office of Regional Activities and Continuing Education, 1974; processed); and Gary L. Appel and Aaron Lowin, *Physician Extenders: An Evaluation of Policy-Related Research: Final Report—January 1975* (InterStudy, n.d.).

61. See, for example, Richard D. Lyons, "Dilemma in Health Care: Rising Cost and Demand," *New York Times,* September 13, 1971.

when the savings from reduced hospitalization and improvements in health are included.

Centers appear expensive at first glance; most are big businesses with big budgets. While the average physician carries a load of about 1,000 patients, the centers have an average registration of 13,000 patients. On average, health centers employ 8.4 full-time-equivalent physicians, 2.8 dentists, 2.7 physician's assistants, and another 38 health professionals including nurses, pharmacists, laboratory and X-ray technicians, dental hygienists, and mental health workers.[62] To provide its wide range of services, the average health center spends about $2.3 million annually. Some large urban centers have budgets as high as $10 million to $12 million; even rural centers often spend as much as $1 million a year.

The centers serve more patients, employ more health professionals, and manage substantially larger budgets than many traditional settings for the care of ambulatory patients do, but their costs per patient served are quite comparable. In 1974 the annual total expenditure per person served by the centers was $238; this dropped to $204 in 1975.[63] HEW estimates that the national per capita cost for the services most comparable to those delivered in community health centers was $214 in 1974 and approximately $240 in 1975.[64] Neighborhood health centers have become both lower-cost providers of outpatient health services and among the few to hold down costs.

These cost comparisons do not include the savings on hospitalization achieved by the centers. By reducing the number of hospital days of the patients they serve by 30 percent, the centers have reduced hospitalization costs per registrant; these costs are $65 less than the average per person in the population as a whole.[65]

Most of the costly image of the centers comes from comparing the average cost per encounter in neighborhood health centers with the standard charge by private physicians for routine office visits. Such comparison overstates the cost of a visit to a health center because each

62. HEW, Bureau of Community Health Services, "Neighborhood Health Centers: Summary of Project Data, First Quarter 1975," report 10 (BCHS, November 1975; processed).

63. HEW, Health Services Administration, internal document.

64. The 1975 figure was calculated by using an estimated inflation rate of 12.5 percent for 1975, based on Marjorie Smith Mueller and Robert M. Gibson, "National Health Expenditures, Fiscal Year 1975," Social Security Bulletin, vol. 39 (February 1976), pp. 12–14.

65. Estimated on the basis of a 30 percent reduction in average per capita hospital costs of $215 in 1975, from ibid., p. 12.

center provides other services besides medical care. And it understates the cost of a visit to a private physician, the average charge for which is customarily higher than the standard fee for the routine office visit, since physicians add charges for laboratory and other services.

Less than half of the health centers' costs go for traditional medical care, laboratory, X-ray, and pharmacy services. Twelve percent is spent on dental care; 10 percent on mental health, home health, and other health services; and 16 percent on supporting services such as environmental health services, social and community services, transportation, training, community organization, and research and evaluation. A limited number of centers also provide hospital services for patients. Administrative costs account for another 17 percent, with the remaining expenditures covering housekeeping, maintenance, security, medical records, and unallocated fringe benefits and supplies.[66]

Average expenditures for medical, X-ray, laboratory, and pharmacy services are $108 per registrant, much less than the $150 spent by the average American for these services in 1975. Dental costs per encounter average about $28, again below the national average of $35 per person.[67]

The average total cost of all services provided by neighborhood health centers is $42 per encounter. While this is higher than in the traditional medical sector, the medical costs alone are competitive. In fiscal year 1975 they were $80 per person registered at health centers (average per capita expenditures on physicians' services for the entire population were $102). Medical costs per person seen by the medical staff were $27 per encounter, of which $17 represented the direct cost of providing services.

The nonmedical services are crucial to the effectiveness of the health centers in meeting their multiple goals, one of which is to foster the use of the centers. The range of services has a distinct effect on this; a higher percentage of registrants use the centers, and these users receive more services, when the centers provide full ambulatory services and home health care than when some services are eliminated. The greatest complementarity occurs for supporting health activities, including transportation and outreach activities. When centers are ranked in quartile groups by expenditure for supporting health services per registrant, both the rate of use

66. HEW, Bureau of Community Health Services, "Neighborhood Health Centers: Summary of Project Data," reports 9, 10.

67. Costs at centers are estimated from ibid. National dental costs are from Mueller and Gibson, "National Health Expenditures, Fiscal Year 1975," p. 12. Inactive registrants and U.S. residents who do not use medical services will distort both costs. Such comparisons must be made cautiously as these figures understate the cost of services per user.

per registrant and the amount of medical care received by each user decline substantially between the highest and lowest quartiles. In centers with the highest expenditures for transportation, outreach, and other supporting activities, 42 percent of the registrants received care during a three-month period, whereas only 25 percent received care in the centers that spent the least on these services.[68]

As comprehensive services attract residents to the centers, the higher registration and utilization rates help the centers and the average cost of care declines. For centers with fewer than 5,000 registrants, the average cost per medical encounter was $29 from October 1972 to September 1973, while the average cost in centers with more than 20,000 registrants was $22.[69]

The costs of neighborhood health centers are comparable to the costs of other large providers of care to ambulatory patients, such as hospital outpatient departments and clinics or large prepaid group practices. Sparer and Anderson, for example, conducted a careful two-year comparison of six centers of different sizes. They found that costs per medical encounter ranged from $16 in a rural center to $28 in a large New York City center, and averaged $23 in all six centers. This was approximately the same as the $22 average medical encounter cost of two large prepaid group practices—Kaiser-Portland in Oregon, and Group Health Association in Washington, D.C.[70]

Financial Performance of the Centers

The neighborhood health centers have demonstrated that they can provide quality care efficiently, but they require substantial federal subsidies to continue operation. Revenues have fallen far short of costs, only about 22 percent of which are recouped through fees charged patients and third-party reimbursement. Another 11 percent comes from state and local government subsidies and private voluntary contributions. The remaining 67 percent is provided by federal grant funds.[71]

68. Derived from sources given for table 6-2.
69. Reynolds, "Improving Access to Health Care Among the Poor," p. 69.
70. Gerald Sparer and Arne Anderson, "Cost of Services at Neighborhood Health Centers," *New England Journal of Medicine,* vol. 286 (June 8, 1972), pp. 1241–45.
71. HEW, Health Services Administration, "Budget Data for Community Health Centers, FY 1975–1977" (August 7, 1975; processed).

The failure of the centers to derive substantial revenue from patients or private insurance plans is not surprising; the goal of the program was to serve needy people who would otherwise be unable to afford or obtain comprehensive health care. But the small share of revenue derived from Medicare and Medicaid threatens the financial survival of the centers.

Several factors account for the failure of Medicare and Medicaid to channel funds to the centers. First, the economic circumstances of the neighborhoods served by the centers are more varied than anticipated. It was originally expected that nearly all residents of the various communities would fall below the poverty level and be covered by Medicaid. Instead, a large fraction have incomes slightly above the poverty level— incomes too high to permit coverage under Medicaid but too low for them to contribute to the cost of care. Furthermore, a sizable proportion of the poverty population as well as most of the near-poverty population are not eligible for Medicaid.[72]

Even when patients are covered by Medicaid, the centers are frequently unable to obtain adequate compensation for their services. The Lee County Cooperative Clinic, for example, receives 9 percent of its budget from Medicaid, even though 22 percent of its patients are covered by the program. Medicaid pays $4 to $6 a visit for medical care that costs the center an average of $20.

Several program characteristics account for this low level of reimbursement. First, Medicaid does not cover the centers' wide range of services— expenditures for transportation, outreach, nutrition, and environmental activities are not reimbursable.

Second, many states will not cover clinic services. This means that many neighborhood health centers are not eligible providers of services and can only receive reimbursement from Medicaid through direct billing by eligible physicians employed by the centers who provide specified services covered by Medicaid. This limits both the services that can be reimbursed by Medicaid and the level of reimbursement per visit. Most states also refuse to pay for services provided by health professionals other than physicians, such as nurse practitioners or physician's assistants. Since the centers depend on such personnel to complement the work of physicians, this restriction works a further hardship on the centers.[73] The 1977

72. See chapter 3 for detailed estimates of the number of low-income people not eligible for Medicaid.
73. Medicare now also covers these services and sets reimbursement rates that are adhered to by the Medicaid program as well.

Table 6-4. Productivity and Efficiency of Community Health Centers, by Selected Indicators, First Quarter, 1975

Indicator[a]	Standard	Median, all centers	Percentage distribution of project compliance		
			In compliance	Near compliance	Out of compliance
Direct ambulatory costs as percent of total ambulatory costs	No less than 60 percent	59 percent	47	43	10
General services and allocable costs as percent of total ambulatory costs	No more than 25 percent	30 percent	24	29	47
Ratio of active registrants to primary practitioners	No less than 1,500:1	2,036:1	62	12	26
Ratio of active registrants to dentists	No less than 2,000:1	4,653:1	80	2	18
Ratio of active registrants to nurses	No less than 1,200:1	1,535:1	54	11	35
Number of encounters per primary practitioner per hour	No less than 2.7	2.4	36	24	40
Number of total surfaces filled per restorative dentist hour	No less than 2.5	2.5	46	12	42

Source: HEW, Health Services Administration, "Budget Data for Community Health Centers, FY 1975–1977" (August 7, 1975; processed), table D.
a. Full-time-equivalent data are used for primary practitioners, dentists, and nurses in the indicators.

amendments to the Social Security Act now require all states to reimburse rural clinics for these services under Medicaid.

Beyond these specific program characteristics, the insurance reimbursement form itself is an inappropriate financing mechanism for the centers. Medicaid and other types of third-party reimbursement plans are oriented toward payment for specific services—individual laboratory tests, minor surgical procedures, and the like. The reporting systems of the centers, on the other hand, are geared to patient encounters rather than to the specific services provided during the encounters. A single encounter may entail many services—blood test, urinalysis, immunization, physical examination, visual and hearing tests, and prescriptions. The failure of the centers to establish accounting and billing procedures to charge third-party plans for these individual services and the inability of the centers to arrange for separate methods of reimbursement suitable to their unique circumstances have seriously undercut their financial independence from direct public subsidies and grants. Financial stability and self-sufficiency will require extensive reforms in financing and methods of reimbursement under public and private insurance plans.

Increased emphasis has been placed on improved management and productivity of medical care services—services traditionally produced in physicians' offices and private medical clinics. This runs counter to the original concept of comprehensive health centers that were also community centers for employment, training, and social services. With the new emphasis on efficiency (dollar cost per service), training funds to upgrade personnel and hire local residents have had to be discontinued.

Part of the emphasis on efficiency is the result of economic pressure on the federal budget in recent years. If better management induces the centers to become more nearly self-sufficient, it will reduce the direct costs of health care borne by the government. Often justification for the emphasis is also based on the argument that the older centers should now be able to produce services at lower cost than in their experimental and learning stage.

Rigid productivity standards, however, often hamper effective delivery of health care and place one more obstacle in the path to self-sufficiency. Table 6-4 shows several productivity and efficiency indicators selected for monitoring health center performance. These include keeping overhead and indirect costs down, keeping medical, dental, and nursing staffing patterns low relative to population served, and ensuring that primary medical and dental personnel see a specified number of patients or render a minimum level of services in a given time period. Standards have been established for each indicator, and they are the same for all centers.

The standards focus almost exclusively on traditional medical and dental services. They do not take into account the effectiveness of nonmedical activities or the complementarity between nonmedical activities and more traditional health services.

The standards for services per practitioner per time period are based on levels prevalent in traditional medical practices. They take into account neither the extent and complexity of the health problems of the poor nor the need for patient education and counseling.

Even more surprising, the standards are not adjusted for the location of centers although rural centers face problems quite different from those of urban centers. Lower population density, transportation barriers, and the limited availability of alternative sources of care in rural areas, for example, may make it important for rural centers to maintain higher levels of staffing per person registered at the center than are maintained in urban centers. Traditional rural problems of recruitment and retention of staff may also affect productivity as turnover of staff affects the ability of remaining staff members to work effectively as a team.

The size of a center and the number of patients it serves are also important constraints on meeting productivity standards. Centers with more than 5,000 registrants provide more patient encounters per full-time medical staff member than do those with fewer registrants, reflecting, in part, the difficulty of obtaining part-time personnel to help provide a full complement of services. Thus a small center may require an obstetrician-gynecologist, for example, and have to hire one full time though half time would be appropriate. Limited space (for instance, few examining rooms) may also interfere with optimal use of personnel in smaller centers. A larger center is likely to schedule its available space more consistently than a smaller center. Furthermore, new centers that have been in operation for a short time typically have fewer patients and thus more staff per patient served.

As program indicators are not adjusted for these important considerations, it is not surprising that a large number of centers are not in compliance with the established standards. Table 6-4 classifies all centers as in compliance, near compliance, or out of compliance with each program indicator for the first quarter of 1975. Twenty-six percent are out of compliance with recommended primary practitioner staffing standards; 35 percent are out of compliance with recommended nursing staffing. Two out of every five centers are out of compliance in the number of hourly encounters for primary practitioners and the number of fillings completed per hour of dentists' time. More centers, however, were in compliance in the last quarter of 1975 than in the last quarter of 1974 as they became aware of the pressure to comply.

Whether greater emphasis on narrow productivity and efficiency standards will ultimately prove beneficial or harmful remains to be seen. Costs may be reduced and centers may become somewhat more economically self-sufficient. Centers that have been unresponsive to local needs may be forced to provide more services.

But focus on medical and dental activities is more likely to undercut the long-term success of the projects in improving patients' health through nonmedical activities. Inadequate education and counseling may cause patients to return with complaints that should have been alleviated if they had followed instructions given them on the first visit. Inadequate outreach activities, especially in rural areas, may result in less emphasis on prevention and community health activities and lead to higher rates of disease and hospitalization.

Since the centers have demonstrated their ability to provide high-quality health care at a cost that is competitive with other types of providers—at a substantially lower cost when the benefits of reduced hospitalization and improved health are considered—insistence on improved management and a different style of activity appears unwarranted. Much of the progress and achievement of the centers may, in fact, be reversed by this change in direction.

Recruitment and Retention of Health Professionals

At first, planners hoped the innovative and challenging programs of the neighborhood health centers would attract physicians from the growing supply of medical school graduates to low-income neighborhoods. The centers used several strategies to enhance their potential attractiveness; some became affiliated with medical schools and residency programs; many offered salaries competitive with other institutions and included continuing education and vacation time as fringe benefits.

These efforts have not met with success. A major affliction of many centers has been the high rate of turnover of physicians; fewer than half of those employed at the centers have remained for more than two years.[74] Administrators have had to engage in vigorous, continuing recruitment efforts to keep staffing at desired levels, taking them away from other urgent administrative duties. Turnover of medical personnel has also been a source of dissatisfaction and uncertainty for patients; they like to develop stable relationships with their health service providers.

Several factors have contributed to this high turnover. Many young physicians feel a public service commitment to spend one or two years in a low-income community before they establish private practices or enter residency programs. In the health centers, which serve as places of training for medical schools, turnover of staff occurs naturally as students move through the centers and faculty members with responsibility for service and training change.

Conflicts with administrators and community boards have also undoubtedly contributed to some of the turnover. Disagreements with decisions made have fostered considerable discontent in some centers.

In recent years, uncertain funding has reduced the attractiveness of the centers as alternatives to private practice. With only a one-year budget commitment, many physicians are reluctant to spend the time and effort required to work in a health center.

Tilson systematically studied the characteristics of individual physicians and centers that were related to high rates of turnover in a sample of forty-four centers.[75] Some findings of his study are reported in table 6-5. The physicians likely to remain at the centers for more than two years tend to be black, older, board-certified, and on the faculty of a medical school. Turnover rates have been high for young physicians, to whom it was expected that working at centers would prove more attractive.

A high level of participation by the community in policymaking, however, does not appear to have prompted physicians to leave more readily. On the contrary, centers in which the community is actively involved have been the most successful in retaining physicians—54 percent of those at centers that the OEO rated high in community participation remained for more than two years, but only 42 percent remained that long at the centers that received low ratings.

Two other organizational characteristics of the centers—the use of paramedical personnel and of a team of health professionals to deliver

74. Hugh H. Tilson, "Stability of Physician Employment in Neighborhood Health Centers," *Medical Care,* vol. 11 (September–October 1973), pp. 384–400.
75. Ibid.

Table 6-5. Probability That Physicians Will Remain in Neighborhood Health Centers for Two Years, by Characteristics of Physicians and Centers

Characteristics of physicians	Probability	Characteristics of center	Probability
Age		*Community participation*	
30 and under	0.30	High	0.54
30–40	0.37	Medium	0.52
40–50	0.57	Low	0.42
50–70	0.67		
		Quality of care	
Board-certified		High	0.51
Yes	0.52	Medium	0.46
No	0.44	Low	0.58
Faculty appointment at a		*Institutional grantee*	
medical school		University	0.51
Yes	0.54	Hospital	0.49
No	0.45	Health department	0.38
		Community corporation	0.55
Race			
Black	0.59	*Use of health teams*	
Nonblack	0.42	Team care high	0.56
		Personal physicians' care high	0.44
Type of medicine practiced			
General	0.42	*Percentage of physicians*	
Internal	0.39	*working full time*	
Pediatrics	0.50	Under 25	0.59
Obstetrics	0.64	25–50	0.56
		50–75	0.34
Monthly salary (dollars)[a]		Over 75	0.43
1,500–1,750	0.26		
1,750–2,000	0.44	*Use of paramedics*	
2,000–2,250	0.52	Very high	0.52
2,250–2,500	0.72	High	0.59
2,500 and over	0.54	Not high	0.40
		Low	0.40

Source: Hugh H. Tilson, "Stability of Physician Employment in Neighborhood Health Centers," *Medical Care*, vol. 11 (September–October 1973), pp. 391, 393–95.
a. Based on 1966–70 salary levels.

care—also correlated with higher retention over a two-year period. Salary levels appeared to influence stability too. The quality of care offered, however, showed no clear relation to the likelihood of a physician's remaining at a center.

These findings suggest that a concern for strong community interaction, intellectual interest in the experimental mode of health care delivery, and salaries commensurate with salaried positions elsewhere are the principal factors that persuade a physician to serve at a center for a prolonged period. If this is the case, the ability of the health center program to expand may depend on the attitudes of medical school graduates and practicing physicians toward public service.

The centers so far have not driven out private practitioners. Hurwitz investigated the place of prior practice for physicians attracted to health centers and compared trends in numbers of physicians in nine urban neighborhoods in which health centers were located with trends in other neighborhoods in the same cities with the same socioeconomic characteristics.[76] He determined that the establishment of health centers had not accelerated the decline of physicians practicing in those areas. The centers had succeeded in their goal of creating a net addition to existing resources. However, over 50 percent of the physicians working at health centers who had previously been in practice had been practicing in other low-income neighborhoods. To some extent, therefore, the centers have redistributed the supply of physicians serving the poor, although they have also increased the ranks of physicians voluntarily serving in poverty-stricken areas.

Since the centers find it difficult to fill their needs for physicians, more use might be made of paramedical personnel. In the South and in rural areas, nurse practitioners at neighborhood health centers have significantly improved the access of the poor to medical care. The centers' wide use of local residents in nonprofessional positions and their relation with medical, nursing, and allied health schools further suggest that they might encourage members of the community to take professional training, either as physicians or as paramedics.

Summary and Recommendations

In spite of adverse publicity, a close examination of the neighborhood health center program shows it to be a surprisingly successful governmental health program. While a few centers have faltered in the face of opposition and internal conflict, the large majority have survived, flourished, and attained considerable success as providers of high quality health care.

76. Elliott Hurwitz, "An Analysis of the Effect of OEO Neighborhood Health Centers on the Distribution of Physicians" (Ph.D. dissertation, Temple University, 1974).

Many centers have taken the challenge of the multiple objectives of the neighborhood health center program seriously and been remarkably adept at achieving several objectives simultaneously while holding down total costs. The accumulated evidence indicates that health centers have been able to:

—improve access to health care of the poor living in impoverished neighborhoods, particularly those often excluded from the traditional medical sector;
—demonstrate that high quality health care can be provided in low-income communities; and
—improve the health of the poor by taking a comprehensive approach to health care that focuses on both the medical and the nonmedical causes of poor health.

Scattered evidence and histories of projects such as the Lee County Cooperative Clinic suggest that the centers have at the same time been able to:

—act as a center for community economic development and investment in human resources;
—develop leaders to represent the poor and disadvantaged; and
—contribute to the social, economic, and political advancement of minorities.

These goals have been attained at a cost comparable with that of providing health care in traditional ambulatory settings. Estimates for 1975 indicated that neighborhood health centers provided a wide range of services at a cost of $204 per person served. The cost in traditional settings for services most comparable to those delivered in community health centers was approximately $240 in 1975. In addition, hospitalization costs of persons served by the centers have been about $65 lower per person than for patients treated in traditional ways.

Despite its demonstrated success, the neighborhood health center program has received little public acclaim and inadequate funding. Instead of the 1,000 health centers serving 25 million low-income people at a cost of $3.35 billion originally planned, in fiscal 1976 the program supported only about 125 centers serving 1.5 million people at a federal budgetary cost of $197 million.

Its demonstrated contribution to health care delivery deserves a much more supportive policy. To furnish this support, current policy should be reformed in the following ways.

—Increase the funding level of the program to permit the creation of new centers in areas with especially serious health and poverty problems and to permit existing centers to continue to provide the same level of services.

—Establish a separate Medicaid reimbursement policy for all centers with federal grant support based on a capitation amount equivalent to what is paid in the traditional sector for the range of services provided by health centers. (Consideration might also be given to bonus payments for documented reductions in hospital services as a result of comprehensive outpatient care.) All states should be required to cover clinic services and to develop this separate method of reimbursement.

—Restore the original emphasis of health centers on economic development and investment in human resources. This should include training funds to upgrade the job skills of community residents employed by centers.

—Develop more flexible measures of performance and effectiveness than the medical productivity standards currently used. Centers should also be encouraged to report quantitative and qualitative information indicating the extent to which they are achieving the goals outlined above.

—Centralize final funding decisions to protect centers from local political pressure.

—Encourage centers to develop local residents as physicians, dentists, and other health professionals and provide financial support for community residents to attend medical or nursing school or take other professional training.

—Pursue national policies that will increase the number of physicians interested in serving in neighborhood health centers. Black and female physicians, particularly, have found health centers attractive places to practice. Health centers should be assisted in the recruitment of qualified health professionals committed to long-term service.

—Authorize long-term funds for health centers to permit rational planning and recruitment of qualified personnel.

chapter seven **Health Care for the Poor:**
Summary and Recommendations

The programs of the War on Poverty and the Great Society promised great changes in American society. Poverty was to be eliminated, and all Americans were to have an equal opportunity in the race for economic well-being. Basic to such promises of equal opportunity was an expansion of health programs for the aged and the disadvantaged. Through equalizing access to health care, curable and treatable illness and incapacity among the poor were to be eliminated, enabling them to take advantage of educational and employment opportunities. National health insurance became the topic of serious discussion for the first time since the depression and World War II years.

Today, health care costs, limited resources, and trade-offs between equity and efficiency dominate policy discussions. An economy suffering from stagflation (simultaneous inflation and unemployment) and disillusionment arising from the failure of increased health care resources and expenditures to reach all Americans (much less to keep them equally healthy) have turned attention away from the health problems of the poor and disadvantaged.

Failure to achieve all that was hoped for is not a cause for despair. A mere ten years brought dramatic progress in improving health despite rising costs and persistent gaps in access to health care. Extending equal opportunity for a healthy life to all is not an easily obtainable goal, nor is it one that can realistically be expected to take place in a decade or even in a generation. Past neglect will take its toll for long periods even if service inequities disappear. Armed with an understanding of past failures and successes, we should be able to solve the problems that remain.

Successes

Assessing ten years of experience with federal health programs is difficult. Although the United States keeps more extensive statistics on the
state of the nation's health than any other country, the information is not
broken down by various population groups, and much remains unknown
about how the poor have been affected relative to other groups. Even with
the most detailed statistics, however, much of the change that has occurred
would not be quantifiable. The difficulties of detecting and documenting
change make any description of past successes tenuous and incomplete.

Furthermore, the United States has become an unhealthier place in
which to live. Increased crowding in cities, environmental and occupational hazards, all contribute to debilitating and stressful living conditions.
Death rates from cancer, alcoholism, suicide, and homicide are rising.
More accidents take place. Rising food and fuel costs increase the incidence of poor nutrition, heightening the vulnerability of the poor. The
physical and psychological stress generated by unemployment and inflation has taken its toll.

The existing evidence, however, gives ample reason for optimism. Death
rates from causes that are amenable to improved health care and that
traditionally have been high among the poor have declined substantially.
Between 1965 and 1974 infant mortality rates declined 32 percent, with
even more rapid reductions in the deaths of babies between the ages of
one month and one year. Deaths from gastrointestinal diseases among
babies fell markedly, from influenza and pneumonia more than 60 percent, and from immaturity over 60 percent. Maternal mortality rates
dropped by two-thirds. The death rates for young children between the
ages of one and four have also been reduced, particularly for cancer (down
26 percent) and influenza and pneumonia (down 48 percent) from 1965
to 1973—although accidents have taken an increasing toll of the young.

There has also been progress in reducing most causes of death in the
adult population. Between 1965 and 1974 age-adjusted death rates from
heart conditions declined 16 percent; from cerebrovascular causes, 18
percent; accidents, 14 percent; influenza and pneumonia, 28 percent;
diabetes, 7 percent; and arteriosclerosis, 37 percent.

The incidence of chronic conditions among the general population, on
the other hand, has increased. In part, this reflects the larger proportion
of the aged in the population. In part, a greater incidence of chronic ill-

ness is to be expected when death rates are reduced. Reporting may also be more extensive and accurate when a larger proportion of the population comes into regular contact with the medical system.

Chronic conditions among the poor, however, have improved slightly relative to those of the nonpoor. In limitation of activity resulting from chronic illness poor children have moved closer to nonpoor children. For some types of conditions, such as visual impairments, for which comparable data are available over a period of time, the poor have made greater gains than the nonpoor.

One of the few health conditions to show a deterioration for the poor relative to the nonpoor is the incidence of acute illness. Acute conditions, including respiratory illness, gastrointestinal disturbances, and injuries, afflicted a greater proportion of the poor than the nonpoor in the ten-year period.

At the same time, the poor have gained impressively greater access to medical care to cope with these illnesses and accidents. Visits to physicians have increased for poor people in general. Low-income families who are covered by Medicaid or other government health programs now use health services at about the same level as middle-income families (after adjusting for health conditions)—reversing a pattern of many decades of greater use of the health system by the relatively healthier high-income population.

The proportion of the poor failing to see a physician over a two-year interval fell from 28 percent in the mid-1960s to 17 percent in 1973. More low-income women were seen by physicians early in pregnancy (up from 58 percent in 1963 to 71 percent in 1970).

Hospital care for the poor increased from fourteen hospital stays for every 100 people in 1964 to twenty-four in 1973. The aged also increased their use of hospital services. In 1964 there were nineteen hospital discharges for every 100 aged persons; by 1973 there were thirty-five. Surgery rates also increased among the poor.[1]

Dental care of the poor has improved somewhat relative to that of the nonpoor, yet a substantial gap persists. High-income people saw dentists twice as often as the poor in 1974 (contrasted with three and one-half times as often in 1964).

1. Caution must be used when analyzing increased use of medical care, especially surgery, laboratory tests, and other services selected by health professionals, as it may reflect unnecessary services as well as a welcome increase in access to needed services. Economic incentives have led to the exploitation of the poor and aged in some cases.

The health programs serving the poor and disadvantaged have undoubtedly contributed to the improvements in health status and access. Medicare and Medicaid have protected many elderly and poor people from much of the financial burden of large medical bills. Protection against the cost of hospital care—the most costly component of health care—has been particularly effective. Many of the aged and their children would be wiped out financially without this coverage.

Comprehensive health centers (neighborhood health centers, children and youth projects, maternity and infant care projects), though carried out on a limited demonstration basis, have been remarkably successful in achieving a wide range of health care goals. They have demonstrated that quality health care can be provided in low-income communities using innovative delivery systems that include the use of health professionals other than physicians, outreach efforts, and community participation in the governance and operation of centers. They have overcome many of the barriers impeding access to health care and better health in extremely poor communities. They have demonstrated that they can improve many dimensions of health—by reducing infant mortality rates or the incidence of serious illness, for example—and have succeeded in reducing hospitalization among the patients they serve by 35 percent below the national average.

In addition to such success in health care delivery, many of the centers have provided the poor with employment and enabled them to upgrade their educational and job skills. They have served as a lever for social, economic, and political advancement of the position of minorities.

Although the centers have taken such a broad approach to solving the health problems of the poor, they have demonstrated their ability to be cost effective. Costs per patient served are comparable to those in the traditional sector, but cost savings from reduced hospitalization and improved health indicate that they actually cost less than traditional methods of providing care.

The Remaining Gaps

While much progress has been made, many problems remain. The health gap has been narrowed, but not eliminated. What modern medicine can do, some of it quite cheaply, has not been disseminated to all. Rapidly escalating costs of care now threaten not only the poor and the aged but many middle-income families as well.

Those most left behind in the current patchwork of private insurance and public programs are the working poor, the unemployed, rural residents, minority groups, and poor children. The elderly, even with Medicare, are not fully protected against the high cost of illness and disability.

Medicaid is the major program financing health care for the poor, covering 25 million low-income people. Yet since it is tied to the welfare system, many are ineligible for benefits. Eligibility is largely restricted to the aged, the blind, the disabled, and one-parent families. Only 40 percent of the rural poor and 55 percent of the urban poor fit these categories. The majority of the rural poor and a large segment of the urban poor are two-parent families, typically unemployed or underemployed in marginal jobs. Consequently, an estimated 8 million to 10 million people below the poverty level receive no Medicaid benefits. They, and many like them just above the poverty level, encounter great difficulty in obtaining even basic health care for themselves at a time when average per capita health expenditures for a family of four are $1,692.[2]

Even for those covered by public programs, inequities remain. Medicare payments for physicians' services are 60 percent higher in metropolitan areas than in nonmetropolitan areas, and twice as high in western metropolitan areas as in nonmetropolitan areas of the South or the north central states. As a result, not only do the people in these areas subsidize the care of the more affluent people in the West and in the cities, but physicians are given one more reason to decide against practicing in rural areas. Medicaid payments in fiscal 1975 for a family receiving aid to families with dependent children (AFDC) ranged from $279 in Wyoming to $1,824 in New York. Even within states, there is wide variation in Medicaid expenditures—they are 54 percent higher per person eligible in New York City than in smaller urban and rural counties of New York. Similarly, in Kentucky Medicaid payments per person eligible are 58 percent higher in metropolitan areas than in nonmetropolitan areas.

Inequitable distribution of benefits by race is also prevalent in both Medicare and Medicaid. Medicare data for 1969, the latest available, indicate that payments per beneficiary were 40 percent higher for whites than for nonwhites. For some services, particularly those of physicians

2. Based on two adults under sixty-five at $547 each and two children at $249 each. Robert M. Gibson, Marjorie Smith Mueller, and Charles R. Fisher, "Age Differences in Health Care Spending, Fiscal Year 1976," *Social Security Bulletin,* vol. 40 (August 1977), pp. 3–14.

and nursing homes, the differences were substantially greater. Extended care benefits, for example, were twice as high for white Medicare enrollees as for nonwhites.[3]

Average Medicaid payments are 74 percent higher for white recipients than for others. Nursing home services are the most inequitably distributed, with average payments almost five times as high for white Medicaid recipients as for nonwhites. Recent data from the Georgia Medicaid program indicate that whites receive an average Medicaid payment of $587 for all services, but blacks and others receive only $271 (see chapter 3).

Most of the major health programs have been geared toward institutional care—the most expensive medical care—and the needs of people after they become seriously ill. Consequently, the bulk of the money is spent on the elderly or the disabled: about 70 percent of all Medicare and Medicaid expenditures are for institutional care. Basic services for poor children receive little attention in existing programs. Although Medicaid has implemented an early and periodic screening, diagnosis, and treatment program for children covered by Medicaid, at most 1 percent of all Medicaid funds are spent on this program and it reaches only about 14 percent of eligible children each year. The one program specifically designed for children (and mothers), the maternal and child health program, has suffered continually from lack of funds, lack of a coherent and integrated child health policy, and failure to adequately connect service delivery with screening and educational activities. During the 1970s grants under the maternal and child health program have almost completely lost out to the mushrooming public health insurance programs' claims on public health dollars.

As a result of this limited attention to children's health needs, poor children continue to lag in access to basic medical services. In 1973 poor children were 1.6 times more likely not to have seen a physician or a dentist for two years than nonpoor children. Immunizations against diphtheria, tetanus, whooping cough, rubella, and poliomyelitis are dangerously low among poor preschool children.

Such lack of access to appropriate care shows up in mortality and morbidity statistics. Infant mortality rates for black and Hispanic babies are still far above the national average. Diseases of the ears, eyes, and teeth in children cause disabilities that could have been prevented.

3. Karen Davis, "Equal Treatment and Unequal Benefits: The Medicare Program," *Milbank Memorial Fund Quarterly: Health and Society,* vol. 53 (Fall 1975), pp. 466–68 (Brookings Reprint 317).

Despite the efforts of Medicare and Medicaid to ease the medical cost burden of growing old, the elderly continue to pay more out of their own pockets for health care than do younger adults. Private payments by the elderly in fiscal 1976 averaged $559 per person (including Medicare premimums); younger people spent $385 of their own money on health care. Medicare and Medicaid have been particularly ineffectual in protecting the elderly against the cost of physicians' services—out-of-pocket costs of the elderly increased from $84 per capita in fiscal 1966 to $172 in 1976 (including the Medicare premium). Exclusion of some services, such as prescription drugs, eyeglasses, hearing aids, and dentures, and limits on nursing home care under Medicare have added to this financial burden. Some elderly people are excluded from Medicare coverage because they are not covered by social security. Open-ended requirements that the elderly pay a fixed proportion of all medical bills and options that permit physicians to charge elderly patients more than Medicare will pay make them particularly vulnerable to the cost of physicians' services. The Medicare deductible and coinsurance features for such services have also contributed to their unequal use by the elderly poor and those who are better off.

Added to all the above gaps and inequities in program coverage, the impact of the rapid escalation in the costs of health care on federal, state, and local budgets now threatens to erase both past progress and any hope of fulfilling the promise of equal access to care. Without widespread reform of the existing health care financing and delivery system, an increasing number of families will join the substantial number who still do not have access to basic health care.[4] Even families with moderate and above average incomes find it difficult to afford adequate insurance coverage and pay for needed services. For them and for poorer families, current public health programs are woefully inadequate.

Medicaid and Medicare have failed to keep pace with the explosion in health care prices. Consequently, their beneficiaries have either had inadequate coverage—only 40 percent of an elderly person's health bill is

4. The rise in health care expenditures since fiscal 1965, when the American people spent 5.9 percent of all their resources on their health, has been phenomenal: by 1976 they were spending 8.6 percent. Hospital costs increased over 30 percent from 1974 to 1976 though the costs of goods and services in general increased only 20 percent. Health insurance premiums jumped 35 percent during the two years in an effort to keep up with such large relative price changes. See Robert M. Gibson and Marjorie Smith Mueller, "National Health Expenditures, Fiscal Year 1976," *Social Security Bulletin,* vol. 40 (April 1977), pp. 3–22.

paid by Medicare—or been unable to find providers willing to accept them as patients for the fees paid by the program. Yet federal and state governments, themselves burdened with rising deficits, have continued to reduce coverage and increase eligibility restrictions, ever narrowing the definition of poverty.

Medicaid and Medicare programs, while in urgent need of reform to stem such cost crisis behavior, have still fared better financially than the comprehensive health centers. Medicaid and Medicare expenditures are to some extent "uncontrollable"; that is, once policymakers determine eligibility and service coverage, the interaction between patients and providers of services, which is beyond the policymakers' control, determines the total expenditure. In contrast, any project grant program is dependent on specific appropriations and yearly funding decisions. When tax dollars are scarce, grant programs are vulnerable to cuts and delays in funding.

In recent years neighborhood health centers, children and youth projects, and maternity and infant care projects have barely been able to compete with Medicare and Medicaid for a share of the public health dollar. The centers continue to be dependent on direct grants for survival because Medicare and Medicaid reimburse an average of only 10 to 20 percent of their expenses, and the incomes of the centers' patients are too low to make up the difference.[5]

To relieve budgets of some health expenditure demands, public agencies and policymakers have pressured centers to move toward self-sufficiency and have used fairly rigid productivity standards as guides for making decisions. This has caused many centers to close their doors. Self-sufficiency has proved an unrealistic goal when large numbers of the users of the centers have inadequate incomes and Medicare and Medicaid coverage is so low.

Despite the evidence presented in all available evaluations that the centers can deliver effective health care at costs below the fee-for-service private sector, few policy proposals have advocated significantly increased support for health centers. The skyrocketing costs of Medicare and Medicaid have absorbed nearly all the increases in public health dollars.[6]

5. Originally, planners expected third-party insurers such as Medicare and Medicaid to provide as much as 80 percent of the centers' total incomes. See chapter 6 for an analysis of why Medicare and Medicaid have failed to finance health care centers.
6. See chapters 5 and 6 for an evaluation of the health center experience.

The Decade Ahead

In coming years, federal health policy faces great challenges. To assure access to adequate health care for all its citizens, programs must combat ever-rising medical care costs and promote an effective organization of health care services. It is no longer valid to assume that minor program changes and new funds alone will solve the country's health care problems. To begin to meet the health care needs of all income groups, and particularly of the poor, there must be systemic changes in health care financing and delivery.

In a time of generally scarce budgetary resources, choices among alternative programs should focus on the greatest needs first. The poor and those caught in gaps between private insurance and current public programs should thus be given first consideration in reforming health care programs.

But policies that assist the poor can promote other objectives as well and lay the groundwork for an integrated health system for all. Experience has taught us that such integration is imperative if we are simultaneously to provide equal access and financial protection and to control the costs of medical care. A brief look at the dynamics of the existing health care financing and delivery system will illustrate how the joint goals of equal access, cost control, and financial protection imply a need for an integrated national health care system.

The present financing mechanisms for health care in the United States are predominantly "third parties" such as Medicaid, Medicare, and Blue Cross–Blue Shield. While these programs make some attempt to protect their beneficiaries against the most expensive health care costs—particularly hospital care—they either fail to cover or only marginally cover less expensive services. As a result, a hospital stay for which the total cost is $2,000 may cost the patient as little as (or less than) an annual $150 checkup. Insurance companies, Medicare, and Medicaid also tend to pay more for specialized services than for primary care services and more for services delivered in urban areas than in rural.[7] Such insurance reimbursement patterns give financial incentives to both patients and providers to use expensive specialists' services even when a less expensive alternative

7. These price patterns are partially due to historical differences in relative prices and partially to the dominant professional status of urban specialists.

is available. Yet private insurance often fails to cover very large expenditures adequately.

In addition to encouraging specialized and institutionalized medical care, the insurance mechanism is generally inadequate and inappropriate for collective health care needs, such as sewage and water purification systems, which no one individual purchases.

Health care resources and workers have responded to such financial incentives predictably. Urban areas in the United States have a proliferation of highly trained specialists and sophisticated hospital facilities alongside a scarcity of primary care and ambulatory resources. Rural and poor areas have few health care services of any kind. The resulting severe maldistribution of resources and increasingly expensive "style" of medicine are beyond the control of any individual patient.[8]

The system is also beyond the control of any one insurance program, public or private. If Medicare or Medicaid tries to hold down physicians' fees, for example, the elderly and the poor will either find few physicians willing to take them as patients or will end up paying higher out-of-pocket costs.

Given the fragmentation of health care financing among different population groups, reform of only one program will ultimately be frustrated or costly unless the whole system of financing and incentives in health care markets is reformed. In their appraisal of ten years of experience with various health care programs for the poor and disadvantaged, chapters 3 through 6 offer three major lessons for widespread reform of health care financing.

First, a better balance must be struck between the delivery and the financing of health care. Financial incentives should deliberately promote organizational and delivery models that provide low-cost, high-quality care. Among the most promising of these are organizations that reduce the incentives for hospitalization, replace the traditional physician's fee-for-service model with salaried methods of payment, and promote the use of paramedical professionals to substitute for physicians where possible. Emphasis must be placed on prevention and primary care—particularly for children and residents of areas with few medical resources.

8. See Louise B. Russell, "The Diffusion of New Hospital Technologies in the United States," *International Journal of Health Services,* vol. 6, no. 4 (1976), pp. 557–80 (Brookings Reprint 322); and Anne A. Scitovsky and Nelda McCall, "Changes in the Costs of Treatment of Selected Illnesses, 1951–1964–1971," Health Policy Program, Discussion Paper (San Francisco: University of California, School of Medicine, September 1975; processed).

Second, any policy that improves access and financial protection must also encompass ways to contain and direct health care expenditures.

Third, major reform of the current network of financing programs, public and private, which can best be accomplished by the introduction of national health insurance, is urgently needed if the low-income population is to have access to adequate health care.

A Better Balance between Health Care Delivery and Financing

When the Great Society health programs began, the Department of Health, Education, and Welfare presented a plan to pursue a balanced policy for developing the delivery of health care for the poor and for its financing. Medicaid was to pay for a broad range of health care services for the poor on welfare. Medicare was to assist the aged in meeting the costs of health care bills. Balancing these programs, with approximately equal budgetary outlays, were to be comprehensive health centers established in low-income, underserved areas. These centers were to pay physicians a salary, use a team approach to providing care, and make use of indigenous workers in a variety of ways. The design of the centers emphasized preventive care, health education, and intervention in nonmedical areas influencing health.

The actual experience of the health care programs was quite different from the plan. The cost of Medicaid and Medicare quickly surpassed original estimates. In fiscal 1976 government expenditures for Medicaid were $15.3 billion, far different from the original estimate of $1.5 billion, and provided medical care for 24 million low-income people. Community health centers, on the other hand, received approximately $197 million and registered 1.5 million patients in about 125 centers, well below the 25 million people in 1,000 health centers at a cost of $3.35 billion originally planned.

The imbalance that has developed is unfortunate considering the success of the health center concept. One of the most striking lessons to emerge from the limited experience with health care centers is that effective health care can be low in cost in impoverished urban and rural communities when it is based on primary health care rather than on specialized, institutional care. This evidence is, in retrospect, neither surprising nor new. Public health services and the general practice of medicine form the cornerstones of every theoretical "ideal" health care system. As points of entry into the system, as coordinators of services, and for services to more than one person at a time, organizations that deliver primary health care are crucial to allocating resources where they will be most effective.

Encouraging the comprehensive care centers, instead of punishing them with narrow definitions of productivity and health care,[9] will require the policy changes listed at the end of chapter 6. But these changes must occur in conjunction with changes in Medicare and Medicaid reimbursement policies if the centers (and other innovative organizations for the delivery of primary care) are to compete successfully for major financial support from public and private insurers.

Neither Medicare nor Medicaid was designed to finance or encourage new forms of primary health care delivery. Instead, both programs sustain and support the patterns and traditions of medical care that existed in 1965. As a result, neither program has been supportive of new organizational forms such as neighborhood health centers or health maintenance organizations.[10] Future financing policy must consider the delivery structure that would avoid similarly undermining innovative organizational forms.

Access, Cost Control, and Financial Protection

Medicare and Medicaid have not only been unsuccessful in curbing program costs, but they have also failed to protect the poor and elderly from devastating medical care costs and to provide all low-income groups with access to care.

Reform of Medicare and Medicaid could begin to remove many of the programs' internal inequities, but it will be unable to control costs if undertaken alone, without broader reform of all health care financing. As noted above, Medicare and Medicaid must pay prices that are competitive with each other and with private insurance companies if they are to serve their beneficiaries adequately. The cuts in services and the increasing financial burden of Medicare and Medicaid in recent years are vivid testimony to the conflict between the provision of services and cost control when programs serve only a portion of the total population.

If federal policy is to begin to influence expenditure levels without hurt-

9. See chapters 5 and 6 for descriptions of the difficulties health centers have in obtaining funds and surviving.

10. HMOs generally involve a prepaid, group practice of medicine. Families and individuals in an HMO obtain all their medical care from the physicians and other health workers in the HMO or through referral. A regular monthly payment covers all the costs incurred by patients under this comprehensive health care system.

ing the poor and elderly, coordinated public and private efforts and a health care policy that affects all population groups will be required. The Carter administration's proposed hospital cost containment bill is the first major policy proposal from the federal government that attempts such coordinated control of costs.[11] Regulation of hospital costs, however, is at best a short-term approach. In the long run, a comprehensive reform of reimbursement policies is necessary for equal access, financial protection, and cost control.

Major Reform—A National Health Program

Experience has shown that guaranteeing physical and financial access to adequate health care for all Americans is beyond the scope of Medicare and Medicaid. Covering the poor and the disadvantaged separately from the rest of the population leads the public program to absorb rapid increases in expenditures and undermines their ability to deliver care to all.

Medicare, Medicaid, neighborhood health centers, and the maternal and child health program have continually been constrained from meeting the health care needs of the poor and the disadvantaged effectively. Their experience shows that separate facilities, delivery systems, and financing programs for different racial or income groups are seldom equal and often cannot meet recipients' needs. Public insurance systems for the poor and the elderly are easy targets when budgets are tight. Health centers that have a reputation for treating only poor people, and that at the same time offer innovative approaches to health care, are labeled second class regardless of the quality of their services. Federal, state, and local officials appear to care less about needed reforms in programs that serve only the least powerful voting groups. So long as only part of the health care system is supported by public funds, demands for equity in the financing, delivery, and distribution of resources end up playing off urban and rural, black and white, and old and young low-income recipients against one another.

Separate programs are also powerless to effect changes in the health care delivery and financing system that would benefit poor and nonpoor alike. Programs that merely attempt to fill in gaps have limited influence on the distribution of resources, on the combination and content of services, on the quality of care, or on the efficiency and cost effectiveness of health care.

11. Hospital Cost Control Act of 1977, H.R. 6575; S. 1391.

The gaps and inequities documented in earlier chapters plus the need to control health care expenditures make the reform of health care financing a national concern. To ensure that this country moves toward a system that provides both the most effective combination of services per dollar spent and access to necessary services for all Americans, reform should meet the greatest needs first while laying the groundwork for integrating all needs into a national plan.

The following discussion highlights early steps in the reform agenda.

First, Medicaid should be expanded to cover all poor people with a full range of benefits, including a mandatory "spend-down" program. Making eligibility dependent on income alone (rather than on family characteristics) and uniform across states would eliminate the major inequities in coverage of the poor. The spend-down program would also reach the near-poor, affording the entire population some financial protection from the costs of serious illness. Depending on initial budgetary resources, spend-down requirements could be limited to some proportion of income above the full-coverage poverty standards. This would avoid abrupt loss of coverage for families that succeeded in marginally raising their incomes.

Medicare benefits should also be increased by eliminating the deductible and the three-day hospital requirement for extended care benefits and by providing a broader range of service benefits in ambulatory care settings—for example, expanded drug benefits. Such expansions in Medicare and Medicaid would close major eligibility gaps between the poor and the nonpoor.

In addition to expanded coverage, Medicaid and Medicare reimbursement policies should be merged to allow coordination and equalization of reimbursements for specific services within localities and among specialties. By requiring providers to accept reimbursement from either program as full payment if they wish to participate at all, the programs should have more control over costs, especially in institutions. Coordination of reimbursement policies would also allow more aggressive support of alternative settings for ambulatory care and alternative resource allocation. For instance, policy could reduce payment differences between rural and urban practitioners, pay equal fees for a specified service whether provided by a generalist or specialist, experiment with capitation payments to settings organized for ambulatory care, and recognize the services provided by nurse practitioners and physician's assistants in qualified urban and rural settings.

A resource development fund should also be created by setting aside a specified percentage of the budgets of both Medicaid and Medicare. This fund would finance resource development in underserved areas and stimulate demonstrations of innovative delivery models. Allocation decisions could be made at federal and state program levels to guarantee flexibility and responsiveness to local problems. Tying the growth of delivery organizations to the growth of budgets could forestall a repetition of the health center–Medicaid history. Furthermore, the system would have a built-in mechanism for stimulating cost-effective reorganizations of services.

Finally, Medicare, Medicaid, and health center programs should enforce the compliance of providers with the requirements of the Civil Rights Act to secure equal benefits for disadvantaged minorities. Stricter enforcement of the rights of minorities to nursing home and other institutional care should be of particular concern. Failure to comply should disqualify providers from program participation for a significant period of time.

These initial reforms of Medicaid and Medicare together with the expansion of grant programs will facilitate the eventual merger of current public programs into a system covering the entire population. A national plan, though costly in public dollars, would clearly result in more control than a comprehensive plan mixing public and private coverage. For instance, a national plan (with regional or state divisions) could coordinate reimbursement policy for all providers in a given community or area, allowing area budgets or other spending controls to be adjusted annually. Regional and area incentives for planning and reorganizing delivery of ambulatory and primary care would, for the first time, be financially reinforced.

Similarly, policy could be used to promote the reallocation of resources from overserved to underserved areas, from specialties to primary care, and from emphasis on acute care to emphasis on prevention. A national resource development fund could make grants available to all communities, including poor and nonpoor residents in demonstrations. Other policy instruments that would be more feasible in a national program than in the mixture of public and private coverage include the allocation of depreciation funds into a community pool for future capital investment; communitywide experimentation with capitation payments for primary care in organized settings and for groups that do not offer a sufficiently broad range of services to qualify as health maintenance organizations;

and creation of a national data system for analyzing the health status and variations in the use of health care services by the population group according to occupation, income, and geographic area.

The Department of Health, Education, and Welfare is currently in the process of developing and planning a national health insurance program that includes major reforms of Medicaid and Medicare as a first phase. However, the implementation of reforms that address and attempt to change present patterns of financing and delivery to control costs and increase access confronts major opposition from those who benefit from the existing system. The long struggle to institute a national health insurance program in the United States shows the strength of this opposition. Strong public support, based on an understanding of structural weaknesses and the potential for change, is critical to the creation of a health care system that will respond to the needs of all income groups without absorbing an ever-increasing share of the national income.

appendix **Methodological Problems with Measuring the Contribution of Medical Care to Health**

The remarkable progress made by the poor in gaining access to medical services from 1965 to 1975, and a corresponding improvement in selected measures of health status that have historically been high in poor communities, were discussed in chapter 2. It seems plausible that the poor's improved access to care also improved their health status.

The research attempting to measure such a relationship, however, is plagued by inadequate data on different population groups' health status, socioeconomic status, and use of medical care services. Despite the inadequate data, several studies have claimed that improved access to medical care can no longer be expected to improve health. In this appendix several of these studies are reviewed to highlight their methodological problems and to urge further research and data collection, thus avoiding such problems in future studies.[1]

Large Area or Group Studies

One approach to investigating the relationship between medical care and health is to compare the average health status of various large groups of people with their average use of medical care services. But these aggregative studies are of limited relevance since the population groups include both poor and nonpoor people; health improvements of any one small population subgroup may be lost in aggregation. Furthermore, these

1. The best studies relating medical care to health outcomes are those conducted for comprehensive health centers. These centers gathered and studied utilization and health status information to a much greater extent than any of the other health care programs. Most of the health center studies found beneficial health effects. These studies are reviewed in chapters 5 and 6.

studies usually do not separate measures of health status that are sensitive to medical care from other dimensions of health; most, in fact, use only total age-adjusted death rates or disability days to measure health status.

Victor Fuchs recently conducted one such aggregate study. His analysis of the factors affecting survival or death is based on two assertions: (1) "the total contribution of modern medical care to life expectancy is large, but over the considerable range of variation in the quantity of care observed in developed countries, the marginal contribution is small"; and (2) in developed countries there is a "disappearance of the traditional relationship between life expectancy and per capita income."[2] He concludes from these general statements that, though the potential of modern medicine for further improving health may be great in developing countries, it is now small in the United States. Citing high death rates from causes linked to personal habits—violence, lung cancer, and cirrhosis of the liver—he argues that the greatest improvements in health could come from changing life styles. As an example, he compares death rates in Nevada with those in Utah and concludes that the Mormon life style—which emphasizes marital stability and the avoidance of tobacco and alcohol—accounts for the lower death rates in Utah.

While Fuchs' argument that life style can and does have a deleterious effect on health is indisputable, many parts of his thesis need qualification. First, he views health narrowly—death rates—and does not comment on the potential of medical care for improving other dimensions of illness, such as intensity of discomfort and functional capability. Second, his examples may be spurious: he neglects to mention that the Morman church has also promoted medical care and adequate income maintenance for members. Third, the assertion that there is no longer a significant relation between life expectancy and per capita income is not supported by the available evidence.[3] In fact, substantial differences in death rates by socioeconomic status persist in relevant health statistics. Although some narrowing of differences has occurred in recent years, life expectancies of certain groups—migrant workers, Indians, blacks, and poor whites—continue to fall well behind those of others.

2. Victor R. Fuchs, *Who Shall Live? Health, Economics, and Social Choice* (Basic Books, 1974), pp. 30–31.

3. This same erroneous conclusion was echoed in the medical care section of the 1976 report of the Council of Economic Advisers, written by a former associate of Fuchs, Barry R. Chiswick, which asserts that higher income actually tends to be positively associated with higher mortality, blaming sedentary white-collar work and (inexplicably) pollution. *Economic Report of the President together with the Annual Report of the Council of Economic Advisers, January 1976,* p. 119.

Fourth, although the United States is a developed country, many sections lag in their share of development and have the severe health and economic problems normally associated with underdeveloped areas. For example, in Leslie County, Kentucky, in 1970 only 16 percent of the adult population had a high school education or better, 64 percent of the families had incomes below the near-poverty level (per capita income of $1,057), 72 percent of the homes lacked plumbing, 62 percent of the homes did not have a telephone, and the median value of owner-occupied housing was under $5,000.[4] This and many similar counties throughout rural America obviously do not fit Fuchs's notion of an advanced, modern, technological society. For residents of such areas, where infant mortality rates are 55 percent above national averages,[5] basic medical care can do much to improve both survival and the opportunity to lead healthy, productive lives.

Finally, Fuchs does not distinguish between the portion of medical care devoted to reducing mortality and the remainder, which he appears to view as of marginal value. Medical care dollars can not only help avert death, but also increase functional capacity and relieve pain and anxiety.

Econometric Studies

Several econometric studies have tried to isolate the independent effects of income, education, and life style variables on age-adjusted death rates. For example, two studies of this type have been conducted by the staff at the National Bureau of Economic Research.[6] These researchers hypothesize that education is the main determinant of health: more educated people are supposedly better able to identify health symptoms, practice good

4. U.S. Bureau of the Census, *Census of Population, 1970, General Social and Economic Characteristics: Kentucky,* Final Report PC(1)-C19 (GPO, 1972), tables 120, 124; and Bureau of the Census, *Census of Housing, 1970, Detailed Housing Characteristics: Kentucky,* Final Report HC(1)-B19 (GPO, 1972), tables 60, 62, and *General Housing Characteristics: Kentucky,* Final Report HC(1)-A19 (GPO, 1971), table 29.

5. Calculated from average infant mortality rates for 1969–73 in Leslie County and in the United States. Averaging produces more accurate comparisons when small population groups form a base for comparison. The Leslie County average was 29.8 deaths per 1,000 births; the U.S. average was 19.2.

6. See Richard Auster, Irving Leveson, and Deborah Sarachek, "The Production of Health, an Exploratory Study," and Morris Silver, "An Econometric Analysis of Spatial Variations in Mortality Rates by Race and Sex," in Victor R. Fuchs, ed., *Essays in the Economics of Health and Medical Care* (Columbia University Press for National Bureau of Economic Research, 1972).

health habits, and use the health system. These analysts also tend to discount the importance of income as a determinant of health and believe that reducing poverty would, in itself, be of little health value. In practice, it is virtually impossible to isolate statistically the individual contributions to health of education, income, or other factors such as occupation, nutrition, medical care, residential location (high or low crime area, nearness to or distance from manufacturing establishments), stress generated by unemployment and low income, marital stability, substandard housing, and inferior public services. Lack of education, low incomes, poor housing, and so on tend to go together.

These econometric studies are further plagued by the use of one year's worth of aggregate state data that make it impossible to sort out the independent effects of contributing factors. At the state level in particular, income, education, personal health expenditures, and alcohol consumption are usually highly correlated with each other.

Despite such flaws in their research design, the Auster-Leveson-Sarachek and Silver studies conclude that (1) income tends to be negatively associated with death rates (that is, that death rates are lower for high-income states) when no education information is included; (2) when both education and income are included, however, states with high educational levels have lower death rates, and for a given education level, states with higher income have higher death rates; (3) medical care tends to reduce death rates, but the effect is rather small; and (4) alcohol consumption, tobacco consumption, and pollution have positive, but generally insignificant, effects on death rates.

Such conclusions are suspect because of their statistical problems. Information that was further disaggregated by cause of death and by smaller subpopulations might show stronger links between medical care and health —particularly for the health conditions of the poor that are particularly sensitive to medical care.

Another econometric study investigated the link between medical care and health status.[7] It analyzed changes in disability days and self-assessment of health status for twenty-eight age-education groups from 1963 to 1970 as a function of changes in the use of medical services.[8] It found that

7. Lee Benham and Alexandra Benham, "The Impact of Incremental Medical Services on Health Status, 1963–1970," in Ronald Andersen, Joanna Kravits, and Odin W. Anderson, eds., *Equity in Health Services: Empirical Analyses in Social Policy* (Ballinger, 1975), pp. 217–28.

8. The study tested health status in 1970 as a function of health status in 1963, changes in medical care use from 1963 to 1970, and other variables.

groups receiving more medical care during the period also had a greater incidence of disability days. The authors concluded from this that positive increments in medical services induced by governmental medical programs did not lead to improvements in health and that a more fruitful way of improving health might be more education.

This conclusion is unwarranted on two accounts. First, as no test for education was included, the authors' hypothesis reflects only their personal, untested beliefs. Second, the study made no attempt to isolate the direction of causality between illness and the use of medical care. Rather, it assumed (1) that death rates across groups did not differ over the period; and (2) that the use of medical services under governmental programs was not affected by changes in health. The first assumption seems to be clearly repudiated by the trends in mortality; the second should have been the object of the inquiry, not an assumption. Failure to investigate the possible link between medical care and health status makes it impossible to derive any causal conclusions from the positive association between the use of medical services and changes in health. The empirical work verifies only that groups with increased health problems or initial poor health received more medical services over the period—which, of course, was one of the major objectives of the health care programs enacted in the mid-1960s. Identifying the direction of causality would require separating the measures of health status that could be expected to change independently of medical care—such as the incidence of unpreventable acute conditions—from changes that are sensitive to changes in medical care.[9]

Medicaid, Medicare, and Health Status

Some studies have attempted to disaggregate utilization and health outcomes into meaningful categories. Only a few researchers, however, have tried to examine utilization and health outcomes for the poor and the elderly covered by Medicaid and Medicare. Friedman and others examined records of women with breast cancer in a Massachusetts area in 1970.[10] They found that variables measuring Medicaid and private insur-

9. Elsewhere the study is similarly beset by statistical difficulties—one set of regressions "proves" that getting married improves health while another set indicates that marriage has no effect on health!

10. Bernard Friedman, Paul Parker, and Leslie Lipworth, "The Influence of Medicaid and Private Health Insurance on the Early Diagnosis of Breast Cancer," *Medical Care,* vol. 11 (November–December 1973), pp. 485–90.

ance coverage were insignificant in an econometric analysis of the stage of cancer at which women sought medical care. Women covered by Medicaid did not necessarily seek medical care earlier than other women.

In another study Friedman found that restricted activity days declined for the elderly after the introduction of Medicare and that the declines were inversely related to the level of personal health care expenditures per capita. His data also indicated that the mortality rates of aged males in 1969 were lower than predicted from a modified cohort model. An attempt to estimate a model relating a summary measure of the elderly's health status to the number of hospital days and medical visits, as well as other explanatory variables, was not successful in separating the relation between health and medical care.[11]

11. Bernard Friedman, "Mortality, Disability, and the Normative Economics of Medicare," in Richard N. Rosett, ed., *The Role of Health Insurance in the Health Services Sector* (Neale Watson Academic Publications for National Bureau of Economic Research, 1976), pp. 365–90.

Index

Aaron, Henry J., 1n
Accidental deaths and injuries, 20
Acute conditions, 38, 39, 40, 205
Aday, Lu Ann, 22n
Administration: of health care programs, 2, 16; of Medicaid, 49, 51
AFDC. *See* Aid to families with dependent children
Age and mortality rates, 27, 29, 30, 31
Aged. *See* Elderly people
Agriculture, Department of, 3
Aid to families with dependent children (AFDC), 52, 59
Albert, Mary A., 65, 66
Alpert, Joel J., 157n, 181, 182n
American Medical Association, 95
Amidei, Nancy, 54n
Andersen, Ronald, 22n, 43n, 77n, 165n
Anderson, Arne, 181, 192
Anderson, Odin W., 22n, 222n
Anderson, Robert E., 165n, 173n, 184
Antonovsky, Aaron, 30n
Appel, Gary L., 189n
Auster, Richard, 221n, 222

Balinsky, Warren, 20n
Ball, Robert M., 112n
Bellin, Seymour S., 173n, 181
Belloc, Nedra B., 23n
Benefits: MCH, 144–47, 157–58; Medicaid, 55, 69–70, 207; Medicare, 94–96
Benham, Alexandra, 23n, 222n
Benham, Lee, 23n, 222n
Berger, Renee, 20n
Bergner, Lawrence, 30n
Berg, Robert L., 20n
Bernard, Sydney E., 50n
Bernstein, Roberta, 180n
Berry, C. C., 20n
Bice, Thomas W., 45n, 66n
Birch, Herbert G., 19n
Blechman, Barry M., 12n

Blendon, Robert J., 170n
Blischke, W. R., 20n
Bonanno, Rosemary A., 180n
Bradbury, Dorothy E., 121n
Bremmer, Robert H., 121n
Brenner, M. Harvey, 23n
Breslow, Lester, 23n
Brody, Jane E., 23n
Brook, Robert H., 47n
Brown, Lawrence D., 164n
Bryant, Thomas E., 161, 177
Bumpers, Dale, 174
Bunker, John P., 23n
Bureau of the Census, 3, 5
Bush, J. W., 20n

C&Y projects. *See* Children and youth projects
Cancer, 29, 223–24
Carlson, Rick J., 23n
Center for Family Planning Program Development, 141n, 145n
Chen, Milton M., 20n
Chiang, C. L., 20n
Children: crippled, 120, 124, 134–37, 143; EPSDT, 84–86; Medicaid, 54, 60, 66, 83, 208; mortality rates, 33–34; visits to physicians, 41. *See also* Maternal and child health program
Children and youth (C&Y) projects, 124–25; achievements, 133–34, 155–56, 157; comprehensive health care services, 132; enrollments, 131; minorities, 145; shortcomings, 158–59; urban-rural distribution, 143
Children's Bureau, 121–23, 125
Chiswick, Barry R., 220n
Chronic conditions, 20, 25, 204–05; restricted activity, 27, 35, 38
Cirrhosis of the liver, 29, 30, 31
Citizens Board of Inquiry into Hunger in the United States, 25
Civil Rights Act, 112, 113, 217